Crichton,

Subway to the Met

Subway to the Met:
Risë Stevens' Story

KYLE CRICHTON

Doubleday & Company, Inc., Garden City, New York
1959

A Few Introductory Remarks by Miss Stevens

When this book was first discussed, it was suggested that it be told by me in the first person, but I fled from the idea with a shudder. My severest critics may be willing to admit that I am a singer, but nobody in his right mind would consider me a writer. I know that many books are written by celebrities and passed off as their own work, but I hardly think this fools anybody. That old devil ghost writer is grinning somewhere in the background. There is another type, the as-told-to books, which are some better but still not the real thing.

Now, I certainly have no smug theories about these matters; it is just that I think a writer is a precious individual, with his own rights and obligations and need for proper credit. I also think the reader has rights—the right to know the truth about how a book is written. When the writer is a superior craftsman like Kyle Crichton, I put myself in his hands with a sigh of relief. I have been as honest with him as I know how; what comes out is my life, but it is his work. It might be held that I am taking the easy way out, avoiding the blame, but this is not the case. I have read the finished job and approve of it. Some parts of my life are not easy to face when seen in cold type, but they are mine. Whether I like it or not, I have been pinned to the printed page. Mr. Crichton has pinned me there like a butterfly, and I have squirmed, but I must admit that he has seen right through me to the girl I used to be, called Risë Steenberg.

However, not even an opera singer lives in a vacuum, and I hasten to add that I might have had no life at all without my

5

mother and father, my son Nicky, and a gentleman named Walter Surovy, often referred to by friends as my Crazy Hungarian Husband. My beloved father is no longer alive, but I still have my wonderful and highly individualistic mother, known as Sadie, and the aforementioned Surovy, who merits a book of his own but has kindly taken a back seat here on my behalf. In short, it is a life of us all and a host of people I have met along the way. Most of them have been good people, some of them have been irritating, and a few have been impossible. I salute my friends, I forgive the others. As someone has said, life is made up of a number of things.

The question most asked of me as a singer is, would I do the same thing if I had my life to live over. I never know how to answer. I was a professional (not very highly paid) at the age of ten. Sadie urged me along when I was young; Walter has used his own highly successful technique on me since. Perhaps I should resent it all, but the very idea seems ridiculous. I have been happy, I have been successful. There were hard bumps in my personal life, but musically it has been a dream. So what have I to complain about? Nothing.

I hope the reader of this book has the same feeling.

Risë Stevens

New York City, 1959

6

Chapter One

An opera singer has to start somewhere, and Risë Stevens started in Prague. It could just as well have been Zurich, Bern, Vienna, Graz, or Basle, and, as a matter of fact, she offered them the honor of discovering her, but they declined politely. They said they were filled up for the season and come around a little later. She didn't have time to wait and was lucky to get Prague.

Not that Prague was anything wonderful at the beginning. She was getting $25 a month and has always maintained that her mother invented CARE packages. If it hadn't been for those monthly cartons of canned goods and chocolate, Risë would have been the skinniest mezzo-soprano in Middle Europe, and that wouldn't have pleased the Prague audiences, who preferred them *saftig*.

There was another slight handicap in that she was singing with a German company and didn't know German. She also didn't know French, although she had learned a few operas in that language and now had to unlearn them. But as Risë has since said, you can do a lot of things when you're young and don't know any better.

The theatre was the Neues Deutches Theatre, and three weeks after her arrival Risë made her debut in *Mignon*. There is a lot of

7

fake sentiment about a debut, and it is supposed to be the most thrilling thing in a singer's life, but in this case it was merely a torture. She was so worried about what she was saying that she almost forgot to sing. The director, Dr. Paul Eger, patted her on the back and said she had done well, but that merely proved that Dr. Eger was a kind man. She knew that she was barely adequate, and she also knew that eventually she was going to be a success in opera. We'll explain that a little later when we get writing about Risë's mother.

No, we may as well tell you about Mother now. Risë has always called her Sadie, has no faintest idea how old she is (for Sadie is very cagey on the subject), and knows that nothing has ever stopped Sadie. If Sadie answers the phone and the party at the other end says, "Sorry, wrong number," Sadie says, "It's a nice day; what's your hurry? Talk a little bit." If she is visiting Risë during the summer at Westhamptom Beach and somebody mentions there is a dance that night at Amagansett, Sadie is halfway to the door before the words are out. "Sadie!" Risë will yell. "It's fifty miles out there!" Sadie will say, "We can all sleep late tomorrow." When people say to her, "Isn't it wonderful your daughter's an opera star?" Sadie looks at them in amazement and says, "What's so wonderful?" It simply never occurred to her that Risë wouldn't be an opera star. She knew it from the time Risë started singing on the "Children's Hour" on radio at the age of ten.

But nobody must get the idea that it was one of those obnoxious stage-mother relationships. Sadie and Risë love one another devotedly, but their temperaments clash like thunder in the night. They are so much alike that sparks begin to fly immediately, and after two or three days Sadie packs her bags and leaves, saying at the door, "I can have more fun at the corner drugstore." If Risë ever had a stage mother, it was this fellow Walter Surovy, who was playing at the same theatre when she arrived in Prague. They have been married twenty years, and Risë feels like killing him at times, but he always talks her out of it. He not only talks her out of things, but he talks her into them, which is often worse. At least, she thinks so at the time; later she has to admit she was wrong.

Almost literally, Risë bumped into Surovy in Prague. In fact, she almost knocked him down; at least she tried. He was an actor and the matinee idol of the legitimate side of the theatre. One day Risë came to the stage door of the theatre and found the entrance blocked by a swarm of teen-agers getting the autograph of this big wheel. She started weaving her way through the mob until she got to Surovy, who kept busy with his autographing and pretended not to see her. She kept saying, *"Pardon, pardon,"* in a pitiful sort of way, these being the only foreign words she could remember at the moment. Surovy looked up in a bland way and said, *"Was wollen Sie?"* He knew very well *was wollended* her, but he was going to make it as tough as he could. She could see at a glance that he was a handsome dog, but that might have been because she was seeing him through a red haze of fury.

So she gave him the "treatment." This consisted of a jab of the elbow calculated to break his ribs. She had picked this up in that salubrious part of New York City known as the Bronx, where she was born and where she discovered that men were men, and women had better learn to be men if they wanted to stay alive. She understands that conditions have become much gentler in that region and that the borough is considered a paradise by thousands of good citizens, but in her early days it was a tough section, and you had to protect yourself in the clinches.

In any event, Surovy said "ugg" in a peculiar voice and fell back in surprise. She went in through the stage door and thought she had seen the last of him, but she might have known better. No European stage star is going to take a thing like that lying down. Either he wants revenge or he wants to rehabilitate himself in the esteem of his opponent. At the time, Risë was living with Harriet Henders, the other American singer in the company, and the sly Surovy used that way of getting to her. He sent Harriet two tickets to a performance of Bush-Fekete's *Jean*, his star part, hoping that Harriet would bring her along. That wasn't hard to do, for otherwise Risë would have spent another lonesome night in the boardinghouse, and by that time she was plain sick of them.

She had to admit that Surovy was at his best that night, but that didn't make her any fonder of him. He was playing a romantic comedy, and the audience—at least the female portion of it—was in ecstasy between laughs and swoons. She could understand only a few words of what he was saying, but the effect was obvious enough. He had those silly *Frauleins* right in the palm of his hand. When it was over, Harriet headed backstage.

"What for?" Risë asked sharply.

"Professional courtesy," said Harriet. "He sent the tickets; we have to go back and thank him."

Risë started to say that he hadn't sent *her* any tickets, but she was intrigued by the idea of seeing the monster closer at hand. She almost backed away again when they reached his dressing room and found another mob scene taking place, but Harriet was firm about their duties. They said the proper pretty words, and the next thing Risë knew they were on their way to supper with Walter and another actor who was squiring Harriet. What she didn't know was that Walter had almost precipitated a riot in the theatre by breaking a date with his steady girl, who happened also to be the leading actress with the company. Only strong hands prevented the actress from following them to the restaurant and hurling crockery at Surovy. Oh, he was a scoundrel, all right; there was no doubt about it.

The language difficulty was bad enough, and Risë sat there like a dummy, nodding her head and smiling in a silly way while the German flowed all around her, but something even worse was about to happen. In her nervousness she was smoking one cigarette after another. Suddenly Walter reached across the table and flipped the cigarette out of her mouth. It was not only an insult, but it was a humiliating physical insult, the kind you instinctively answer with a slap or a kick. She was furious, all right; she flared up inside like a volcano—and just as quickly simmered down.

"I should have known right then about Walter and me," she now says wryly.

From all this, one might get the idea that Risë is rather a combative female, but in truth she is completely unsure of herself and always has been. If pushed hard enough, she can get her back up and be stubborn, but she would much prefer to let things slide. In the early operatic days people were kind to her, and she got along much better than she really had a right to. Since that time Walter has been around to do the battling, and what he doesn't know about theatrical intrigue and infighting hasn't been invented. He started in the most obscure and bedraggled little theatre companies and scrambled to the top. In that Middle European atmosphere it is not so much dog eat dog as the law of the jungle, where any sign of weakness calls for a general onslaught on the victim.

Since the Prague days Risë has sung in Cairo and Alexandria, at the Teatro Colón in Buenos Aires (a wonderful place), at Glyndebourne in England (a small fairyland), at La Scala in Milan, at the Paris and Vienna Operas, and at the very best of them all, the Metropolitan in New York. During that career she has learned a great deal and become what some might think a bit excessively case-hardened, but in essence the Bronx still has her in its grasp. That was a bad time for her family, and to this day she wakes up out of terrifying dreams in which her whole life has been a mirage and she is back on Bergen Avenue in poverty. The scene in the dream never changes. She is in a tiny room in a cheap boardinghouse. There is a narrow iron cot, a single uncovered light hangs from a cord in the middle of the room, there is a book where the leg of the dresser belongs, and the curtains at the window are sleazy and tattered. It takes a great shaking of the head after this harrowing experience before Risë can reassure herself that they have money in the bank, a house on Long Island, an apartment in New York, a good annuity, and an arrangement with a record company that will give her a steady yearly income.

In the face of all this, it can be said that Risë has done rather well. When Rudolf Bing arrived in 1949, preparatory to taking over direction of the Metropolitan, he asked what artists were getting the top fee. When he found Risë Stevens among them, he had a small Viennese fit.

"But it's impossible!" he cried. "She's a mezzo-soprano."

He said it like a dirty word and had every right on his side, for in other famed opera houses it is the tenors and the high-flying sopranos who get the red-carpet treatment. The mezzos are supposed to be nice reliable ladies, content to blink in the effulgence given off by dramatic sopranos and coloraturas. Risë has never really thought about the matter one way or the other. If she did *Carmen* and *Rosenkavalier* and *Orfeo* and *Dalila* and they turned out to be smash hits, she was happy enough about it without wondering whether it made her top dog. Opera is like every other entertainment medium: it doesn't matter whether you're a nice fellow and vote right in presidential elections; all that counts is the box office. If you drag in the customers, you can beat your grandmother and still be a big name.

And now to Risë's strange name, which needs a bit of explaining. She was born Risë Steenberg and took the Stevens from an aunt who had the good sense to marry a nice man with a nice name.

The Risë gave her fits at the start and would perhaps still be doing so if it wasn't for movies and television. From hearing it often enough, people got used to it, but in the beginning printers either didn't have the two little dots for the "ë" or preferred to ignore it. The result was that people called her "Rise" (like getting up in the morning), and printers thought it was a typographical error and made it "Rose." Risë's European friends almost invariably called her "Ree-zay," but around the Steenberg house it was always either "Rees-uh" or "Reez-uh."

Since the Metropolitan is the only permanent opera company in this country, and every singer in the world is trying to break into it, nobody needs to be told that you have to stay on your toes if you want to keep up in that competition. A glorious voice may get you in, but you had better develop all your potentialities if you want to stay in. It is still possible in some European opera houses to plant yourself on a favorite spot on stage and raise your voice in a well-tempered bellow, but that won't get you far in New York. In fact, the example of the Metropolitan has changed opera everywhere. You must learn to sing with distinction and with the proper phrasing and shading and coloring of the voice; you must learn to act; you must learn to use the stage as if you really believed you were the character you were playing. And good looks and a good figure aren't exactly going to handicap you.

There was never any chance that Risë would be anything but a rounded singer, because Walter was always at her elbow to prod her. His favorite phrase was: "We have to stretch you." He stretched her so far at times she thought she was going to snap. It was then she started saying: "But you're so wrong, Walter!" Sometimes he reasoned her out of it, sometimes he ridiculed her out of it, but in the end she always found herself doing it. This was true in her operatic work, although she had ambition enough for eight people and was just as determined as Sadie ever was, but it was even more true in her general career.

"Figure it out for yourself," Walter would say patiently. "You have personality, and you're a success as an opera singer. But that isn't enough; you have to be a national celebrity. So we stretch you."

He stretched her into movies, into radio and television, and into a fabulous concert career. He did this by what he calls "cooking." If that wasn't enough, he resorted to "knitting." He was "cooking" when he got her to the play in Prague with Harriet Henders. He got the idea, cooked it a bit in his mind, and contrived a way of carrying it out. If that hadn't worked, he would have started "knitting," which means scheming and plotting. He knits to perfection, although often Risë would be just as happy if he didn't bother.

But there is another talent he has that Risë calls "goofing." For instance, one night after a concert in Toronto, Walter left her to come back to New York. He had ducked out of the hall after her first number and only reappeared when she had finished. Between times he had been having dinner with a group of his convivial friends. When he said good-by to her at the hotel, Risë won't swear that he was crocked, but he was sailing nicely on an alcoholic cloud. It was late and the thing he wanted to do on that plane was sleep, but he happened to run into Ed Sullivan, and nobody sleeps when Ed has an idea on his mind. He sat down beside Walter and immediately began to talk.

"Can Risë roller-skate?" asked Ed.

"Sure," grunted Walter, out of a haze of sleep and wine. He would have been just as positive if Ed had asked about her pole vaulting.

"Could she appear on the show two weeks from next Sunday?" asked Ed.

"Why not?" replied Walter, and turned his face to the window and went to sleep.

By the time he woke next noon in their New York apartment, Walter was having second thoughts, but it was too late. A messenger had already showed up with a contract from the Sullivan office, and a secretary had called to confirm the date. In a sense the whole thing was Risë's fault, for she had once made the mistake of bragging to Walter that in her early Bronx days she was the Sonja Henie of her block. Ice skating was confined to frozen mud-holes on empty lots, but roller skating was a year-round business, and Risë was really pretty sharp at it.

Walter is a master of attacking when he is in the wrong, and he now went at her with his face beaming with fake elation.

"I've got a wonderful date for you on the Sullivan show!" he cried. "Skating."

"Skating!" Risë screamed in horror.

"Roller skating. You've told me yourself what a whiz you were."

"But that was twenty years ago," she shouted. "I haven't been on a skate since."

"It'll be a cinch for you," he said soothingly. "When you once have it, you never forget it. Two or three days and you'll be skating all over the place. Besides I've promised Sullivan."

"*You* promised him!" she cried. "Well, why don't you go on and do it yourself?"

And that's where he had her. She could tell by the strange elated look that came in his eye.

"Now who would want *me* on a show like that?" he asked with tender modesty. "It's the great Stevens they want to see— the Stevens who can do anything and do it good."

So in due course she was over at some rink near Madison Square Garden and sure enough the skating came back to her and the appearance on the "Ed Sullivan Show" was considered one of her finer theatrical accomplishments. She had to admit that she got a kick out of the skating after she had worked the kinks out of her legs, but for those two weeks she gave Surovy a decidedly cold shoulder. As if he cared! He had stretched her again, and when it was over the newspaper notices were glowing and letters poured in and she had added another small stroke to the picture of herself the public was getting.

In her darker moments she sometimes feels that the public is getting the wrong picture of her, but the results don't seem to show it. Where the effect is most readily apparent is in her concert tours. The Metropolitan is a great showcase for a singer, but no artist will get rich from opera alone. In the days of Caruso phonograph records were a gold mine, but that is no longer true. Part of the cost of making operatic records is now charged against the singers, and great financial returns are not possible. But when a singer has established a concert reputation, there is no end to what can be done. It's a little trite to say that the money rolls in, but that's the truth of it.

But here again . . . there's a trick to it. Some of the finest opera stars are failures in concerts; as the theatrical saying goes, they can't draw flies. What a singer does at a concert is vitally important, but the greatest artist is not going to do much in concert if nobody comes in to listen. Everything being equal, concert audiences prefer to hear artists they are acquainted with. The roller skating neither helps nor hurts Risë as a concert star; it merely makes her better known as a personality. The wise Surovy was aware of this from the beginning and kept stretching her even when she didn't want to be stretched. The result is that for the last fifteen years Risë has averaged forty concerts a year. That means a lot of wearying travel, a lot of work, and a lot of strain, but it also means about $150,000 a year in fees. This is far from being net profit, but it adds to that nest egg that makes her dreams about the Bronx pleasanter.

But when Walter preens himself on his success, Risë has one sure way of bringing him up short.

"What about the 'All Star Revue' with Martha Raye?" she asks maliciously.

This is a curious episode in Risë's life, for the proposition had looked good at the start. Martha Raye was at the peak of her television fame, and her program was a great showcase for a guest star. There is the further circumstance that Risë considers Martha one of the finest of comediennes, and they've had a close personal relationship through the years. But Risë has a sixth sense about audience reactions, and the first rehearsal gave her an intimation of disaster. She found herself working in a sketch with Martha about tossing a salad. Something told her that Martha would never stop with a mere exhibition of herself as an elegant society hostess. She would eventually be tossing that salad all over the landscape. Risë expressed her fears to Walter; perhaps there still might be time to get out of the contract.

"Don't worry," said Walter easily. "Martha'll take care of it."

This was small comfort for anybody who knew Martha. She was not only a hilarious comedienne, but she was a small deadly projectile to boot. If tearing down the scenery got a laugh, she was quite prepared to kick out a wall of the theatre to build the laugh to a roar. But she was moderation itself during rehearsals. Risë retained her doubts, but Walter was there on the side lines with warm support.

"You're *sure*, now?" Risë would ask pleadingly.

"Of course, I'm sure," said Walter. "It'll be a riot."

The performance started quietly enough, with Martha making faint, elegant stabs at the salad—and then it turned into a shambles. Martha belabored Risë with salad; Risë belabored her right back. The audience was in an uproar of delight. The reviews next day were laudatory.

Risë sank back with a sigh of relief—and then the first mail started coming in. It swelled to a tidal wave and was filled with denunciation and reproof. The writers were willing to admit that Martha Raye was funny, but they didn't want Risë funny in the same way. They added that the whole thing had been in bad taste; they had felt squeamish; they resented having their idol tarnished.

Risë was shocked and baffled. The studio audience had been ecstatic; this mail was something else again. It was flattering to find her followers so loyal and concerned, but it was small comfort in view of the avalanche of protest. Walter had got her into the mess. She went in search of him. He had locked himself in his office and was presumably going over the awful evidence. Starvation would eventually get him out; she sat down to wait. When he finally came forth, he had a sheaf of letters in his hand and a calf-like look of repentance in his eyes. Risë said not a word, seething inwardly. He gazed at her for a long minute with an air of transfixed admiration.

"You were brave," he said in a low solemn voice, and bowed his head in reverence.

It was an act right out of the Corn Belt, and instead of hitting him over the head with a candelabra, Risë burst out laughing.

"What can you do with a man like that?" she wants to know.

Chapter Two

The news is of small importance to anybody but Risë, so she will merely say that she was born in a fourth-floor walk-up at 1286 Stebbins Avenue, the Bronx, New York City, on a Wednesday at 7:45 A.M., June 11. The apartment house sat on the corner of Chisholm and was near Westchester Avenue. It was no thing of beauty. Sadie doesn't remember what rent was paid but says that if it was more than $20 a month, they were being robbed. But Stebbins couldn't hold a distinguished family like the Steenbergs for long; they moved to Bergen Avenue, the Bronx. And this time to a *third*-floor walk-up. Real progress.

You will note the precise reference to the birthdate above, June 11. Everybody has to be a little wacky about something, and Risë centers on the number "eleven." Her friends laugh at her, Walter holds his fingers to his nose in derision, and there is general agreement that she is touched in the head, but that doesn't move her in the slightest. Everything good that has ever happened to her has had eleven mixed up in it somewhere. Black cats don't bother her, she would just as soon start a journey on Friday as not, she walks under ladders with aplomb, but she is convinced she would die in room ten if room eleven was available.

The Bronx was vigorous enough, and it was healthful. Risë takes a high line toward people who complain about the confining influence of the city on their children. That may be true about Manhattan, but in her neighborhood on Bergen Avenue they could only have got in more exercise if somebody had invented a forty-eight hour day. They skated right around the clock—either roller skating or ice skating; they played handball and softball till their tongues hung out; they played stickball in the streets; they climbed fences and trees, and when they got a little older, they played basketball till the cows came home. Risë was not only a tomboy, but she had already learned all there was to know about the elbows and the straight arm. She was tall and far from thin. Anybody taking a whack at her got a whack back. In fact, she must have been a sight; rather like the Powerful Katrinka of cartoon fame.

That was a great neighborhood on Bergen Avenue, and the block spirit was terrific. Nobody dared venture far out of his own territory, but within that small area they had a world of their own. In summer everybody hung out their front windows and talked to people in the street or to friends across the street. Fourth of July was simply tremendous. The block was roped off; clotheslines with flags and bunting were hung across the street; lampposts were decorated with flowers. In retrospect it seems to Risë that dancing went on from dawn to midnight, but she admits her memory is probably playing her false. At any rate, there was plenty of dancing when it got started and plenty of drinking, too, and everybody had a hilarious time. The Germans and Irish predominated in that neighborhood, but Risë was never conscious of any prejudice because she had a Lutheran Norwegian father and a Jewish mother. She thinks this was generally true in New York till the Hitler days.

What started her singing was the pianola they had in the parlor. Papa would play it, and Risë would sing along with him. The words were on the rolls, and the favorites were "When Irish Eyes Are Smiling" and "Sylvia." One day Papa looked up and said to Risë almost in amazement: "Why, you know, Risë, you've got a very nice voice." Sadie had been ironing in the kitchen, with the board in the open doorway so she could take part in the fun.

Sadie said in a loud combative voice: "She certainly does!" As if they had been arguing about it in private and she wanted to get her views on record. Pa was always a bit of a defeatist about Risë's singing. She remembers him once saying: "If you can't make best, you can make second best." Sadie almost took his head off for that. "She'll be BEST!" she yelled.

Risë doesn't know where Sadie got all the confidence, because there was no musical background in either of the families that would seem to warrant it. But Sadie was a great one for illusions, and she invented a background. She first began talking casually about singers in general, letting the hint drop that Risë came from a long line of them, and then she actually invented a few mythical aunts who were great opera singers. Pa laughed till he choked.

"Name a few of them," he demanded.

"Well, I can't name 'em," said Sadie, "but I heard about them from my grandmother. They were Poles. They were the toast of Warsaw."

He couldn't very well deny it, but he didn't have to believe it, and he didn't. Sadie went a little easy on him after that, but she kept bearing down on Risë about their musical heritage.

"Why, everybody in this family is musical," she said hotly.

"Who?" Risë asked.

"Your father," said Sadie promptly.

"*Pa?*" Risë cried, not believing her ears. "What does *he* do?"

"He plays the pianola," said Sadie, holding her head aloft proudly.

Pa never really wanted Risë to be a singer. He wanted her to be a commercial artist or a designer. The idea exasperated Sadie.

"She sketches well, huh?" said Pa one day, tentatively.

"She can't draw a straight line!" cried Sadie flatly, which was supposed to be the squelch of all time.

As a matter of fact, Risë wasn't thinking about it at all. Around the corner from the apartment was an Armour packing plant, and that's where her gang spent the Saturdays. The refrigerator room was a three-story structure at the back of the building, and there was a trolley-like affair that went from the top of the refrigerator to the floor. The beeves were taken out of the refrigerator, hooked onto the wire, and sent hurtling down to the trucks below. The plant was closed on Saturday, and if they could sneak by the watchman, they climbed up to the refrigerator, took a tight hold on the hooks, and came down with a crash to the ground.

"By all rights, we should have been killed," says Risë with a shudder.

When they couldn't outwit the packing-plant watchman, they hung by their legs from the iron bars that extended from the sidewalk to the basement in the old brownstone fronts. This is a little hard to explain in print, so we will merely say that if their legs slipped on the bar, they'd land in the paved areaway on their skulls. They were a hardy group and proved it by the mere fact of going to school. They were safe enough in their block on Bergen Avenue, but the school was ten blocks away in alien territory. Along that route there were toughs on every corner, and by the time school was out and they were coming home, there were drunks rolling out of the speak-easies. The gentry that frequented this obstacle course seemed to make no distinction between girls and boys. The children tried to vary the route, but that did little good, and almost every day some girl would get beaten up.

"We met this by traveling in groups," says Risë. "I was the heftiest girl and the target of most of the insults, but I didn't mind so long as we got to school all right. My pet abominations were the speak-easies and the drunks, because I knew about them from personal experience. My father was one of the gentlest men that ever lived, but he drank heavily. His full name was Christian Carl Steenberg, and he was born in Christiania, now Oslo, Norway. His grandfather had been in the importing business and had operated his own ships. The fact that my father was brought over here by his parents at the age of five seems to mean that something had gone wrong with the family business.

"It was a real love match between Sadie and Pa, and that was easy to understand, because he was a fascinating man. Not only was he gay and clever, but he was a romantic figure because of his work. He was a crack salesman and was often away for six months at a time. Sadie would cry her eyes out when he left and cry just as much with joy when he got back. Those happy homecomings are what I remember best. I can still see him on a Sunday morning, getting out the ironing board to press his suit. He would sing and shout while he pressed, and I would be capering around in front of him. Sadie would be getting breakfast and beaming with happiness. He was a small, trim man and always immaculately dressed. He wore starched white shirts; he took a cold shower every morning of his life; he pressed his suits so often you'd have thought he would wear them out.

"He would take us for walks on Sunday afternoons, and those were wonderful affairs. I had no hope that I would ever get farther from home than Trenton, New Jersey, and here was Pa talking along gaily about Chicago and Detroit and Cincinnati. It was pure romance to me, right out of the fairy books. I suppose drinking goes with a traveling man's life, or at least did in those days, but there was also a heritage of drinking in the family. I am told that the Scandinavians are all heavy drinkers, and I guess that's natural in those cold countries. Pa fought hard against it and would be on the wagon for months. Then something would happen, and he'd fall off. He was a fine salesman and could always get a job, but the fact that he changed jobs so constantly seems to be the tip-off. It made a strange life for us. There were weeks when we seemed to be rolling in wealth and others when we had very little. He had weekly commissions as high as $250, an enormous sum in those days. And then there would be the lost job, the hard struggle with the new job, and the bad weeks. It doesn't take a psychologist to figure out where I got my sense of insecurity.

"It was much worse when Sadie sent me to the speak-easies to bring him home. At first I flatly refused to go. I knew those saloons from the daily battle along the streets, and I knew they were no place for a young girl. More than that, I hated them almost with a Carrie Nation zeal. I felt that if I ever passed through those doors, I'd want to break something or hit somebody. Strangely enough, I was willing to go when I had my brother Bud with me. When I had his hand in mine, I took on a new sort of courage. In a symbolic sense I suppose I considered him a man who belonged in a saloon; also I probably realized that they wouldn't hit an infant. None of these rationalizations can hide the fact that the whole thing was a torture for me. I not only loved my father, but I admired him, and the sight of him helpless before those bums and thugs was almost more than I could stand."

This started when Risë was seven or eight years old and continued till they left the Bronx. She still doesn't know whether the moves they made in the Bronx were to better themselves or were steps down. To this day Sadie will not admit that Pa was a drinker. "Oh, a little beer once and a while," she'll say. She thought he was the most wonderful man that ever lived and continued thinking so even when he wobbled in after drinking up his pay check.

Sadie came from a very loyal and close-knit family, which was ruled by the iron hand of her mother. This was the Grandma Mechanic, who had such an influence on Risë's early life. When the Steenbergs moved to Sherman Avenue, Grandma Mechanic had lived across the court. Grandpa Mechanic had died at an early age, leaving Grandma with seven children. The youngest was one year old; the oldest was fourteen. Grandma Mechanic had held the family together by her own efforts—scrubbing floors, working as a housemaid, cooking for the more affluent Bronx families.

By the time Risë got to know her, the oldest Mechanic boys were working and Grandma was installed in the family flat as a matriarch. She read the newspapers faithfully and was informed on everything. She had warmth, good judgment, and authority. Even when the boys were married, they were careful to do nothing that would displease her. If one of them got out of line, she slapped him. Even after her death the family continued to live by her lights. To this day they omit no opportunity for a family reunion; not a day goes by without the members being in touch by telephone.

Sadie had defied her mother's judgment in marrying Chris, but Chris had become her favorite son-in-law. On her deathbed it was Chris that she called to her side. This was her way of showing the family that she had given him the stamp of approval. But in the troublesome days in the Bronx he had been a source of grief to Grandma. She supported Sadie with all her great strength, and she thought hard about the problem. There came a point when she decided that action must be taken. A gathering of the clan was called by Grandma. The sole topic was: what is to be done about Chris?

"I've thought it over, Sadie," said Grandma, "and for the sake of the children and for your sake and even for Chris's sake, there will have to be a separation and probably a divorce."

Sadie simply shook her head in negation.

"But even the children think it's the right thing to do," said Grandma.

To Risë's eternal shame she must confess this is true. Bud was too small to have anything to do with it; she was the one who agreed when Grandma proposed the idea to her. She was torn to pieces by the internal struggle. It seemed to her that Pa would have to go, or she'd go herself. She's forgotten how old she was when this happened, but she couldn't have been much over ten. She was large for her age and wise beyond her years, but she shrinks now at the thought of having been that cruel as a child. But the provocation must have been great if she could even consider running away from a father she loved so well.

But these are useless post-mortems, for there was never any chance that Sadie would leave Pa. Her usual loquacity had deserted her in the family conclave, but she had something even better: a quiet obstinacy that baffled them. They presented the most irrefutable arguments, they appealed to her common sense (of which she had always had a full supply), they pleaded and demanded and threatened—and Sadie merely shook her head.

"You don't understand him," was all she said.

The relatives could certainly agree on that, but they didn't consider it an argument in his favor.

During the Sherman Avenue interim Risë got her schooling at P.S. 10, P.S. 35, and P.S. 38. Why she was shifting around like that, she doesn't remember, but she did all right with the books, and there were fewer speaks and wandering drunks to worry about in that neighborhood. During this time she got her start in show business. Sadie saw an article in the paper about a man named Orry Parado, who took an interest in children, taught them songs, and put them on WJZ's "Children's Hour." Sadie announced that she was going to take Risë in to see Parado forthwith. Pa still had his doubts about matters like this and put up a fight.

"She's too young," he said.

"If she was any older," said Sadie, "she wouldn't be a child."

It was hard to buck an obvious truth like that, and Pa simmered down into a series of grumbles. So Sadie lugged Risë off to Parado, who didn't seem to be doing his selecting with any great particularity, for he accepted her as soon as she got there. It turned out that he was selecting the others the same way, for she found herself in a regular army of ambitious kids. Parado was a kindhearted man who felt that every human being had talent if it were only brought out. He was quite meticulous, however, when he started picking kids for the radio show. A great many of them fell by the wayside, but Risë was in the groove from all that singing with the pianola and got selected right off the bat. Both Pa and Sadie had been right about her from the start: she had a good natural voice. Even then she had a low voice, which was good for Parado's purposes because most of the kids had the high piping yips that were natural for their ages. Risë was a good contrast and was in like a charm.

Every Sunday morning Sadie and Risë went down on the Third Avenue "El" and got off at 42nd Street. They walked across 42nd Street to a building between Fifth and Sixth avenues. The show was on between nine and ten, and she got $5 a week for the labor. Milton Cross was the announcer, and Mr. Parado handled the singers. The kids did solos and joined in such war horses as the "Quartet" from *Rigoletto* and the "Sextet" from *Lucia*. The show must have been pretty good, for it went on for years. Risë doesn't think she got much from it except not to be afraid of a microphone, but fate was to see that she didn't put it entirely behind her. When she made her debut at the Metropolitan years later, whom did she find there as announcer of the Saturday broadcasts? Milton Cross, of course. They had a tearful and joyous reunion, and the effects were still apparent in Cross's voice when he started his broadcast.

You could say that Sadie was a stage mother in the "Children's Hour" days; she had to be. It was either that or hiring an armed guard for Risë. The mothers were there to see that other mothers didn't steal all the good numbers for their children. It sounds much worse than it was, for children are quick to catch on to the lore of show business. The show must go on, they must all be good troupers, they must smile at the success of a rival even when their hearts are breaking.

The mothers didn't take much stock in such nonsense. *They* were the ones the show's producers had to worry about. They were quite prepared to be fair about everything, provided their child was in first place. Otherwise, daggers at dawn. Sadie did all right in that competition, but Mr. Parado was rather a genius at keeping harmony. His platform was very simple: One wrong move, and off the show you go! Losing the five bucks a week was bad enough, but the dishonor was worse. There might be grumbling in the ranks, but there was never open revolt. The resentments of the week disappeared when they went on the air on Sunday morning. To the studio audience they were the happiest little band of juvenile troubadours in captivity.

"We smiled, we bared our teeth in happy jollity, we simpered, we bowed, we were cute and charming. In short, we were the brave hypocrites that all good performers must be in the face of that court of last resort called the audience," recalls Risë.

Several things happened in Risë's Sherman Avenue days that had a direct influence on her life. Her best friend in grammar school was Florence Hynes. They were together so constantly that anybody might have thought them twins, but Risë was very conscious of their differences. She adored Florence and also knew that Florence was better than herself in every respect. Florence was prettier, she was a better dancer, she was far smarter in school, and even Sadie couldn't deny that she was a better singer. Never was there a girl who seemed more certain of being a success in some professional field. And then her mother died, and Florence's ambition died with her. She was seized by a conviction that somehow she had failed her mother. Nothing could have been further from the truth, but Florence had a guilt complex that could only be eased by giving to others the help she felt she had failed to give her mother. Sadie not only had the fullest sympathy for her but understood what she was going through.

It was not hard for her to talk Florence's father into letting her come to live with the Steenbergs.

Sadie hoped that by having the two of them interested in music, Florence would get over her complexes, but she failed. Music became for Florence a form of self-indulgence, a selfishness. She didn't want to do anything that would help herself; she wanted to help others.

"But nobody sings for herself alone," pleaded Sadie. "They sing for everybody."

Florence just shook her head sadly.

After that she refused to sing duets with Risë, and when Risë and Pa sat down at the pianola, Florence went into the other room. It made a great impression on Risë, but mostly as a warning. She remembers saying to herself, in a grit-your-teeth way, "Nobody's ever going to keep *me* from singing."

Not that anybody was trying to keep her from singing; the shoe was now on the other foot. Sadie was determined that she was going to be a singer. While she was sympathetic with Florence's state and refrained from pointing the parallel between the two girls, Risë was quite aware of her feelings.

"I knew that if Sadie died and I gave up singing because of it," says Risë, "she'd come back to haunt me."

The other thing that hit Risë was a blow that got the family out of the Bronx. One afternoon a policeman came to the door of the apartment when Sadie was there alone.

"Are you Mrs. Steenberg?" he asked.

"Yes," said Sadie, her heart beginning to sink. Policemen could only mean bad news to people in that neighborhood.

"There's been an accident . . ." began the policeman hesitantly.

"To my husband?" asked Sadie flatly, never being one to beat around the bush.

"Well, I'm not sure," said the cop, looking at Sadie intently. "He's a pretty old guy. . . ."

It turned out to be Grandfather Steenberg. He had been picked up drunk, as a vagrant, with both legs broken. They had taken him to Welfare Island, and he had died there. They hadn't seen him much over the years and knew he was a big drinker, but this was a shock that couldn't be shaken off lightly. Sadie made up her mind on the spot. They were leaving the Bronx. Her family set up an immediate uproar.

"Where are you going!" they cried in agonized chorus.

"Jackson Heights," said Sadie.

"But we'll never see you again," they wailed. Jackson Heights was only a few miles away across the East River, but to them it sounded like Alaska.

"I don't care where we go," said Sadie, "just so I get Chris away from these men he runs around with."

Pa himself didn't need any convincing: he had been shocked to his shoes by his father's death. He never said in so many words that he had taken the oath, but the move to Jackson Heights proved to be a magical action. He never took a drop of liquor again in any form. He died in Risë's arms in 1952, a much-beloved man.

Compared with the Bronx, life in Jackson Heights was idyllic. Sadie's family found that by making one simple subway change they could get to Jackson Heights with no trouble whatever. They never quite approved of the place, considering it remote and a bit primitive, but they had to admit that Pa was a new man. The Steenbergs were still living on the wrong side of the tracks, 88th Street across Northern Boulevard, but Risë's school (P.S. 127, Queens) was only a few blocks away. There was plenty of open space in Jackson Heights in those days, but Risë was now a grown-up young lady in junior high, with a proper scorn for tomboyish things like baseball on a vacant lot.

She also met another major influence in her life: Jacob Greenberg, principal of the school. Making the change to Jackson Heights had not been easy for Risë, for she still had the Bronx accent that bedeviled her for years and didn't much appreciate the snickers of her new classmates. But if Pa could make the move without complaining, she figured she should be able to take a little riding, so she was quiet like a mouse in class, attentive and very willing. She was at the awkward stage, rather gawky and gangling, and had the misfortune to be tall enough to stick out in a crowd, but she also had been appearing publicly on radio and was not too self-conscious. One day Mr. Greenberg stopped her after class.

"You sing on the "Children's Hour," don't you?" he asked.

"Yes, sir," said Risë.

"Well, there's no reason why you shouldn't be singing here, too," he said almost aggressively, as if he had taken a great decision.

Next morning he had her singing at assembly, and that was her job the rest of her time at P.S. 127, Queens. She often felt a little queer in her homemade dresses, but once she opened her mouth she was all right.

But Mr. Greenberg didn't stop at that. He wasn't a music teacher or an authority on music, but he somehow got the idea that Risë had a future as a singer. He didn't go so far as arranging private lessons for her, but she could tell from the way the music teacher at school treated her that she had been tipped off by the principal to give her a little extra of whatever it was she had. And then one night he came over to the house to talk to Pa.

"Mr. Steenberg," he said, "you have an exceptionally talented child here—and, I think, a potential opera star."

"Pooh!" said Pa.

"You have, too!" said Sadie, just as promptly.

Mr. Greenberg turned in happy amazement to this new source of strength.

"I quite agree with you, Mrs. Steenberg," he said.

"The odds are a thousand to one," said Pa.

"Even so!" said Sadie combatively.

"Even so," agreed Mr. Greenberg, looking at her with admiration.

At the time, it struck Risë as being rather an inconclusive discussion, and it certainly led nowhere while she was still in junior high, but it put the idea in Sadie's head. She had always thought of Risë as a singer, but now she got opera fixed in her mind, and nothing ever after got it out. Risë might never be any good as a singer, but if she sang at all, it was going to be in opera.

Sadie bided her time, and Risë, having nothing better to do, bided it with her.

Chapter Three

Risë's rush to fame was halted abruptly when she started going to Newtown High in Queens. It was in the Elmhurst section and near her old school, but it might as well have been on another planet. It was a huge place, one of the largest high schools in the country, and so crowded that classes were on double shifts. Hundreds of students milled through the corridors, and for the whole first year Risë had a desperate feeling that she had been washed out beyond her depth and would never reach dry land again. It didn't seem possible that an individual could stand out in that mob, but she went to assembly and saw young gods and goddesses performing with success and to acclaim.

This made Risë unhappy, but it made Sadie furious. She couldn't understand why carrier pigeons or semaphore signals hadn't heralded Risë's approach to Newtown High. She seemed to hold Mr. Greenberg responsible, but that poor man was probably as baffled by Newtown High as Risë was. Even if he had friends there on the faculty, it was highly unlikely that they could untrack themselves long enough to welcome a mere freshman. And you might just as well address a letter to a hurricane as to that wild institution. Risë explained all this to Sadie, but it had no effect on her. One morning she announced that she was going right over to that school and tell the principal himself what a treasure they had in their midst.

"If you do," Risë said promptly, "I'll run away and never come back."

Both of them knew that the truant officer would yank Risë back soon enough, but Sadie also knew that Risë could get mulish under pressure. She was having trouble enough getting adjusted without being the center of a controversy over her modest artistic talents. Mr. Greenberg had bolstered Risë up and Newtown High had knocked her down, and she was quite prepared to accept the latter judgment as the sounder. In short, her old inferiority complex was working full time, and she was less concerned with her dubious singing future than in getting established in the school on any basis.

Worst of all, she had grown out of the "Children's Hour" and had nothing to take its place. That had been her stock in trade, the one thing that gave her confidence, and now she felt like a member of an Our Gang comedy who had suddenly grown a mustache. Sadie clung grimly to Risë's past fame and let hints drop among the neighbors that she was merely at liberty, trying to make up her mind about which of several lucrative offers to accept. On a more practical level Risë was carrying on a running battle with Sadie about her clothes. She wanted the hems of her skirts let down; she wanted to look like every other girl in school. Sadie was subconsciously trying to keep her on the "Children's Hour." She never put it that way, for she knew Risë would protest violently, so she always made it a matter of style.

"Don't you want to look a little different?" she asked. "Don't you want to stand out in the crowd?"

"No!" cried Risë tearfully.

What Risë wanted more than anything in the world was to make good at Newtown High. She wanted to look like everybody else, act like everybody else, feel like everybody else. Sadie shrugged her shoulders resignedly—and let down the hems another notch.

Sadie was even more miserable than Risë was during this period. It seemed that her child's musical career was over. There was some talk of getting Risë a private teacher, but one look at the family exchequer put an end to that. Sadie also tried getting jobs for her, but that also failed. The best she could do was singing at the wedding of a neighbor's daughter. Risë did "Oh Promise Me," and the bridegroom later slipped Sadie a five-dollar bill. A small confusion followed, in which Sadie was saying, "We wouldn't think of it; just a favor for a friend," etc., but when they left she had the money firmly in hand.

Sadie then saw an item that there was to be an audition for the chorus at Roxy Theatre, and Risë found herself on her way into the city for that. How Sadie figured that Risë could sing at the Roxy and still keep up classes at Newtown High is a mystery. The chances are she didn't think of it at all; she merely knew that this was a chance for a job, and she wanted Risë to have it. There was another mob scene at the theatre, and the great Roxy himself was handling the auditions. When they worked their way up to him, he said to Sadie in a bored voice:

"What do you want to sing?"

"Me?" said Sadie in astonishment. "Nothing. It's the little girl."

Roxy worked his eyes around to Risë in sad reflection.

"Well, go ahead," he said.

Risë sang, and Roxy rendered his decision to Sadie.

"Not bad, and not good, either," he said. "This child is still wet behind the ears. Get her back to the books."

With the beginning of sophomore year things took a turn for the better. Risë had made a few friends, and her confidence was slowly returning. During the summer gangs of girls would make up parties and go over to Main Street Theatre in Flushing, which was running pictures and vaudeville. They took the streetcar on Northern Boulevard, and it was a great lark. It was a tiny car, the tracks hadn't been repaired in years, and the motorman drove like mad. The girls clung to their seats, yelled with delight, and had a wonderful time. But it was the vaudeville that got Risë back on the track about singing. She said secretly to herself that if she couldn't sing better than some of those up there getting paid for it, she'd eat her hat. So Sadie didn't have to pressure her to go out for the school chorus in her second year; she was going out anyway.

From the look of the first rehearsal it seemed that everybody in school had the same idea. The room was jammed with applicants, and the musical faculty got jittery. Auditioning the singers individually would have taken months, so the pianist struck up a song they all knew, and they were off in a cloud of dust. Just what they felt they were going to get out of an idea like that, Risë doesn't know; but it wasn't long before one of the teachers picked her out—and it wasn't in a nice way, either.

"Who is that singing the wrong note?" she asked sharply, and Risë was more than a little upset when it turned out to be her. She was just starting to say something in extenuation when Miss Anderson broke in.

"That was not a wrong note," she said. "The girl is a mezzo . . . she was singing an octave lower."

As a matter of fact, Risë *had* been singing an octave lower and knew exactly the effect she was trying to get, but with Miss Anderson saying it, it sounded as if she had scored a touchdown in the last minute of play. The other girls seemed to fall back in awe, giving Risë enough space to push out her chest, and the next thing she knew she was off to one side having a private conversation with Miss Anderson.

She was "in" at Newtown High at last. Miss Anderson took her under her wing and trained her in sight reading. She would flash a card, Risë would read the note on the card and sing the note. In no time at all she could do it like lightning. She was also trained in "think tone" method (you think A and sing A) and later taught how to follow hand directions. Most important of all, she was taught how to "hear" music when it was first played. It is much like learning a poem at the first reading. When you have mastered it, you can take in an aria at one gulp and fix it in your brain forever. Without that talent it would take forever to learn an opera and a lifetime to get up a repertory of operas.

Miss Anderson's work led Risë directly to Cornelius Valentine, head of the music department, and that soon got her on the platform of the assembly hall. When she joined the gods and goddesses she had so long worshiped from afar, she found that Newtown High wasn't so large and impersonal after all. Her last months of school were a romp. She sang at assembly, at recitals, and in operettas. Her academic career might be less than spectacular, but she was doing all right in music.

Her high school days ended in a blaze of glory. She was one of the stars of the Band Box Revue, in which she wore a yellow dress, princess style, with one shoulder bare and the other with a flared sleeve. Sadie had worked for weeks on this triumph. Not only did Risë sing, but she did a dance with high kicks. She felt wicked, and she was also sure that she was now a complete success in show business. Mr. Greenberg changed their minds about that. He had attended the performance and now wrote Sadie a letter.

"Risë was very good in the little revue, but she mustn't let that go to her head. Her future is in opera, and she must never forget it."

Risë might forget it, but there was never any chance that Sadie would. Risë thought she had been pretty hot stuff in that revue, and it wouldn't have been hard to talk her into musical comedy, vaudeville, or anything else at the moment, but Sadie had her sights higher. And fate was right at hand to look after things for her: she read in the papers about an organization known as the New York Opéra-Comique, Inc., which was just being started by a group in Brooklyn. Sadie didn't know *opéra comique* from an opera hat, but whenever she heard about anybody giving auditions, Risë was right there.

Opéra-Comique was a serious attempt to establish a second opera company in New York, and it had important financial backing. It was a copy of the Opéra-Comique in Paris, which operates on a more intimate basis than the Paris Opéra but is no less highly regarded because of that. The difference is in the number of performers involved and in the fact that spoken dialogue is permitted in *opéra comique* but that all recitatives in grand opera must be sung. Bizet's *Carmen* was originally produced at the Opéra-Comique in Paris, and it still is a classic production of the theatre. Bizet was dead by the time the Paris Opéra deigned to do it, and a new composer was engaged to write music for the recitatives.

The New York Opéra-Comique had an excellent director in Kendall K. Mussey and a first-class organization in general. It played in two houses: the Little Theatre on St. Felix Street in

Brooklyn, next to the Academy of Music, and the Heckscher Theatre on upper Fifth Avenue in New York. The auditions were held at the Little Theatre, which turned out to be a toy auditorium seating 122 people. There was the usual mob scene, with people milling about and threatening to push over that tiny structure, and this time Risë was in real competition: most of the singers and dancers were experienced and of what she considered a fabulous age. They were in their twenties, but seemed to her to have the maturity of world figures. She was fifteen, and prepared to swear she was eighteen, but her heart sank at the thought of competing with these established professionals. Sadie must have felt the same way, for she became excessively belligerent when they reached the head of the line.

"This girl is a very fine singer!" she blurted out to Mr. Mussey.

"We'll see," said Mr. Mussey sourly.

Risë has forgotten what set piece they were singing, but she remembers very plainly that she felt she had botched it. She didn't follow the accompanist very well, and at one point her voice gave a little quiver out of sheer nervousness.

"Leave your name," said Mr. Mussey. "We'll let you know."

That was the finisher. Risë had been around long enough to know this was the polite way of saying you hadn't made it. The trip home was long, and Sadie must have heated the subway a few extra degrees with her fumings.

"That fellow at the piano," she kept snorting. "Couldn't play a lick."

About two weeks later a letter arrived saying that Risë had been hired for the chorus and the ballet. The salary was $25 a month.

"*Ballet!*" hooted Pa.

"Why not the ballet!" answered Sadie, just as vigorously. "She danced at school."

"High kicks, if you call that dancing," said Pa. "You don't do high kicks in the ballet."

"She'll do something," cried Sadie.

As a matter of fact, the dancing didn't worry Risë too much, even though she was scarcely the perfect ballet type. She might be tall and skinny, but she had the co-ordination that comes from

35

athletics and was as adaptable as a lump of clay. If they said move the left leg, she moved it properly at the first attempt and kept on moving it properly forever after. When Risë told this story to Walter years later, he roared in derision.

"You must have been a sight," he said.

"Maybe so," she replied, "but I could hoof it."

The Opéra-Comique was the best experience of Risë's career, but she had to be in health to stand it. Winter and summer, day after day for two years, she had to be in Brooklyn at nine o'clock every morning for rehearsals. This went in hand with the regular season of performances. After singing till midnight at either the Little or the Heckscher Theatre she made the long haul back to Jackson Heights and was lucky if she got to bed by one o'clock. At seven she had to be up again for breakfast and the endless walk to the subway at 90th and Roosevelt Avenue. If she got a seat on the subway she was lucky. Most of the time she hung by a strap and bumped her forehead against the heel of her hand to keep herself awake. The train made every local stop into Manhattan, and she can still recite the station names like a litany. It was sheer torture. She was young, she was still growing, and she was desperate for sleep. She always had a faint hope that she'd get a seat when she changed trains at Times Square, but there she ran into the crowd headed for Wall Street and only rarely was fortunate enough to slip into an empty place.

She would be more dead than alive when she reached Brooklyn, and on the walk from the subway station to St. Felix Street she would debate with herself whether she preferred the ballet lesson right away or later. She had no choice in the matter, but the routine sometimes varied, and it was a question of doing it in the early flush of dawn or later when she had got her second wind. The morning session was divided into half-hour periods, and there was no dawdling. There were no excuses for being late, and they worked without a break from nine till twelve. Everything was done with professional precision and thoroughness, and only a dumbbell could have gone through it without being affected by it. After she got warmed up, Risë enjoyed every minute of it and forgot all about being tired and sleepy. In addition to the ballet, there were sessions in Shakespeare and acting, sight reading, counterpoint, and harmony. Risë remembers that they had discussions at home about the Shakespeare. Pa thought it was rather a nice idea, Sadie couldn't see what the purpose of it was, and Risë had her doubts about it. When she once told this to Walter, he looked at her in astonishment.

"What kind of people were you, anyway!" he demanded.

"Well, it really didn't seem to have much to do with singing," she said in an aggrieved tone.

"It was a chance in a lifetime," he cried. "If you couldn't make it as a singer, you could have been an actor. You'd have been a great actor."

Maybe so, but at the time she couldn't see the point of Old Bill of Stratford. She read the plays and eventually acquired a nice round way of saying the lines, but she was only going through the motions. It was only later that she understood what they were trying to do. It was part of the general culture that any artist needs who wants to get the most from a part. The broader you are as a personality and the more you have to impart intellectually, the better you do whatever it is you're doing. That holds true in life as well as in opera. Risë lays no claims to being a Shakespearean scholar, but she wouldn't give anything for that experience in the Opéra-Comique. If you're never going beyond high school, Shakespeare is a pretty good substitute for college.

Sadie is convinced that Risë was a star the minute she stepped into Opéra-Comique, but she did the chorus and ballet stint a long time before she got her first small part. She learned how to carry herself, how to walk, and how to stand gracefully. By degrees she picked up that indefinable thing known as "stage presence." Some performers have a mildly successful career without ever really acquiring it. It's the quality of knowing exactly where you are every minute you're on stage. It has a great deal to do with balance and vision and animal instinct. Great athletes have it: they are always in the right place.

At the noon break for lunch Risë usually had a ham and swiss on rye and a glass of milk at the corner drugstore. On $25 a month you don't eat at a Stork Club; you're lucky to eat at all. She was not only sleepy, but she was hungry. Sadie had wanted to pack her a lunch, but Risë put up a howl of protest at the very idea. A member of the Opéra-Comique eating out of a paper bag! She would rather perish of malnutrition. But she didn't kick too hard when Sadie slipped an apple or an orange in her handbag when she left in the morning. At first she ducked around to the side of the drugstore and munched the fruit in secret, but she stopped that when she found that her associates were either enjoying home snacks of their own or wished they had them to enjoy.

The afternoon session was her meat: that is when they learned the operas. They were doing *Orpheus in Hades, La Vie Parisienne, The Chocolate Soldier, The Marriage of Figaro, Beggars Student, The Poacher, The Bartered Bride,* and *Die Fledermaus.* Risë's primary job was to learn the chorus parts, but she never stopped at that. She learned her own part and all the other parts. She is not particularly a "quick study," but she is an everlasting retainer. But in the meantime she was stuck in the chorus. She wasn't complaining, but she knew she had to escape. Having a good voice and being young and beautiful didn't seem to be any good; the months passed, and she was still in the chorus. She began to do a little thinking.

In a musical comedy a chorus girl can attract attention by her looks or her big smile or by the way she wiggles her rear. That doesn't go in opera, even comic opera. There had to be another way, and Risë was determined to find it. She knew that mugging would get her nowhere except back to Jackson Heights, out of a job. She knew that jazzing up her chorus routine would have the same result. She kept her eyes open; she gradually began to catch on.

"What does it is intensity of feeling," Risë says. "If you feel it hard enough, it somehow comes through."

She has since had confirmation of this theory from an old friend, who has been an inveterate theatregoer for the past fifty years. When she asked him what stuck in his memory after that long experience, he laughed apologetically.

"You'll not believe this," he said, "but when I close my eyes and think back on the theatre, it isn't Mrs. Fiske or John Barry-

more or Miss Cornell I recall. I always see a little, blond, plump
Russian girl who sang in the chorus of the *Chauve-Souris,* that
wonderful show they brought over from Moscow at the end of
the First World War. The star of the show was the droll master of
ceremonies, Bailieff, but I can scarcely remember him. But I see
that girl as plainly as if I were still in the audience. She sat on
the floor in a rollicking song number and was so gay and intent
and dominating that I don't think anybody saw the other members
of the cast at all!"

Risë certainly never had this effect on the audiences, but she
could feel somehow that she was getting across. Sadie had been
saying all along that she was not only the best in the chorus but
could sing rings around most of the cast. That might have been
true, but it evidently wasn't getting back to the management.
Then one morning at rehearsal the stage manager waved a hand
generally in Risë's direction and said:

"You there in the second row . . . Skinny! Come down here!"

That is how she discovered she was going to get a small part.

The opera was *The Poacher* by Albert Lortzing, and Risë
played Countess von Eberbach. It was nothing to write home
about, but it was a start. Sadie and Pa were on hand for opening
night, and Risë sang well enough, but the anti-climax that followed was rather painful. Her success obviously called for a
celebration, but the combined family assets were on the light
side. They settled for a little hole-in-the-wall restaurant near the
theatre, where Sadie and Pa had hamburgers and coffee, and
Risë had two crullers and a glass of milk. They then took the
subway back to Jackson Heights.

Her next role was Prince Orlofsky in *Die Fledermaus,* the
Johann Strauss operetta, which she later sang at the Metropolitan
with somewhat better success. But she was making progress with
the Opéra-Comique and now began to cash in on the work she
had done on the operas. When anybody failed to appear at rehearsal, she was right there to volunteer her services. The high
point was when she filled in for a tenor. Everybody laughed,
but it saved a rehearsal, and that did her no harm with the big
shots. Risë doesn't want anybody to get the idea that she did

nothing but work. That company was great for social life, and she had a couple of boy friends who felt that sleep was something that should be reserved for the afterlife. The result was that she began getting home later and later, which made the morning arousal excruciatingly painful.

"Oh, Sadie," she would moan. "Call 'em and tell 'em I'm dead or something."

"No, sir!" said Sadie firmly. "You get right up. It's your own fault if you want to run around half the night."

Since she couldn't very well deny it, she would drag herself out and start the long trek to Brooklyn. The rest of the company could sleep on Sunday, but she didn't even have that break. In her senior year at Newtown High she had got a job in the choir at the St. James Episcopal Church in Elmhurst, and later she had been made soloist. That brought in $20 a week, and there was no possible chance that she could give it up. Since he had stopped drinking, Pa had a steady job, but this was barely enough to keep their heads above water. Risë was at an age when she needed better clothes, and had a figure that was hard to fit. They needed every cent they could get in the house, and she appeared every Sunday morning in church with what she hoped the pew-holders would consider an angelic expression. Half of the time she was so tired she could barely see the organist.

At the theatre she was making progress, but the theatre itself was not doing well. The Little seated 122 people, as has been said, and the Heckscher had 700, but expenses were so great that even with sold-out houses the company lost money. The singers tried to close their eyes to the inevitable, but the handwriting was on the wall. The backers kept putting up new capital bravely, but it was only a question of time till the theatre would have to close. It was a dilemma that couldn't be solved: if the company took a larger house, the intimacy of the performances would be lost; staying as they were, ends could never be made to meet.

In short, Risë was just hitting it right with the Opéra-Comique when the sad news came at the end of the second season. The Opéra-Comique was through, and Risë was through. She spent two days in bed catching up on sleep and then started the weary rounds. It was summer, and there were no openings for a singer. She landed with a dress house on West 37th Street, modeling coats. The pay was $28 a week, she specialized in fur coats, and it was one of the hottest summers in the records of the New York weather bureau.

Chapter Four

Along about July she thought she was going to die at the modeling job, but she stuck it out. As a matter of fact, it wasn't much worse than the usual New York summers, and they had never bothered her before, but those fur coats got heavier and more suffocating by the day. She kept doggedly at it, managing the fake smile and the long slinky walk of the good model, but she thought the summer would never end.

One night she dragged herself home after a particularly humid day, and all she could think of on the long walk from the station was a cold bath and an hour's nap before dinner. Sadie met her at the door in some excitement to say that there had been a telephone call for her.

"Madame Shenn something," she reported. "I didn't get it good. She had an accent. The number's there."

"Madame Schoen René?" Risë cried in agitation.

"I don't know," said Sadie. "You'd better call her."

Madame Schoen René was one of the best-known voice teachers in New York. Everybody in the profession looked up to her, and she had been pointed out to Risë at performances of the Opéra-Comique. She was a small, compact, manly-looking woman who resembled a miniature Field Marshal von Hindenburg. The stories about her in musical circles were legend. She conducted her classes like a military campaign, and anybody who didn't like it got thrown out on his ear. Risë was a twittering wreck when she called, and Schoen René didn't waste any small talk on her.

"I'm offering you a scholarship for next year," she said bluntly. "Do you want it or don't you?"

"Of course, I want it," Risë said in a flutter, "but I——"

"If there are any 'buts,'" said Schoen René brusquely, "come in and see me about it."

The "but" was that Risë couldn't afford to take a scholarship. It would take care of her education, but it wouldn't help at home. Even going in to see Madame was costing her a day's work at the dress house. On the way down Risë had debated how she could break the news to Madame without offending her. One look at her was enough to show that this was one individual you didn't shilly-shally with: Risë laid her cards hastily on the table.

"Simplest thing in the world," said Madame promptly, and began writing on a little card. "Take this over to the man and tell him I sent you."

The man turned out to be Marshall Bartholomew, later to be a professor of music at Yale and then director of the chorus for the "Palmolive Beauty Box Theatre" on radio. The studio used six boys and six girls in the chorus, and Gladys Swarthout was star of the show. Mr. Bartholomew listened to Risë sing, but she could tell she was going to get the job anyhow on Madame's recommendation. The pay started at $80 a week, and she almost ran back to Jackson Heights with the news. Sadie tried to keep a level head on her shoulders, but she didn't object too strongly when Pa went out with their last money and bought a steak. They couldn't celebrate Risë's debut with the Opéra-Comique, but this was another matter: she was now in the upper financial brackets. At least in those circles. They laughed, and chewed away happily at the steak, and considered that the world had opened up in most pleasant fashion.

Risë stayed two years with the Palmolive show, raising her salary to $100 a week and eventually working into small roles. Gladys Swarthout was not too happy about this, for their voices

lay in the same range, but there was never any real conflict about
it. Swarthout was a satellite among opera stars, and Risë was a
mere flickering light in the sky. She was content with what they
gave her and certainly was no opposition for Swarthout. They
did an exceptionally good *Madame Butterfly* together, in which
Risë sang Suzuki and Gladys—although she never did Cio-cio-san
at the Met—was at her best in the star role. Risë enjoyed every
minute on the Palmolive show and was sorry when it was all
over for her. The money made all the difference in the world
at home.

In the meantime, she was being put over the jumps by Madame
Schoen René. She was a martinet, a Prussian drillmaster, a ty-
rant—and she changed Risë's life. Risë might not have been able
to take the beatings if it hadn't been for a short speech Madame
gave her at the beginning. Fixing her with an eagle eye, Madame
said, "If you weren't good, you wouldn't be here. I don't have
failures in my class; I get rid of them. Now, do you want to work,
or is singing merely a fad with you?"

"I said I wanted to work," reports Risë, "and I said it in a hurry,
too. She had me so hypnotized by that eye, I was afraid she
might leap at me if I said the wrong thing. And, of course, I was
sincere; I needed work and wanted to work. And she was as bad
as Mr. Greenberg at hammering opera, opera at me. 'Anybody
can be a singer,' she would cry. 'You're going to be an *opera*
singer. You're going to be a *big* opera singer.' She always looked
at me defiantly, as if I were going to talk back, but I never had
the nerve for that, and in truth I agreed with her perfectly: I was
going to be an opera singer or bust. There was never any doubt in
my mind about that after the Opéra-Comique experience. Everything about opera suited me. I felt at home in it; I liked the
combination of orchestra and conductor and singers and chorus
and costumes and scenery. And I never really had any doubt
about making good in opera. That sounds boastful, but it is the
truth."

The meeting with Schoen René marked the end of Sadie's reign
as Risë's guiding light. They never talked about it, but Sadie
was wise enough to realize that in higher musical matters she
was out of her depth. When Rise needed a bit of hardheaded

practical advice, she went home to Sadie, but Schoen René had become her new musical mother. Without really being conscious of it at the time, Risë became a dedicated character. Schoen René furnished the knowledge and pulled the strings, and Risë did the work. Under Madame's critical eye it never occurred to Risë to balk at her orders or to resent the routine she was going through.

Schoen René came by her sense of discipline naturally: her father had been state forester in Prussia under Bismarck. Really he was under the government in Berlin, but Schoen René always spoke of Bismarck, as if there was a personal relationship between her father and the great man. Her father was in charge of the Black Forest, accountable for the planting, cutting and replanting. She once said that her father had made the Black Forest famous, but that may have been stretching it. She had been an opera singer in Europe herself until her career was cut short by an attack of scarlet fever. After vainly trying the usual cures, she went to the famous Spanish teacher, Garcia, who was then in Italy. Her musicianship must have made an impression on him for after she had tried to sing, he had shaken his head sadly and said:

"No, no; the voice is gone, but that is not the end of the world. You must teach. Everything about you tells me you have a genius for it."

That didn't make up to Schoen René for the fact that her last chance as a singer was gone—in truth, she never got over it—but it was something to have the great Garcia encourage her as a teacher. She quickly acquired a reputation in Europe and brought it intact to New York with her. It was a lucky break for Risë when Madame took her on, but she sometimes wonders if she'd have jumped at it so eagerly if she had known what she was in for. That whole first year with Schoen René she did nothing but practice scales: La-la-la-la-LAH; LAH-la-la-la-la. Once a week on the Palmolive show she had a chance to sing—and then back again to the blasted scales.

Secretly she had a feeling that Madame was carrying it a bit too far. Hadn't she sung major roles with the Opéra-Comique? There were even clippings to show that she had been treated well by the New York critics. But if she uttered so much as a light sigh of impatience, Madame fixed her with a murderous eye and she hastily la-la-la-la'd some more. Madame was determined to extend the range of Risë's voice and kept hammering at her day after day to that end. There finally came a point when Risë blew up.

"I can't do it!" she wailed. "I simply can't do it!"

The next thing she knew, Madame had yanked her elbow viciously, given her a thunderous push from the rear, shoved her through the door, and slammed it behind her. Risë stood trembling in the corridor. Her first reaction was rage and resentment; her next was tears. She huddled against the wall and sobbed. It was as if her whole physical system was shattered; she couldn't stop crying. But when she had cried herself out, she knocked timidly at the door.

"Come in," said the stern voice.

Risë opened the door slowly and looked around with fear. With an impatient wave of the hand Madame motioned her to come back to the piano.

"Never say 'can't' in my presence again," she said sternly.

That was all. Risë went back to doing the scales.

It could be said that Schoen René was Risë's Svengali, but she was also the best friend she ever had. She taught her poise and dignity. She propounded questions to her about public issues and literally withered her with scorn if she answered sloppily or with the usual clichés.

"Think!" she would cry, tapping her brow furiously. "Think with your own mind. What is your head for!"

Risë never became an authority on national affairs, but to this day she is careful about not making a fool of herself in discussions. If she doesn't know the answers, she refrains from pretending she does.

And Madame simply pounded the Bronx accent out of Risë. Risë doesn't think she talked like one of Arthur Kober's Bronx characters, but she must have had the lilt and the intonations. Whenever she used a word or expression that marked her as Bergen Avenue, Madame mimicked her most disagreeably. Since Madame had a German accent of her own, Risë wasn't inclined to consider her the last authority on the subject of pure speech, but she was eventually forced to admit that Madame was right and she was wrong. So far as Risë knows, there isn't a trace of the Bronx left in her. That is, of the Bronx accent; the Bronx itself is with her every minute.

Once a week she had dinner at Madame's apartment, and that was another step in her development. Madame had a wonderful cook, and the dinner was always served as if she expected a grand duchess to drop in. Since the Steenbergs generally ate in the breakfast nook at home, this was an advance for Risë, and she wasn't too comfortable at the beginning. Madame was tact itself in overlooking her awkwardness, and Risë learned by watching. Madame always had other guests for dinner, and they were intellectuals like herself. They talked casually about books and paintings, theatre and opera, and it was months before Risë dared open her mouth. Madame pressed books on her and watched her other reading like a hawk. Risë has always liked detective stories, but it was almost a capital offense if Madame caught her with one. She would snatch the book from her and hurl it across the room—much as if she had just picked an asp off her collar.

Although she was a hard taskmaster in the studio, Madame was a mother to Risë in other ways. She worried about her health, she worried about the boys she went out with ("not good enough for you; they'll just distract you"), she wrote out elaborate diets for her ("the figure must be just right; someday you will do *Rosenkavalier*"), she never let her leave the studio without looking out the window anxiously to view the weather ("take this scarf; I don't need it any more; it's an old one"). Although she had got Risë the Palmolive job, she never approved of it and was fearful that they'd ruin her voice. Risë doesn't know what she'd have done without the radio work; those infernal scales had worn her down to the point of screaming. In addition to the lessons, Madame piled her high with musical study homework, but it wasn't satisfactory. Risë had been used to studying in a group and couldn't concentrate when alone.

"No," said Madame, at the end of a year. "It won't work. You'll have to go to Juilliard."

"How?" Risë asked.

"Get a fellowship!" said Madame heatedly.

"How?" Risë persisted.

"I'll get it for you, you *Dummkopf!*" Madame exploded furiously.

And, of course, she did, since she was one of the top teachers at Juilliard. As far as Schoen René's services were concerned, the change meant nothing at all to Risë. Madame was the only voice teacher she ever had at Juilliard; she simply carried on the old routine in a new setting. But Risë had a full scholarship in the other branches, and that was what counted. She took languages, counterpoint, harmony, theory, history of music, and piano. She still plays a bad piano and doesn't know why. She had the best teachers and tried hard enough, but at the end of the first year they threw up their hands and said: "Forget about it: *sing!*"

By this time even Madame Schoen René was letting her sing. She still "vocalized" till she was blue, but the class began studying operatic roles and Risë started playing them. As a matter of fact, she had begun to arrive when she reached Juilliard. The Opéra-Comique had been invaluable experience, and the year with Madame had put a new polish on her. She knew how to sing, and she knew how to make people notice her. After a few performances Albert Stoessel, the music director, began hunting parts for her. Under Schoen René's pounding, she was now a full-fledged mezzo-soprano instead of a contralto, but leading roles for mezzos are limited. She managed enough of them, however, to get an established place in the company, and it was only a question of perfecting the parts. Of course, that wasn't possible in the limited setting of Juilliard, but it added to her Opéra-Comique experience and gave her the foundation that she still depends on.

The Palmolive engagement ended after two years, but this time Risë wasn't afraid of starving to death. Bread-and-butter money for most of the Juilliard singers came from church work. Risë had given up her Elmhurst church job after going with Schoen René, but the New York positions were even better. They paid $25 and $35 a Sunday, and singers who were later to be international celebrities were then living on it. Most of the bookings were handled by a Mr. Price, a kindly little man in a tiny cluttered office in Steinway Hall. Risë put her name on his list and almost immediately began getting engagements. Mr. Price was a little hurt that she wouldn't take a permanent post in a big Newark church, but she was weary of travel by this time, and New Jersey seemed on another continent. He spotted her around town in various churches, and she began to find that she felt most at home with the Episcopal service. She had been raised a Methodist and in her Bronx days had won a pin every year for steady attendance in Sunday School. Those were the happiest of her Bronx memories and she can still recall with pleasure the little Easter entertainment and the Christmas shows, but now suddenly she knew that she wanted to be an Episcopalian.

"This is probably important only to me," says Risë, "and I mention it because I discovered for the first time that I had a deep religious nature. I had always liked going to church, but now I realized that religion meant a great deal to me in a fundamental way. I don't carry it about like a flaming torch, but it has helped me through some bad spots, and I am in essence a religious person."

Curiously enough, the first effect of this new feeling was a defeat. She wanted most desperately to sing at the Cathedral of St. John the Divine. Mr. Price arranged for an audition, the musical director at the cathedral said he would let Risë know, and after some nervous waiting Risë called Mr. Price for the decision.

"Not yet," said Mr. Price. "Maybe later."

After six months she tried again, and the verdict, if anything, was worse.

"Not good enough yet," reported Mr. Price. "That's what they said. Maybe later."

There never was any later, for she was busy enough without it and recognized a beating when she saw it. Juilliard was buzzing those days, and she had plenty to do. And Madame and Risë had plans for the future that didn't include Juilliard. Risë had been hoarding her Palmolive money like a squirrel. Part of it went for the household budget; the rest she delivered almost intact to a savings bank. At intervals she would take out the bank book, look at it with a frown, and begin counting on her fingers. Schoen René was in on the secret—in fact she had put the idea in Risë's head—and she kept checking on her.

"How much now?" she would ask, and Risë would report the

49

latest audit, with interest as of to date. Madame would look dole-
ful, gaze off into space as if making calculations in her head,
and then say: "Well, keep on."

At the end of the second year at Juilliard she called Risë in
one day, looked at her severely, and said with decision:

"The time is now!"

"But I haven't got enough," Risë cried.

"We'll make it enough," Madame said sternly.

They sat down with the little bank book and began to figure.
Round trip on the ship, tourist class, so much. Tips, so much.
Railroad fares in Europe, so much. *Pension* in Salzburg, so much.
Clothes, so much. Incidentals, oh, *far* too much.

"I will make up the difference," said Schoen René promptly.

"Oh, but, Madame——" Risë protested.

"You will pay me back when you are famous, no?" said Madame, trying to look fierce, and failing. Risë paid it all back after
she was famous.

Madame would never listen to any discouraging talk on the
subject. She had been disappointed in other promising pupils and
was determined that Risë was going to make it. The slightest
mention of doubt infuriated her.

"But I'm doing pretty well here," Risë once said, and thought
Madame would take her head off.

"It is nothing!" she cried in rage. "It is for children. You have
not begun to learn."

This was an unjustified knock at Juilliard, and a reflection
on her own abilities as a teacher, but such considerations never
swayed Madame. She would just as well announce her views at
a Juilliard board of directors meeting.

"It is Gutheil-Schoder you need," she went on. "There you will
really learn."

Maria Gutheil-Schoder was the great Viennese soprano who
was the greatest of Octavians in *Rosenkavalier*. Illness had halted
her career and she was now teaching in Salzburg. Schoen René
had her own pride as a teacher, but it never occurred to her that
she was in Gutheil-Schoder's class as an interpreter of Richard
Strauss. She had no envy, no pettiness; on the contrary, Risë

thinks Madame would have dragged her physically to the presence of Gutheil-Schoder if she had balked.

It turned out that Risë's meager savings would pay only for the passage; Madame would provide the rest. She next proposed that Risë give up the idea of traveling tourist and come up with her in first class: she would pay the difference. Risë refused, there were weeks of heated discussion about it, and Risë finally won. In all the years of their association, Risë had only two victories over Madame. The last came much later and will be treated in the proper spot. In their arguments about first class and tourist Madame made a priceless remark. In a mild way Risë had hinted that possibly Madame's insistence on going first class proved that she was too conscious of social position and reputation. Madame replied in all wonderment and sincerity: "Why, I'm a very simple person; I merely want the best."

As a matter of fact, the arrangement made little difference, for Madame invited Risë up for dinner in first class every night. She ate in elegant surroundings, danced demurely with elderly gentlemen in the lounge, and then at midnight, like Cinderella, disappeared into the bowels of the ship. Down there she was bunking in a small cabin with three schoolteachers from Ohio. They were nice girls, and Risë could see that they were hurt by her nightly escape into fairyland: it seemed a reflection on them. All day long they ran around together, happy as bees; at night Risë turned her back on them. That night at dinner she suggested to Madame that it might be fun to go down and watch the dancing in tourist. Madame laughed a little sarcastically.

"I wondered how long you would be," she said. "Go along now and join the barbarians; you won't be happy any other way."

Risë was happy enough to get out of first class. Tourist class was jumping in those prewar days, filled with gay and handsome college students, and she knew she was missing a lot. When the orchestra packed up and left around midnight, a young fellow from Penn State with an accordion kept the riot going until they finally dropped from exhaustion. It was a wonderful trip, and it ended with Risë a wreck. She chased around all day at shuffleboard and deck tennis; had a formal dinner with Madame; charged back down for the dancing, and tumbled in bed around dawn. As if that wasn't bad enough, the time changes were killing her.

"You'd think it was midnight," says Risë, "and then you'd see the clocks had been put ahead an hour and it was one o'clock. I've been trying ever since to get back the sleep I lost on that voyage."

But a week in Paris revived her, and she was in high spirits when Madame led her off to Salzburg. Madame introduced Risë to Madame Gutheil-Schoder, entered her at the Mozarteum, established her in a small *pension*—and went off to Vienna to see old friends. The *pension* was clean and nice, but Risë was alone and utterly helpless in conversational German or French. She had learned operatic roles in those languages, but that didn't help her when she needed a direction from a policeman. At the Mozarteum she held up the whole procession by requiring an interpreter for anything that went on, and she could see they didn't have high hopes for her future. Aside from the fact that they specialized entirely on Mozart, the Mozarteum was something like Juilliard. They had the usual harmony and counterpoint, but they particularly stressed the interpretation and stage direction of the Mozart operas.

She did much better with Madame Gutheil-Schoder. Gutheil-Schoder had a heart condition and hid her paleness with excessive rouging, but she was a tall, handsome, fascinating woman. She was thin and held herself stiff as a ramrod, but she had great elegance and charm. She concentrated on two operas, *Rosenkavalier* and *Salome,* in both of which, her adoring followers assured Risë, she had never had an equal. After a few lessons Risë could quite believe it. Madame's first words about the role of Octavian in *Rosenkavalier* convinced her.

"It is almost impossible to sing," she said. "You MUST act it well."

One day when she was explaining to Risë what was necessary for a woman to play a man's role like Octavian, she suddenly pulled her skirts well above her knees, exposing a beautiful pair of legs.

"Madame!" screamed her associates in horror.

"Pfui!" cried Madame, in disgust. "A leg is a leg. Nobody ever died over a leg."

She then gave Risë a full explanation of the differences between man and woman.

"The stance is different entirely," she said. "When a woman walks, she sways from the hips; a man walks directly, straight, with the full foot on the floor. You must *rearrange* your legs when you play Octavian. They are no longer your legs; they are a man's legs. Your brain must know it; your body must feel it. Your shoulders must not move; your legs must be straight; your body must be straight. You must *never, never* think you are anything but a man."

There was an amazing transformation before Risë's eyes. Striding about the room with her skirts held high, Gutheil-Schoder's legs miraculously became a man's legs. They turned inward and seemed to become firmer and more masculine. She walked with the decisive clump of a man, but with the nonchalance and slight pomposity of the fake Octavian. It was an astonishing performance; it made Risë know once and for all how the part must be played.

Risë can't say that the Salzburg experience was one of the happiest times of her life, for the language barrier made her miserable, and she was very homesick. She worked harder than was necessary, had almost no social life, and came away with a feeling that she had failed. It was only later, in New York, that she had repayment for her labors. Madame Gutheil-Schoder wrote to Madame Schoen René.

"Have no worries," she wrote. "Risë is one of the most interesting pupils I have ever had. She already shows signs of being a great Octavian."

She had no idea what this would mean for Risë, and Risë would never have a chance to tell her. Madame Gutheil-Schoder died a year later.

Chapter Five

The Salzburg experience ruined Risë in a certain sense: she could hardly wait to get out of Juilliard and back to Europe. Ordinarily, she would have been pleased with the job she now had on the Sigmund Romberg radio show, but she was bored with it. She liked the money she was getting and began hoarding her share of it again in the savings bank, but she felt she was trapped in a gilded cage.

"It was the most unhappy year of my life," she says now.

And she knew she was going to have trouble with Juilliard. They wanted her for a fourth year, and she didn't see how she was going to last out the third. She wanted the Juilliard diploma, but she wanted Europe even more. She finally finished the three-year course, which entitled her to a diploma, but she didn't get the diploma itself until years later.

"I've forgotten whether they held it back," says Risë, "or I ran away so fast they hadn't time to give it to me. I know they were angry with me for not staying the fourth year."

And there were other serious matters to be decided. Through the grapevine she knew that Edward Johnson, head of the Metropolitan, had his eye on her and had shown a decided interest in her for *Rosenkavalier*. The idea that he might offer her a contract at the Metropolitan never occurred to her, but she kept her head when it happened. She said she would let him know, and went off to confer with Madame Schoen René.

"Well, you'll take it, of course," said Madame, fixing her with a hard and questioning eye.

"No," said Risë.

"*Ooray!*" cried Madame, throwing up her hands in delight. "I knew you wouldn't."

Risë's heart was set on the Metropolitan, and one might have thought she would have leaped at the chance to get in at an early age, but she knew that when one entered as a minor artist, it took superhuman effort to get to the top. Since she had no warning of the offer, and had not talked to Schoen René about it previously, it must be admitted that she showed courage in making the decision.

"Oh, I was scared, all right," admits Risë, "but I just knew I wasn't ready for it. I was too young, and I didn't know enough. Afterwards, I had qualms about it, and felt I had probably lost a chance that wouldn't come again, but by that time I was on the boat for Europe and too happy to care much."

During the year another incident occurred that has since led to some small controversy among her friends and family. Juilliard urged her to enter the Metropolitan Auditions of the Air, and she reached the finals without too much trouble. She lost to Anna Kaskas in the finals, and it has since been hinted that she lost deliberately out of fear that she might be committed to the Metropolitan if she won. Risë scoffs at this.

"I got licked," she says inelegantly. "Anna won it, and that's all there was to it. The Met couldn't have hog-tied me and dragged me in, if I hadn't wanted to go."

So she was set for Europe, and there was the usual small thing to worry about: finances. This time it wasn't a matter of a few months' vacation; she would stay until she had either made good or had failed and given up. There wasn't much chance of the latter happening, for she had long since made up her mind that nothing was going to stop her singing, even if she was reduced to work in a country choir. But these lofty sentiments meant little in the face of the financial crisis. She went into the usual huddle with Schoen René, hinting that her ambitions might be a little too high for her abilities. Madame was immediately furious.

"You will get no more lessons from *me!*" she said heatedly. "That I can assure you. You must *go!* You must *get out!*"

"Yes, but how?" asked Risë.

Madame yanked her by the arm and practically threw her into a chair.

"Show me that bank book," she demanded.

Short perusal of the document proved that there was little to be expected from that source. Madame looked off into space, as was her wont.

"Come with me," she said decisively.

Their destination proved to be the Corn Exchange Bank, where they huddled with sundry blackcoated gentlemen and arrived at a deal. The loan was made on Madame's signature, and a line of credit was extended with a top limit of $5000. The gentlemen asked what Madame would like as a starter.

"One thousand dollars," she said promptly.

Risë was stunned and came out trembling.

"Why so much?" she asked, seeing her fortune already melting away.

"You may not eat, but you're going to look nice," said Madame decisively. "Come along now; we'll get you some clothes."

Risë was determined not to use the money except for emergencies, but it went fast enough when they reached Europe. To the disgust of Madame, Risë again went tourist on the ship, but Madame resolutely put her foot down at anything but first class on the European trains. After a few days in Paris they went on to Germany, where Risë was thrilled by seeing Geraldine Farrar having tea at the Hotel Adlon in Berlin, the scene of her early triumphs. Madame deposited Risë temporarily at Salzburg again, where she attended the Mozarteum for special classes in stage direction with Dr. Herbert Graf, who has now been stage director at the Met for many years. This took two months' time and more of her money than she liked to think about, and then she was hauled back to Paris, where Madame awaited her.

"From now on," said Madame in a sepulchral voice, "it will be you against the Fates. I will not be here to help you. Before I go, I will do the last thing for you."

The last thing was introducing her to Eric Simon, prominent in musical affairs in France and talent scout for the Metropolitan in Europe. The Simons proved to be a second family for Risë. She lived in a *pension* but took her meals at the Simon house and met their friends. This was highly pleasant and flattering to a young American girl, and the world was justified in thinking that all her problems were solved now that she was under the wing of Simon, but the facts proved to be otherwise. Simon might propose, but the directors of the European opera houses had ideas and complications of their own. Because of the two months at Salzburg, Risë had started late in seeking a connection. She traveled down to Zurich with Simon for an audition and was turned down because all places in the company were filled. The same happened at the other cities already mentioned. Risë's money was running out in small rivulets, and she became panicky.

"Now, now," said Simon consolingly. "They all say you sing well, and *I* tell you you sing well. It is only a question of time."

This was small consolation for Risë, who faced the oncoming winter with a sense of bleakness. She had a bitter feeling that she was letting down her family, Madame Schoen René, the Corn Exchange Bank, and the United States of America. Simon partially revived her spirits by insisting that she do her practicing in the Simon home, and in fact he went further by playing for her and coaching her. One day they were going at it hot and heavy in the music room when George Szell, now of the Cleveland Orchestra and at that time conductor of the Prague Philharmonic, entered the drawing room with Madame Simon.

"Who is that?" he asked.

Madame Simon told him, and added the facts about Risë's hard luck in finding the European houses filled up.

"Well, heaven knows I don't believe in coincidences," said Mr. Szell, "but this is a coincidence if I ever heard of one. The girl is obviously a good mezzo, and the Neues Deutches Theatre in Prague is desperate for a mezzo."

He wrote out a few lines to Dr. Eger on his card, and that night Risë was packed and off for Prague. Here again, her auspices were of such high order that one might assume her way would be easy, but she seemed to run up against a stone wall in Prague. She had picked up a little German in Salzburg, but now she had to face Czech on the streets. She found the theatre with difficulty and was received by Dr. Eger with surprise. He had never heard of her, there had been no advance warning of her coming, and he had nothing to go on but this card from his friend Szell, who might have been carried away by French wine and the beauty of this young American.

It was an awkward situation because of the language barrier, and for a few minutes Dr. Eger seemed at a loss what to do next. He finally motioned for her to follow him, and she eventually found herself in the auditorium of the opera house. From somewhere there appeared a pianist, and Risë was soon doing arias from *Mignon* in French. She was comforted by the fact that the pianist spoke enough English to be understood, but she was not too happy about the reaction of Dr. Eger. When she finished, he looked off in the distance in a reflective way and said nothing. Her heart sank, and she turned and started for the door. She had seen that look before on Madame Schoen René's face and knew that it meant no good.

"Kommen Sie zurück!" cried Dr. Eger sharply, and at her elbow was the little pianist, showing her by smiles and motions that she was to come back. From the halting translation of the pianist she found that Dr. Eger had thought she had done extremely well. There would be a contract in kronen at the usual rate for beginners. It was later she got the shock of finding it was only $25 a month, but it didn't matter in any case: she was getting a chance to sing with a professional company.

"But I don't sing German," she said.

"It doesn't matter," said Dr. Eger, through the translator. "We will teach you."

It was a testimony to German thoroughness and Risë's receptivity that they had her ready for *Mignon* in three weeks. As has been hinted, it was not the most finished performance of the opera ever given, but the Prague pewholders were much taken by the striking good looks of the newcomer, found her voice surprisingly good, and were not too annoyed at her mangling of the umlauts. The experience had left Risë a bit shattered, for she had studied assiduously by day and sat up most of the night memorizing what she had learned. She was not greatly helped by an opening-night gift from the irrepressible Surovy. He sent her a tiny live bunny in a crate.

"What's the idea of the animal?" asked Risë suspiciously, through Harriet Henders.

"Why, it's an American custom, isn't it?" cried the ebullient Surovy, his eyes filled with what Risë felt was false sincerity. "The rabbit's foot for luck? Well, you got four rabbit's feet."

Rise felt at the time, and still feels, that the man was indulging himself in a sarcastic gesture calculated to revenge himself for the jab in the ribs. Those European stage stars are like elephants, with a long memory.

But if this was his intention, his subsequent actions failed to bear it out. He launched a whirlwind campaign with the intention of rushing Risë off her feet, and succeeded. There was no resisting the charmer when he got under a full head of steam. He knew all the tricks of bowing low over the hand, sending the flowers, ordering the proper wines at dinner, and listening with lightly concealed ecstasy to her few halting words in German. His glowing countenance showed that such jeweled words had never been heard before by mortal man. They were together so constantly that it eventually became an opera-house topic of conversation.

"It's none of my business, Risë," said Harriet Henders, "but you really should watch your step with Walter."

"Why?" asked Risë.

"Well, he has an awful reputation as a rounder, and any girl who goes out with him is stamped right away."

Risë replied with some sadness that she would have to be regarded as a ruined woman, for she had fallen hard for the monster and couldn't conceive of being without him. What followed was a hilarious courtship which bordered on the ridiculous. Risë was the lowest paid of the singers, and Walter was the highest paid of the actors. Risë managed to stay solvent, with the help of her mother's packages, and Walter was constantly broke.

"It wasn't what he spent on me," says Risë, "but he just spent it. He bought me meals, but I wouldn't take anything else. On

Saturday night he'd have a wad of kronen in his pocket, and by Wednesday he'd be hitting up his friends for loans."

Surovy's reputation in this respect was a source of merriment for Prague, where the rules about debt were strict. As a way of warning her about Walter, Risë had been told he had been twice in jail for debt, getting out through the intercession of Dr. Eger, who needed him at the theatre and advanced the money for springing him from the dungeons. Risë took this lightly, as being a quaint medieval custom retained for its humorous possibilities. She took a different view of it when a telephone call informed her around noon one day that Walter was again in the clink.

"I'll go right over," she said in a panic.

"Don't bother about that," said her informant easily. "He's *there*, all right. What he needs is some money to get out. You'd better see Dr. Eger."

Risë took only time enough to pick up Harriet Henders as an interpreter and hurried over to Dr. Eger's office. The good doctor heard her out quietly, tapping his pencil reflectively as if the tidings were not new to him. He turned to his secretary.

"Is Mr. Surovy playing tonight?" he asked.

"No," she said.

"Then I think we'll let him stay there a while," he said, mouthing the words with pleasure.

Half of Prague went down to look at Walter through the bars, and Risë shed tears of exasperation and pity, but he stayed where he was till Dr. Eger sent around the money next morning.

Walter swears that his Prague reputation was a press-agent invention to stir up interest in the theatre. It was the day of matinee idols, and he had a positive duty to act the part of an off-stage Don Juan.

"We were a repertory theatre and did a new show each week," says Walter. "The comedy roles were easy for me, but I had an awful time with tragedy and worked myself into a stew over them. I was in the theatre from ten in the morning till midnight. What time did I have for being a Don Juan?"

There is competent evidence that he succeeded against the stiffest odds, but all that stopped when his friendship with Risë began. They were together constantly, Walter's old girl friends in the company had given up in disgust, and the Stevens-Surovy combination was the talk of the town.

It was then that Risë discovered Walter's mania for practical jokes and general mischievousness. Every night after the performance Walter took Risë home by streetcar. There was a strict law in Prague against carrying animals on public conveyances. Among other things Walter had learned in his wandering days was a touch of ventriloquism. He would seat himself demurely, and soon thereafter a most disturbing medley of whines, yips, and small yelps would break out, which seemed to center on a man in the front seat who was asleep on the shoulder of his wife. The conductor would leap aloft like an avenging diety and fall on the poor victim with force.

"All right, now, wise guy!" he would shout irately. "Get the pooch out of here, or get out yourself."

In the midst of the altercation that followed, with the victim protesting indignantly and the conductor roaring threats, the piteous puppy cries would break out in the back of the car. When the conductor reacted to the new crisis with a rush to the rear, he would be confounded to find that the dog was now evidently riding on the roof.

But Risë's and Walter's happy idyll was upset by two circumstances: (a) Risë had a disastrous experience singing in *Aida*, and (b) she received an offer for a two-month engagement in Cairo and Alexandria. Even to this day she has a feeling that the two things had a connection. If she hadn't been so bad as Amneris in *Aida*, why had Dr. Eger been willing to give her two months' leave to sing in Egypt?

"I was confused," says Risë, "but Walter was really on a spot. He didn't want me to go to Egypt, but he couldn't say so without sounding selfish. Out of loyalty to me, he was forced to say that I had been wonderful in *Aida*. But in selling me on that, he gave me the support I needed to believe that the Cairo offer was really an advancement and not a form of exile."

The offer was from a Viennese company, starring Richard Tauber, the famous lyric tenor. She was to have all expenses, but little salary, and she was to sing only *Rosenkavalier* and *Orfeo*. She approached Dr. Eger with no hope that he would agree to the plan and was unpleasantly surprised by the promptness of his acquiescence.

"You are established here now," he said, "and for the next few months you would merely be repeating your successes. The Cairo experience will be good for you and good for us; you will learn a great deal from Tauber."

"He never breathed a word about my *Aida*," says Risë in retrospect. "That's what I call a tactful man."

Walter had hidden his chagrin well, but he couldn't resist a last barb when he saw Risë off at the train.

"Be sure to send me a post card," he said with a mocking glance. "I'm collecting stamps."

Risë gave him a murderous look and turned away without saying good-by.

Risë recalls the Cairo trip as one of the pleasantest times of her life, but there had to be a fly in the ointment. The company was to appear in the theatre where *Aida* had been first sung, and it was unthinkable that the opera shouldn't be given. The company was not equipped for it, and it would stretch the efforts of the troupe to the limit, but *Aida* was the Egyptain national opera, almost the country's anthem, and there was nothing else for it. They suggested that Risë do Amneris and ran up against the true stubborn Stevens.

"You can throw me to the crocodiles of the Nile," she said, "but I'll never do that part again."

She has bucked some very tough impresarios since that time, but she has never again done *Aida*. She has a phobia on the subject, and is willing to admit that her stand makes no sense, but wild horses couldn't drag her onto the stage again as Amneris.

"But *Aida* is the most popular of all operas, and Amneris steals the show," they protest heatedly. "You're just cutting yourself off from a great role."

"Maybe so," says Risë, "but I'm not doing it."

But Dr. Eger had been right about the good that would come from the Cairo experience: her *Rosenkavalier* improved immensely, and she was a sensation in *Orfeo*. In both of these roles she was playing men's parts, and the Egyptians were as appreciative of a handsome pair of legs as any other race. As is always true in musical circles, the grapevine rumors of her Cairo success had preceded her to Prague, and she returned to a heightened fame. The trip had done nothing for her financially, however, and she now began picking up $5 and $10 for performances in provincial opera houses around Prague. She also resumed the Surovy romance where it had left off. She was willing to forget the crack about the stamps, and he was happy enough to see her again. However, nothing was ever going to curb his tart opinions on her career; nothing has to this day.

"I see where you scored a great triumph last night in the famous city of Pumpernickel," he would say ironically, after one of her excursions into the hinterlands. "Who did you expect to find there —Toscanini?"

Risë merely gave him one of the enigmatic smiles she knew exasperated him, and otherwise ignored him. She still pursues this policy and finds it extremely effective. Their firm relationship is the marvel of the musical world, and it was never for a moment based on the saccharine emotions of childish romance. Walter considers Risë a woman first and a prima donna somewhere down the line. Risë lets herself be led as far as she wants to be led and then can't be moved by a bulldozer. Walter plans the campaigns, makes the preliminary moves, and issues the orders. Risë listens, reflects, and finally speaks.

"People hear us arguing," laughs Risë, "and wonder when we're going to start drawing the knives. They needn't worry. If I had ever wanted to be a coy ingénue, Walter knocked it out of me from the start. We were mature people from the beginning! What a relief it is!"

After her first season in Prague, Risë tapped the Corn Exchange till to get home for the summer—and landed in New York broke. She had a contract for a second season in Prague and knew she would get back if she had to swim, but the financial picture wasn't rosy. There was still some elastic in the Corn Exchange line of credit, but she was resolved not to put Madame Schoen René any further in debt. Madame pooh-poohed the notion with some asperity but ran against the impermeable Risë that nothing could move.

"Well, then," said Madame, "we'll get you a loan from Juilliard."
This was a stunner for Risë.

"But they're sore at me for going away," she said.

"Sensible people know when to forget," said Madame sagely.
This proved to be true. Accompanied by the redoubtable
Madame, Risë had a pleasant conference with John Erskine and
Ernest Hutcheson, president and dean, respectively, of Juilliard,
and came away with a loan of $500. This would get her estab-
lished again in Prague, and the gods would simply have to be
kind thereafter. A sentence dropped by Mr. Erskine at the meeting gave her hope that a turn was coming in her affairs.

"I don't think we'll have to wait long for the return of this, Risë,"
he said significantly.

Since Mr. Erskine was a director of the Metropolitan as well as
head of Juilliard, Risë took this as meaning he knew something
that would eventually be imparted to her. One night in Prague
an excited colleague approached her backstage.

"Did you see the American in the audience?" she asked eagerly.

"How do you know he's an American?" asked Risë.

"By his clothes; how *else!* He's in the fifth row."

A lively and handsome-looking Edward Johnson visited Risë
in her dressing room after the performance.

"Do you think you're ready for it now?" he asked.

"Yes, if you do," she laughed a bit uneasily.

"Oh no; you don't get me that way," he said. "I thought you
were ready two years ago. The question is, do *you* think so?"

She admitted that she did. She was to have a contract with the
Metropolitan, which would bring her the munificent sum of $150
a week. Her debut performance would be in the winter of 1938.

As if this wasn't enough, she was now hit by a second fall of
manna from heaven: Erich Kleiber, the famous maestro, offered
her a season at the Teatro Colón in Buenos Aires.

Professionally, she was on her way; privately, she was sunk.
Buenos Aires and New York were open to her; Walter was
trapped in Prague. Hitler had started the agitation over the
Sudetenland that would eventually bring on the Second World
War. Walter was a cork bobbing on the surface of that turmoil.

Chapter Six

Although Madame Schoen René had hammered constantly at her about current affairs, Risë arrived in Prague with no interest in politics. The fact that the Sudetenland was a German enclave in Czechoslovakia meant nothing to her. Hitler was already stating in threatening tones that these unfortunate people were being held in bondage by the iniquitous Czechs; he would never rest until they had been freed and made a part of the Third Reich. Risë's thoughts were entirely on her career and on her desperate efforts to conquer the German language.

With Walter it was different. He had been raised in Hungary, and his mother now lived in Vienna. His father had been General Imre Szurovy of the Hungarian Army. Walter's career as an actor had been entirely in the German theatre, and for a time he had been one of the rising young men in Max Reinhardt's company. What happened in the Sudetenland was of immediate interest to him because of the position of the Neues Deutsches Theatre in the heart of Prague. Within the theatre itself a political split was already coming to a head. Many of the actors were political refugees who had fled Germany when Hitler came to power. Others were avowed Nazis who were merely waiting until Hitler could take over Czechoslovakia.

The anti-Nazis had formed a club in the theatre in 1937, and Walter was a member of it. Most of the participants were Jewish, and Walter was non-Jewish, but his political views had always been on the liberal side. Because the company was operated with strict discipline, the inner tensions were not allowed to ruin the performances, but there was no way of avoiding the controversy raging outside.

Risë was only dimly aware of what was happening, but the matter was brought forcibly to her attention one night when she arrived with Walter at the theatre. They could see the crowds as they came up the street, and Risë was elated at the thought of a packed house, something not too prevalent in the last troubled months. A look at Walter's worried face dispelled this idea promptly, and she could then hear the shouts and the angry growls coming from the crowd. The play was Schiller's *Don Carlos,* a revolutionary document containing a stirring defiance of tyrants. The Nazis of Prague had preferred to take its presentation as a direct slap at Hitler; hence the mob.

When Risë and Walter had pushed their way through the stage door, they found a frightening state of calm backstage. There was not an actor in sight! At Walter's questions the stage manager shrugged his shoulders helplessly.

"The Nazis have refused to act," the stage manager explained, "and the Jewish actors have been warned that they'll be manhandled if they try to get in."

"Where are the police?" asked Walter.

"You tell *me*," said the man.

Walter went to the peephole in the curtain and looked out into the auditorium. It seemed to be filled.

"How did *they* get in?" he wanted to know. "They must be eighty per cent Jewish."

"That's part of the trick," said the man. "What do those Nazi bastards care if they get in; they're not going to see anything anyhow, and they'll probably get bumped around a bit when they go out."

As Walter discovered later, this was not strictly true. The Jewish audience had showed up despite threats of violence. If the Nazis considered *Don Carlos* a test of allegiance, the Jews were just as determined to accept the challenge. This was in the early days before the world had decided Czechoslovakia should be sacrificed to Hitler; the Jews were fighting with their backs to the wall in the one refuge of freedom that remained to them in Central Europe.

While Walter was looking through the peephole, the manager of the theatre arrived and showed by his actions that he felt the situation was hopeless.

"Well, there you are," he said, throwing up his hands. "No actors; no performance."

"I'll give the performance," said Walter, making up his mind suddenly.

"*What!*" cried the manager in amazement.

"I'll read the play," said Walter. "It won't be much good, but they'll get it."

The manager was reluctant but not hard to convince. Not only would the reading keep the company's record clear of never missing a performance, but it might quiet an audience that otherwise could easily get out of hand. The tension in the auditorium was ominous, and there were already loud foot stampings and shouts at the delay of raising the curtain. He went before the curtain to explain the circumstances, the curtains parted—and there was Walter prepared to read. When he came to the great speech where Posa defies the King and cries, "Give me freedom of thought!" the audience broke into a riot of applause.

"I thought the house would come down," says Risë, who had stood trembling in the wings. "I've never known anything like the violence and intensity of those cries. It was as if their very hearts were coming out of their mouths. They had stood everything, and they knew what the future held for them. This might be their last chance to echo the cry for freedom. They shouted with utter defiance; they defied the Fates and Hitler and the powers of darkness everywhere. It was the most stirring thing that has ever happened to me in the theatre, or in life either. It was desperation, and it was sublime."

It was a triumph for Walter, but it did him little good in certain circles of Prague. As an Aryan and a member of the ruling establishment of the old Austro-Hungarian empire through his father, a different attitude had been expected of him. Some of his friends tried to excuse him on the ground that he was merely doing his job as an actor, but the others could see—and they were perfectly right—that Walter had taken a definite stand on the anti-Hitler side. Risë had been shocked to the depths by the experience, but she has always been able to lock herself into anything she was doing. "Old one-track mind," as Walter calls her, was soon wrapped up again in the problems, labors, and successes of the opera.

This was proved in even more startling fashion when she was given a week's leave of absence for two guest performances of *Rosenkavalier* with the Vienna State Opera. She was so engrossed in her work that the presence of great numbers of troops in the center of Vienna made no impression on her. Her first performance went off well, although she was somewhat at a loss to understand the fickle reactions of the audience. At curtain call a very good German singer was received almost in silence, while a mediocre Italian tenor was greeted with something approaching ecstasy. Her own reception was a bit too frenetic to convince her of its sincerity. During her second performance she was amazed to find actors and stagehands giving the Nazi salute in the wings. Her first feeling that this must contain a touch of burlesque was shattered by a look at the frenzied eyes of the saluters. She hurried off between acts to notify the management of what was happening.

"Do you realize," she expostulated, "there's a lot of Nazis in this company? They're giving the salute backstage."

"My dear lady," said the manager sadly, "there are indeed a lot of Nazis in the company. Hitler took over Austria three days ago, and where were you?"

There was no mistaking the tension in the air in the spring days of 1938 when Risë prepared to leave for Buenos Aires, but the personal problems that faced Risë and Walter seemed much more important to them. Walter knew all too well the situation around him, and it took all his courage to keep smiling at Risë's enthusiasm over her change of luck. The future was opening wide before her; his past was closing around him. They toasted the Metropolitan Opera contract; they toasted the unexpected windfall of the Teatro Colón engagement. In the midst of her preparations for leaving, it suddenly struck Risë that Walter might not be as happy as herself.

"But I'll be back next season," she said in reassurance. "I've signed the contract again."

"Of course, you will," said Walter hastily. "Look . . . see what I've got for you."

It was a doorplate for the apartment they had been furnishing for her return for the season 1938–39. It read:

Walter Surovy

Risë Stevens

"Top billing for yourself, eh!" cried Risë indignantly.

"When you make it, you get it," said Walter.

This was a light moment, and they had few enough of them, but they then took an action which set the theatrical world of Prague by the ears: they announced their engagement to be married. This had followed an interview with Eger, who had called them in unexpectedly and said to them without preliminaries: "I have been thinking it over; you must get married." Risë is still not sure what prompted this, unless the good doctor felt that their relationship was ruining the reputation of the theatre, but the reaction to it was rather unnerving. A roar of laughter went up over the city.

"If Surovy stays married a week," said the most quoted witticism, "you can count it a lifetime of happy matrimony."

But worse was to follow when Risë received a peremptory order from Madame Schoen René to meet her in Paris. Risë had carefully refrained from sending Madame an engagement announcement, but news travels fast in musical circles. The word had reached Madame in New York, and she had immediately taken boat for France. From the tone of her note it was plain that she was in a towering rage. Risë had nothing to look forward to but misery in the interview, but it never occurred to her to refuse to go to Paris. She owed her career to Madame and now recalled belatedly that she had once promised Schoen René that she would take no definite personal step without consulting her.

Madame was in her sternest Prussian mood when Risë arrived.

She submitted coldly to Risë's light peck on the cheek and got down to business immediately.

"You are a naughty child!" she said tensely, "and I can't for the life of me understand what has come over you. An *actor!* A poor miserable actor with the worst reputation in all Europe."

"I love him," said Risë.

"Love, *bah!*" cried Madame. "What is love! A fancy you'll regret the rest of your life. Have an affair, yes, if that's what you want . . . but marriage, NO! Your career is too important to you."

Risë tried to defend herself, but Madame cut in furiously.

"I won't have it, do you hear! I have put all my strength behind you, and I'm not going to have everything ruined now by a silly love affair!"

Risë could recognize the symptoms of an attack of stubbornness coming over her. The line of the jaw hardened, she could feel her back begin to stiffen. But the mood changed quickly. There was never a chance that Madame would talk her out of her love for Walter, but she realized that she had a debt to Madame that couldn't lightly be tossed aside.

She sat down to talk quietly with Schoen René. Risë soon found that her defense of Walter meant nothing whatever to Madame, who considered him not as an individual but as a symbol of the hated thing called matrimony. Risë's future had become a mania with her, and there was no possibility of a meeting of minds on the subject. In Madame's eyes marriage could only be a disaster. The talk lasted for hours and ended where it began. Risë would not budge, and Madame refused to be reconciled.

Risë has sometimes thought of this as her second successful defiance of Madame, but it was a standoff rather than a victory, and she derived no satisfaction from it. The trip back to Prague was sad, and Risë was torn by the realization that she had little time left with Walter. Their plans were for a wedding when Risë returned for her third season with the Prague company, but both knew in their hearts that what might be facing them was a final farewell. The world was upside down, war was almost certain. When friends hinted that immediate marriage might be a solution, Risë perked up and showed interest, but Walter merely shook his head grimly.

"What's the use?" he asked sadly. "I'm here, and Risë will be ten thousand miles away."

On this point he was on the side of Madame Schoen René. Marriage in these circumstances would be a sentimental gesture. If they were mature people, this was the time to show it. Unless they were to be together, what was the purpose of a compact that would merely be a dragging anchor on them both?

They decided to spend their last weeks together as if they were to be the last. After the Prague season ended, they left for Trieste to spend a month before Risë sailed on the *Vulcania* for South America.

"I was so happy to see sunshine and water again," says Risë, "that I lay out on the sands of the Adriatic the whole first day. What it got me was a sunburn I thought was going to kill me. I spent the entire first two weeks in bed."

But the last two weeks were an idyll that Risë has never forgotten. They walked and swam, ate at queer restaurants, and sat on a hill at sunset watching the change of colors over the sea. Once on a walk in the hills they came on a deserted church, sitting on a peak overlooking the bay. When they explored it, they found a tiny altar still intact. As by a common impulse, they sank to their knees. They held hands and looked into one another's eyes.

"I will love you forever," whispered Risë.

"I will love you forever," said Walter.

Risë suddenly broke out in sobs, throwing herself in his arms.

"I know," said Walter gently. "We will love each other forever, but we will be apart."

"I'll come back," cried Risë. "I swear I'll come back!"

"You will never come back," said Walter softly.

They played out the role of happy lovers as long as the Trieste stay lasted. They said good-by with a smile as they embraced for the last time on the pier. Anybody who saw Risë as she waved joyously from the deck of the departing liner would have thought she was merely off for the weekend. Walter kept up his happy waving as long as her figure could be seen on the top deck of the ship. When it was over, she threw herself on her bunk in her cabin in despair, sobbing convulsively. In an endeavor to stop crying she kept saying to herself desperately, "I *will* come back; I *will* come back," but she knew that a phase of her life had ended.

When the ship reached Genoa and she was joined by the other members of the company headed for Buenos Aires, they looked at her in astonishment.

"What's happened to you?" asked a girl she had met in Vienna. "You look like a ghost."

For answer Risë broke into another storm of sobbing.

"When I say that I was treated better than I had any right to expect in my early days in opera," says Risë, "I mean it started on that ship. Nobody needs to be told that there are jealousies and cruelties in an opera company, but they couldn't have been nicer to me. They treated me like a child who has been handled roughly by life, and at the end of two weeks I began to come out of it. Up to that time, I couldn't even enter the dining room without breaking into tears."

With Risë on that trip were Anny Konetzni, Emanuel List, and Karin Branzell. The extraordinary thing about their treatment of Risë was that they knew Walter's reputation and couldn't for the life of them understand why she wasn't jumping with joy at getting away from him. But as opera singers who dealt only with the rawest emotions, they recognized the genuine thing when they saw it, and spent their efforts in weaning Risë from her grief.

By the time they reached Buenos Aires (a journey of four weeks), Risë was in a mood to take up her career again. One look at the Teatro Colón was enough to elevate the spirit of any artist, for it is acknowledged to be one of the most beautiful theatres in the world.

The theatre was not only a joy to behold, but it possessed mechanical wonders that made it a treat for singers. There were revolving stages and elevator stages; there was lighting equipment enough for a small city. The dressing rooms were large and clean and elegant; the scenery was sumptuous and lovely; the acoustics in the theatre were a dream for an artist. And the first-night audience was a revelation even for the singers who had performed before the crowned heads of Europe. Surely not since

Risë's mother at the time of her marriage.

Risë says she didn't copy her mother's attire as the Merry Widow on TV, but . . .

Risë's mother and father,
better known as Sadie
and Chris.

Risë and her brother Bud,
who was killed on
Normandy's Omaha
Beach in World War II.

A shipboard candid not only became Walter's favorite picture of Risë but also got her into Hollywood.

Risë and Walter on their belated honeymoon to South America.

Risë seems to be
bolstering the morale
of her soldier husband.

An early family
picture: Risë,
Walter, and Nicky.

The Surovys in
Hollywood, with the
ubiquitous swimming pool
as background.

Juilliard School of Music
spared no expense
in trying to hide Risë's
youth, in this
world-première school
production of
Maria Malibran.

BENEDICT FRENKEL

Anna Amelia Schoen René, the iron-willed teacher most responsible for Risë's success.

Risë (just seventeen) plays
Prince Orlofsky in
Die Fledermaus, in the
New York Opéra-Comique
production, with
William Hain.

The same role at the
Met in Rudolf Bing's
first popular success.

As Herodias, Risë
puts the hex on Salome
in the La Scala world
première of Mortari's
La Figlia del Diavolo.

Risë's private moment
of triumph: after any
important performance she
collapses with the
ever-present tea, here in her
La Scala dressing room.

the days of Louis XIV at the palace of Versailles had there been seen such gowns and jewels and beautiful women.

On the practical side Risë was well pleased with her situation. She was getting $1800 for a three-month season, and a chance to sing with a superior company. Ahead of her was the engagement with the Metropolitan in New York. She found, in addition, that the social life of a singer in Buenos Aires was far different from what it had been in Prague. The Argentinians overwhelmed the company with attentions, inviting them into their homes, entertaining them with Lucullan feasts in settings of fabulous beauty. It was a bit too much for Risë, however, who was still self-conscious about her poverty and no sartorial match for the Argentinian women. She was relieved to find herself taken in by the United States Embassy group, who were elegant enough in their own way but not necessarily awed by wealth.

In this company she had a delightful round of afternoon teas, cocktail parties, dinners, and days at the seashore. Her performances at Teatro Colón had made her a town celebrity, and the young secretaries of the Embassy were all too happy to be seen leading her in to dinner at one of the famous restaurants. It was at this time that she met an American who, for want of his real name, will be called Mr. John Smith. He was young, handsome, wealthy, and a devoted follower of the opera. His interests called him often to South America, but in New York he was on the board of the Metropolitan Opera, a backer of the New York Philharmonic, and a considerable figure in musical circles. When Risë found herself becoming interested in him, she suddenly took stock of herself and then remembered one of her last talks with Walter.

"Now, don't be silly," he had said. "We've taken vows of love, but that doesn't make you a nun. Life will go on whether you like it or not; you might as well join it. I'm certainly not going to sit alone brooding in my room, and there's no reason why you should."

This was all very well, but Risë continued to have doubts to the point where Mr. Smith became excessively weary of talk about Mr. Surovy. In the glamorous setting of a restaurant, with the mountains behind and the sea glowing fitfully below in the moon-

73

light, Mr. Smith would find himself being regaled by another story of Walter's capers in Prague.

"I'm a little sick of the fellow," he said one night. "Would you mind very much talking about something else?"

Risë thought this was fair enough and piped down on the ubiquitous Surovy, but he was never far from her mind. But Mr. Smith pressed his suit assiduously, and everybody agreed there couldn't be a pleasanter fellow or a better catch. Risë was not yet in the market for a catch, but she couldn't deny that the Smith attentions were flattering. In short, it was a wonderful summer all around. Her success at the opera house was outstanding, and only lack of time kept her association with the Embassy crowd from being one long house party.

When she boarded the ship for New York in September, she could look back on a summer of accomplishment and success. The Erich Kleiber productions at Teatro Colón had been of outstanding quality, and Risë was confident that she was ready at last for the big time. Her newspaper notices had been enthusiastic, and she could tell from the feel of things around the company that she was accepted as a finished artist. There was a great party at the pier when the company sailed, and in the midst of it was Mr. Smith, with the usual candy, flowers and fruit and—a little something more. Something that Risë was not too eager to see: it was plain that Mr. Smith was serious in his intentions.

"I'm sorry I can't get away with you," he said, "but I'll be following you."

She sat down on the ship to consider matters. Europe was falling apart, Walter was 10,000 miles away, and there was no certainty that she would ever see him again. On the other side, there was no question of the Smith qualities. He was an American, they would have a common bond in music, and her future would be assured. The only certainty in a future with Walter was that it would be exciting. Her career was in America, and particularly at the Metropolitan Opera, if she made good. His could only be in Europe. They had once discussed the possibility of Walter making a new career in New York.

"No, no," he had said. "It won't work."

"Others have done it," she protested, naming European stars who were in the American movies.

"Yes," he admitted. "They start well, and then they fade. When you lose your language, you lose everything."

Risë refused to believe this and still doesn't believe it, but it helped her analysis very little as the ship slowly crept up the Atlantic toward New York. At last she managed to get the matter out of her head. It was a happy ship, the voyage was calm, and her friends were as kind as ever. And, most important of all, Mr. John Smith had been left behind in Buenos Aires, and the decision, if there had to be a decision, could be postponed.

When she arrived at the dock in New York, Mr. John Smith was there to greet her. He had flown up from the Argentine, a thing not so simple then as it has now become.

Chapter Seven

Risë's mind was in a turmoil as she began preparations for her debut with the Metropolitan. Her work gave her an excuse to slow the pace of the Smith courtship, but his attentions never ceased, and she was forced to admit that he afforded a form of moral support she badly needed in the ordeal she was about to face. Buenos Aires was one thing; New York was another. Her confidence had been at its peak in Argentina; she now found it oozing away by the day. Instead of being comforted by the fact she was back with her own people, she felt the Bronx enveloping her again with iron bands. She had terrifying dreams in which she made her opening-night entrance by stumbling and falling flat on the stage; in the middle of the second act she lost her voice and stood foolishly gasping like a fish out of water.

Smith was a help in getting her out of her moods, but in the back of her mind she knew she needed Walter. In Prague it had been Walter who had given her pep talks before her performances, and criticized her roughly for her mistakes, and defended her from the attacks of others. But from him now came nothing but gloom and distress.

"It is only a matter of time," he had written in his last letter from Prague. "The black cloud is on the border."

And then, abruptly, Hitler had marched into the Sudetenland —and there was silence from Walter. His letters had been coming regularly, and now they stopped. For two weeks Risë was in a state of panic. Her letters to him disappeared into a void; a frantic cable to Prague was unanswered. She recalled the theatre club of liberals; she remembered all too well the reading of *Don Carlos* on the stage of the Neues Deutsches Theatre. And then a letter arrived from him in Vienna.

"When Hitler marched in, I marched out," he wrote. "Hans and the others said I was foolish, but I think *they're* foolish."

He had simply picked up a small bag and left. Behind him was everything he possessed—the furniture he had bought for the new apartment, his theatrical wardrobe and books, his friends, his career in Prague. He took a train for Bratislava—got off at the first suburban station outside Prague. The train was alive with guards looking for escaping Jews. Walter had a Hungarian passport—a suspicious thing when all foreigners were suspect. It could mean a manufactured passport; its holder would be in serious trouble.

"I started hitchhiking," he wrote. "In your country I understand it is quite simple; it is not so here. It took me seven days to get to Vienna."

With all Europe in a state of terror over Hitler's moves, cars were few on the roads. People stayed close at home, eyed their neighbors nervously, and hoped that somehow the storm would blow over. Strangers seeking rides were not welcomed gladly, and, in fact, Walter found it difficult to get a lift even when he offered to pay for it. Payment was suspicious; it meant that the traveler was desperate. Everybody was conscious of the blow that might fall on them for abetting the escape of what Hitler might consider a criminal. For most of the seven days Walter traveled by peasant carts and trucks. The truck drivers seemed less afraid of the authorities. They lived on the open road, they were used to freedom, and they were not afraid of black shapes in the dark.

"The hell with them," said one gay fellow who gave Walter a thirty-mile lift and spent most of the time whistling tunes from Viennese operettas.

The nights gave Walter great trouble, for he was passing through a section with few inns, and twice he was left off a peasant cart in an area far from a town. Once he slept in a hayloft, and on the other occasion he only broke down the resistance of a farmer by paying him more for a bumpy straw bed than it would have cost him at the Hotel Sacher in Vienna. It was travel through one of the loveliest parts of Europe, and it was travel through a wasteland. Stark fear had seized Europe, and no man trusted any other man. As he walked along, he entered sizable towns in which not a human face was to be seen. Leaving at the other end of town, he was always seized with a feeling that he was to be shot in the back. They would shoot him out of panic, in a conviction that this would somehow mollify the dark gods that had enveloped them.

When he stumbled at last into his mother's apartment in Vienna, his appearance shocked her into speechlessness. This soon gave way to relief at seeing him again, for she knew his anti-Nazi views and was fearful at the news from Prague. Although the Nazis were established in Austria, the Surovys were in no danger. Their lineage was impeccable; their background was of the old royal court. The Nazis were inclined to be lenient with actors, considering them amusing children who were not responsible for their wayward views. Under the old Roman view of "bread-and-circuses," they also realized that the theatre could be an asset to them. Feed the people and amuse them; their minds would then be free of dangerous political thoughts.

Walter had already been signed for an engagement at the Josefstadt Theatre in Vienna, but this was to start during the Christmas holidays, still almost three months off. From what he had learned in Prague when signing the contract, the Josefstadt had been strictly left alone by the Hitler regime, but there was no way of knowing how things were since the brutal actions in Czechoslovakia. Hitler was going from one triumph to another; he might have decided that the time had come to whip the cultural forces of the satellite countries into line.

There was one way to find out: go down to the theatre and see. Walter might prevail on them to advance the contract and start him to work at once; or he might find that they didn't want him at all. It was with trepidation that he approached the stage door of the Josefstadt. His experiences on the rough trip from Prague were not calculated to bolster his confidence. He was prepared for anything, and what he found amazed him.

The doorkeeper eyed him roughly, took his name without sign of interest, and watched his every move. Just as nervousness was beginning to seize Walter, the doorkeeper suddenly waved a hand toward the stairs and said:

"Dr. Hilpert will see you."

This was something new in Walter's experience, and he approached the door of the manager's office in a state of bemusement. Something was happening, but he didn't know what it was. When he entered the reception room, the secretary had evidently been forewarned of his coming. She smiled warmly, cut him short when he started to give his name, and ushered him into a second office. Another secretary met him there and passed him along with the same friendly smile. It was all strange and amazing. In the European theatre the position of the manager is so exalted that it is far easier to get a royal audience than to procure an interview with the head of a theatre. He is protected by dozens of secretaries and assistants; access to him is by a process of protocol which would have discouraged an ambassador of Venice in the days of the doges. He sits in a faraway suite, in an atmosphere of reverence and adulation. Walter had expected this—and now he found himself in Dr. Heinz Hilpert's presence almost as if whisked on a magic carpet.

"Ah, you wonder, eh?" said Dr. Hilpert. "Well, I will tell you. If anybody comes to the stage door and says 'Heil Hitler,' he does not get in."

The Viennese theatres were keeping their independence despite Hitler. Hitler had not perfected his program of world conquest; it was good politics for the Nazis to go easy on a country like Austria, which had close historical associations with Germany. With a common language the Nazis hoped to win over Austria without the need of force. Their attitude toward the theatres was based on this and the knowledge that the Viennese regarded their theatres on the Ringstrasse as sacred institutions. Even the comedians in the political cabarets continued their hilarious parodies of Hitler, playing to audiences of the Nazi hierarchy, who outwardly managed wry smiles to show their tolerance of art and inwardly gnashed their teeth in rage.

On the theory that nations never outlive their great periods, even the Socialists of Austria had a nostalgic feeling for the Emperor Franz Josef era, fustian and fake though it was in many respects. When Mary Watkins Cushing visited Vienna in 1910 with Olive Fremstad, the famous prima donna, she reported on the scene in this manner in her book, *The Rainbow Bridge:*

"Vienna was heaven. The old Kaiser was still alive and his imperial touch animated the life of the city. The aristocracy still dashed through the streets in open carriages with galloping horses and outriders, and the few who possessed motorcars had their coats of arms emblazoned on them, with coronets or crowns, as the case might be, hanging where license plates are now attached. The air was full of music: the carriages had buglers; the royal automobile horns played snatches from Brahms or Wagner; even the postman had a horn (a curly one with yellow tassels), and a special boy in a top hat to blow it for him. On all important corners were cafés where the orchestras played day and night; in the side streets were beer gardens gay with the sound of accordion and fiddle, of yodeling and rhythmic clapping. In every public park and garden from twilight on, orchestras and bands played waltzes or selections from the classics; and at least two opera houses and a dozen theaters were functioning full blast."

The first attempt of the Nazis to impose themselves on the Viennese theatres had been a failure. Hitler had issued orders for a command performance at the Burgtheatre. It was a gala evening in the historic old house, with Hitler in the royal box surrounded by the most important figures of the Nazi regime. The audience had been carefully hand-picked from among Nazi sympathizers and members of the old court who were grateful that Hitler had saved them from the Socialists. The theatre was a blaze of uniforms, medals, tiaras, and diamond chokers. Goering, his broad chest filled with decorations, strutted by the side of the limping Goebbels and his handsome blond actress wife. The nobility of Vienna, slightly moth-eaten from years of frustration, had blossomed forth again in all their glory.

From somewhere there had been resurrected the old Austrian

officers, who now appeared in their spiked mustaches and side-burns, garbed in their skin-tight breeches and glazed boots, much like toy soldiers trotted out for Christmas festivities or a holiday celebration. The lobby and great staircase were filled with the happy chirping voices of women, who had dug out of wardrobe and closet their Worth creations of 1914 and now appeared dripping with feathers and lace. The gorgeous males clicked their spurred heels and bent with automaton-like precision over daintily gloved hands. It was the New Coming, a shining light presaging the return of grace, position, and order to the famous old town and state.

Gustav Gründgens, manager of the Burgtheatre, had been carefully instructed in the line his curtain speech was to take. He was to herald the arrival of German *Kultur* in Vienna. Two sister Germanic states had been reunited in glory. Germany had come to share its artistic wealth with its poorer relation. When Herr Gründgens appeared before the curtains, his speech proved to be brief. Waiting until the tumult of applause could die down, he had merely said in a firm voice:

"This has always been a great theatre and will continue to be a great theatre."

He bowed and disappeared into the wings.

What this proved, temporarily at least, was that men like Hilpert and Gründgens were so powerful that even Hitler couldn't touch them. The fabric of Austrian life was so tied up with the Viennese theatres that any attempt to curb them would have brought such an uproar of resentment that the German policy in Austria would have been embarrassed.

This was comforting to Walter, but he had seen enough in Prague to know that this would change with the outbreak of war. His letters to Risë became increasingly gloomier. It was only a question of time till Hitler absorbed Hungary, making Walter's Hungarian passport of dubious value. As a citizen of the Greater Reich, he would be subject to German military service, provided he escaped the concentration camp. Being an actor in the arrogant Viennese theatre would merely compound his guilt. Hitler would turn the screws on these institutions, as he had done with everything else that stood in his way.

Risë was torn with conflicting emotions. She had a sinking feeling that she would never see Walter again; the omnipresent Mr. Smith was conducting his suit like a military campaign—and he now had Madam Schoen René on his side. Madame maintained her violent views on matrimony, but if it was to come for Risë, she preferred the wealthy music-loving Mr. Smith to the vagabond actor of Prague. Risë was not thinking of marriage; she was thinking of her Metropolitan debut, and that was giving her endless trouble. Since the depression days, when the Metropolitan had almost been forced to close its doors for lack of patronage and backing, the opera house had been operating on a restricted budget.

Edward Johnson was performing miracles with his limited resources, but this was small consolation for a young singer who needed guidance and preparation. Risë was terrified at learning how little rehearsal time she would have for her opening in *Rosenkavalier* in Philadelphia. There were reassurances from the management.

"You've done the role dozens of times; what is there to be worried about?" they asked. "The part never changes, and you have the great Artur Bodanzky to conduct for you."

Mr. Bodanzky was indeed a great conductor, but Risë was to see him at only one rehearsal with orchestra before opening night in Philadelphia. Before this she had several sketchy meetings with sub-conductors and *corépétiteurs* (coaches) in a small rehearsal room at the opera house. These seemed mainly concerned with making sure that the cast hadn't somehow prepared the wrong opera. Certain passages were discussed that, from time immemorial, had given trouble in the production of *Rosenkavalier*. Since this procedure was followed by every opera company in the world, it presented no problem for Risë, but she couldn't help being annoyed by the original assumption of the gentlemen that she was a novice getting her first experience of the mysteries of backstage life. Plainly they had never heard of her and considered her a new American *Wunderkind* that Edward Johnson had begun to present at this period out of a burst of what the foreign element of the company considered an excess of patriotic zeal.

Risë kept hoping that everything would be ironed out at dress rehearsal, but this proved to be an event almost too exactly named. Various seamstresses and wardrobe mistresses hovered about her, making last-minute corrections in her costume. The stage manager moved the cast about the stage into their positions. These varied little from standard procedure in *Rosenkavalier*, which by this time had become as ritualized in production as a morris dance.

When Risë wended her way home after this event, she had a strange hollow feeling in her midriff not occasioned by lack of food. She kept telling herself that everything was going to be all right but had nothing substantial to back up the theory.

The family was now living at 105th Street and Broadway in Manhattan, a move promoted by Risë when she signed her Metropolitan contract. When she had written Sadie from Prague about the great news, she had added:

"I can't stand the thought of that subway ride, and that awful walk from the station. Get a new apartment somewhere else, provided it's Manhattan. It might not be any better, but it'll sound better."

That was practically all that could be said for the new apartment. It was larger, more expensive, and thoroughly disagreeable. The rear faced on an air shaft; the front faced on Broadway, which provided a roar of traffic, bus backfirings, and assorted turmoil well into the night. Risë's way to work was still by subway, but her hours were now different, and she was generally assured of a seat. With a few exceptions the Steenbergs were still living with the furniture that had started Sadie and Pa on their married career. The only good piece in the house was a beautiful old chair built by Sadie's father, Grandpa Mechanic, who had been a distinguished cabinetmaker in his time.

After the glamour of Buenos Aires it was a wrench for Risë to settle back into the old home routine, but she was soon too busy to worry about it. She was particularly fond of her brother Bud, who was growing into a handsome boy with an equable disposition and talents that seemed to point to an engineering career. By herculean efforts, including the curbing of her own bubbling nature, Sadie tried to make the apartment a refuge for Risë, but

83

her success was limited. As the time for the opening approached, Risë disappeared into the netherland that seems to envelop all artists on the eve of performance. She was on this earth but not of it. She rode the subway in a daze and at home sat in brooding silence.

At this juncture Sadie provided a comic interlude by stating flatly that she had no intention of going to Philadelphia for the opening. In her view it was a small place somewhere in the Amazon Basin. Also, it would be expensive in the Steenberg meaning of the word. It was only ninety miles away, but there would need to be a little party after the opening and perhaps hotel rooms overnight. And she had a low opinion of the Philadelphia critics.

"Pfoo, *that* little town," she cried indignantly. "What do *they* know? Will you be a different Risë there? No. We'll just wait for you here."

"Well, Bud and I are going," said Pa, promptly.

They were all on hand for the afternoon train to Philadelphia, including Madame Schoen René and the ever-attentive Mr. John Smith. Risë sat down on a seat in the chair car and immediately swung it toward the window, with her back to aisle. When the kindly Mr. Smith reacted to this with an attempt at comforting persiflage, Madame fixed him with a look and placed her finger on her lips. She knew from experience the feelings of a prima donna on the way to her debut; it was much similar to the ride of the French royalty in the tumbrels. Risë gazed moodily out on the Jersey meadows and tried to think of anything but what was facing her. She failed. Phrases from the score raced through her head. She had a definite conviction that her mind would go blank as she started to sing.

Memories from her childhood flashed through her head, and she found herself saying through clenched teeth, "This is the big league; this is the big league." In emergencies she has always had a tendency to lapse into baseball phraseology. When you hit the big leagues, you are at the top. In baseball, there is sometimes a second chance; in opera, never. When you fail at the Metropolitan, there is nowhere to go but down.

She spent the afternoon in seclusion in her hotel room, a practice she has followed religiously since. At six o'clock she left the Bellevue-Stratford Hotel and walked next door to the Academy of Music with Madame Schoen René. Here again there was seclusion, while she worked on her make-up and vocalized for an hour with Madame. This consisted of scales, trills, and arpeggios, and again the baseball comparison is apt: it is exactly like a pitcher warming up before a game. During the last hour she was in the hands of Jennie, the wardrobe mistress, and the seamstresses, who made last-minute alterations in her costume. Half an hour before curtain time she went on stage and made a check on props, the setting of the furniture, and any obstructions that might prove fatal later.

"What big star is *this?*" asked a caustic voice in the wings as she came off.

If she heard the voice, she paid no attention. She had acquired the habit of checking the stage in Prague, where it had also been taken as an indication of arrogance. The stagehands took it as a reflection on their competence and were not amused. Young artists were expected to be heard and not seen. There had also been raised brows in Prague at her relationship with directors.

"You will stand here," the *régisseur* said.

"Why?" asked Risë.

"Because I tell you to," shouted the director.

But that had never proved to be enough. Even at a time in the first season when her fate was doubtful with the company, she had insisted on being given logical reasons for movements that had a crucial importance for the story line. If she didn't feel natural in the action, she held up the rehearsal until matters could be adjusted.

"*Prima donna assoluta*," they said in Prague, which is the greatest compliment that can be given an opera singer but which was not intended that way by the sarcastic Prague wits. She might *think* she was the top singer, but they had another view on the subject. They considered her a bumptious young American who was a bit too big for her boots. This also failed to sway Risë, who has the mulish stubbornness in music that she often lacks in life.

The side-line comments in Philadelphia bothered her no more

than they had in Prague. Back in her dressing room after the tour of the stage, she experienced a metamorphosis that would have startled anyone not knowing opera singers. In that terrifying calm before the rise of the curtain, she ceased being Risë Stevens of New York City and became Octavian. Her face seemed to alter; a change came over her body; the spirit of another being seemed to enfold her; the sounds about her faded away, and she entered an artistic world in which existed only Octavian, the music—and her future.

At the ten-minute warning call she arose like a dazed and dedicated character, while the dressers fluttered about with last-minute ministrations. There was the last fleeting combing of the wig; the last pin inserted to hold a wayward flare of the jacket; the last dab of the powder puff on her painted cheeks. At the five-minute call Madame Schoen René threw open the door of the dressing room with a regal gesture and stood back in reverence while Risë swept out and into the wings. If this was Risë's big moment, it belonged as well to the little Prussian, who had trained her, protected her, financed her—and now thrust her forth into the great world of opera.

"Madame suddenly raised herself to her full height and pecked me on the cheek," says Risë. "She had never done it before and never did it again."

Lotte Lehmann, Emanuel List, and Friedrich Schorr were members of a notable cast at her première. Lotte Lehmann was to be her inspiration, her protector, and the greatest influence of her operatic life. This will be discussed at a later point in the book. At the moment, Risë's heart was in her throat; she trembled with the fear that strikes even the greatest actresses on an opening night. She was on stage as the curtains parted. Before she could sing a note, there was a prolonged burst of applause. She waited patiently, knowing that this was standard procedure having nothing to do either with her previous reputation or her singing. In the program it was stated very plainly: "Risë Stevens (debut)." The reception would have been the same for Arabella Clapsaddle or Mata Hari. What followed was what would count. But all nervousness fled from Risë at the delay, and suddenly she knew she was going to be all right. At the first notes her voice rang forth unhampered and clear. The prompter was in his little box in the center of the footlights; the handsome, eagle-beaked Bodanzky was waving his baton energetically from the conductor's box; God was in His Heaven, and all was right with the world. Risë was at home.

Risë came back to her room at the Bellevue-Stratford to find that it was filled with Mr.-John-Smith flowers, and a table had been set for an after-theatre supper. Seven people finally sat down to this repast under the elated but ever-watchful eye of Madame Schoen René, who regarded the popping champagne corks as missiles aimed straight at the throat of her treasure. After Risë had downed two glasses in exuberance at leaping the Philadelphia hurdle so successfully, Madame had lifted a warning finger.

"No more," said she sternly, and Risë shrugged humorously in the direction of the sympathetic Mr. Smith, and obeyed. The incident established for the evening a sedate tone that Mr. Smith had not anticipated, and the occasion will not go into the annals of the Bellevue-Stratford as one of its wilder affairs.

On the daring side could be accounted the fact that they stayed up for the first newspaper reviews. Risë was dying for sleep and could very well have waited for the newspapers next day, but Sadie would not hear of it. Sadie might not be an expert on the opera, but she was a bred-in-the-bone New Yorker who knew that after any first night it was a duty of the performers to join the Death Watch and wait for the newspaper verdict. It was a struggle to keep going until the first newspaper arrived about two-thirty, but it was worth it. Among other things, it permanently altered Sadie's opinion of Philadelphia. She has held ever since that it is one of America's finest cities.

"A New Star Is Born," said the first review. "Glorious voice, distinguished stage presence, youth, beauty . . . Miss Stevens hit with great impact last night . . ."

The other reviews reinforced the opinion: Risë's debut was a smash success. They all pointed out that, among other assets, Miss Stevens was soothing to the eye. They refrained from the obvious comparisons with mastodonic sopranos of yore, merely intimating that the Metropolitan was on the right track in adopting pulchritude as a general policy.

But Philadelphia comment, no matter how accurate and pro-
found, had little to do with the case. New York was still to be
faced, and there the final verdict would be rendered. The opera
was *Mignon*, the conductor was Wilfred Pelletier, and in the
distinguished cast were Richard Crooks and Ezio Pinza. There
was only a short time for preparation, and the ordeal was trying
for Risë, but the Philadelphia bloodletting was behind her, and
she faced New York with hope. From the backstage reaction
during the Philadelphia performance, she could sense that she
was being accepted by the tribe. Rival mezzos might pray de-
voutly for her collapse, but she could see that the crew was filled
with the quiet satisfaction of having launched another career with
success. Nobody patted her on the shoulder as she came off
stage, but the warmth was there, the friendly smiles were there.
The stagehands make no pretense of being critics, but they know
a good job done in a professional way. Risë had the satisfaction
of knowing that, from their point of view, she was solidly established with the company. She belonged.

Mr. Smith had been at his best for the Metropolitan opening.
He had sent a limousine and chauffeur for the Steenberg clan
and had been on hand in Risë's box when they arrived. Sadie
had worn his orchid with the proper pride of the mother of a
great diva. Mr. Smith had pointed out the celebrities for them
and, in fact, had waved to many of his personal friends in the
boxes of the Diamond Horseshoe. Between acts he had strolled
with them in the promenade behind the boxes, bought them
drinks in the restaurant, and examined the pictures of former
great stars along the walls.

"Risë will someday be here," said Sadie positively, and then,
looking at the crowded condition of the collection, had added:
"They'll have to push somebody else back."

The party that followed Risë's successful debut had erased from
the Steenberg memory the sad occasion in Brooklyn. Mr. Smith
had taken a private room at the Ritz, the guests were large in
number, and even Madame Schoen René could not dampen the
enthusiasm. As parents of the new star, Sadie and Pa were treated
with deference and affection. It was the great night of their lives,
the culmination of the long trail of struggle and worry. When

Mr. Smith at last deposited them in the lobby of their apartment house and departed into the night, Sadie turned to Risë with a happy sigh.

"He's a very nice fellow," she said, and added eagerly and significantly: "*Very* nice."

The New York critics were kind to Risë, accepting her as a distinct addition to the company and predicting a happy future for her. There were no hallelujahs or dancing in the streets, but the critics agreed that the new mezzo sang well, looked stunning, and had style. Since the New York critics were renowned for their refusal to do handsprings, Risë's reception could be regarded as both an ovation and a vote of confidence. She settled down in happiness to work out her future.

The New York debut had been December 17, 1938, afternoon. On the morning of December 21 of the same year, Risë answered the telephone in the Steenberg apartment. At first there was silence from the other end, and she jiggled the receiver with annoyance.

"It's me," said a voice finally.

Now it was Risë's time for silence. Her heart leaped into her mouth, and for a long moment she couldn't speak.

"Walter!" she said in a trembling whisper. "Where are you?"

"I'm here," said the impish Surovy.

Chapter Eight

During his last months in Vienna, Walter was faced with the possibility that both his career as an actor and his love affair with Risë were at an end. The Nazis were still driving with a light hand, but whole areas of dramatic literature were no longer permitted the Viennese theatres. The radical plays of Georg Kaiser and Ernst Toller were of course unthinkable, but now it was gently suggested that the German classics might well be re-examined with a view to excluding those that could possibly "excite the public." As the list of available plays narrowed and the pressure of the Nazis became more apparent, it took no seer to predict the end.

As for Risë, Walter had been aware of what was happening almost from the time of her first Buenos Aires letters. Nothing had ever been said about Mr. John Smith, but Walter knew without being told. Risë had beauty and charm and was embarking on a career that was bound to make her famous. Short of barricading herself in a cave, there was no possible way for her to avoid the life around her.

"I could read between the lines," says Walter wryly.

Walter made up his mind to leave Vienna, but it was easier said than done. When he quietly canvassed the chances of getting out of the country, he ran against a thousand obstacles. His first goal was Switzerland, where he could still carry on his work in a German-speaking theatre, but brief examination of this idea brought him the realization that he was merely evading the main issue: what he really wanted was America and Risë; anything else was a waste of effort.

But in the present condition of Europe, America lay out beyond nowhere. Unless sent on official business, Germans were not permitted to roam the world at leisure. When the first bombs began to fall, Hitler wanted his own people and his satellite allies close beside him. The borders were being sealed; the lock would soon turn in the door. When that happened, Walter would be trapped along with the rest. He stepped up the activities that might possibly get him out in time, and by chance he had a stroke of luck. On taking one of his friends into his confidence about his plans, that worthy had responded with a happy shout.

"What you'll need above all else is an American visa," he cried, "and I'm just the boy who can get it for you. The American consul. Wonderful fellow. One of my best friends. Comes to the theatre every night."

This turned out to be far more difficult than the jolly one had predicted. The American consul was indeed a pleasant fellow, but he had serious problems of his own. His office was besieged by people seeking a way of escape from Hitler. United States immigration quotas from Central Europe had long since been filled up. What were left were temporary visas and visiting permits. These needed to be scrutinized with care. Were the departing Austrians genuine refugees, or were they Nazi agents being subtly planted in democratic countries?

Hungary was still officially a neutral country, and it was this that finally got Walter the visa. Although the Iron Guard—the Hungarian reactionary equivalent of the Nazis—were established in power in Budapest, the regime maintained a pretense of independent action. They had stubbornly resisted attempts to include them in the Rome-Berlin Axis, and there was a faint hope in liberal circles that Hungary might remain a neutral island in the middle of Europe. In short, Hungarians were temporarily in a different posture from other Middle Europeans, and Walter benefited from the fact. He was issued a temporary American visa, good for thirty days.

"Good luck, old fellow, and all that sort of thing," said the consul in a friendly way, "but you still have to get out of Germany."

"I know," said Walter grimly.

He needed a German *Ausweis* (exit permit) and was afraid to apply for it; it would merely draw attention to him. In his background were his Prague political activities, his reading of *Don Carlos* in defiance of the Nazis. He thought of going over the Swiss border illegally but dismissed the idea. The Nazis guarded every inch of that frontier, and they shot to kill. For six weeks Walter fluttered helplessly against the walls of his cage. A letter from Risë brought matters to a head. For the first time he heard about Mr. John Smith. He had given the opening-night party in Philadelphia. Walter had known instinctively that he had a rival; he knew now that this was the man.

He took a definite resolve; the time for going was now. He applied to the Hungarian Embassy in Vienna for help in getting the *Ausweis*. For fifteen years he had scarcely set foot in his native country; there was no certainty that the Hungarian intercession would influence the Germans. What project had he in mind in New York? the Embassy asked. Walter put his cards on the table: he wanted to get to New York to marry the woman he loved. Delay might be fatal to his chances.

"It's not exactly a project," smiled the Hungarians, "but we'll try."

The *Ausweis* was issued two days later.

"They're still treating us pretty gingerly," explained the Hungarians. "You're lucky. It may not last long . . . and you're still not out."

Walter next went to see Dr. Hilpert, the theatre director. The Nazis would check to see if he had plans for returning, as had been asserted in his application for the exit permit.

"Dr. Hilpert, you will do me a great favor if you will allow me a two-weeks' vacation during the holidays," he said. "I want to visit New York."

"*New York!*" said Dr. Hilpert in astonishment. "You'll hardly get there and back in two weeks."

"One day will be enough," said Walter.

Dr. Hilpert looked at him quizzically.

"You're not coming back, are you?" he asked softly.

"No, but you're not supposed to admit it," said Walter.

"I *don't* admit it," said Dr. Hilpert stoutly. "I'll expect you back after the holidays." He allowed his eye to droop slightly in what might be taken as a wink. "Good luck," he said.

Walter started on his pilgrimage. He had his American visa, his Hungarian passport, and the German *Ausweis*. They looked formidable, and they might mean nothing. Between Vienna and the freedom of America was the whole width of Germany. There were borders to cross, inspectors to face, and the whole hypersensitive distrust and suspicion of the Nazi hierarchy to combat.

The crucial moment came at the German border. When the train halted, he joined the group before the little table of the custom officials. At his turn he handed over his passport, which the official regarded with a cold eye. He then looked up with a challenging air, and barked:

"Your name!"

The name was on the passport plainly enough, but evidently there was a purpose in the demand.

"Walter Surovy," said Walter.

"*Walter Surovy*, eh!" cried the man in a loud voice.

What followed was an extended silence, while the official again examined Walter's passport and seemed to be waiting for something. It was then that Walter noticed the black curtain behind the desk. After what seemed an interminable wait, the official suddenly stamped Walter's passport with a loud bang and handed it back to him. The first great step had been taken.

"I was too confused to realize it at the time," says Walter, "but of course there was another man back of the curtain checking on a black list. If my name had been there, my permit and passport and visa would have meant nothing. I'd never have got out."

At Hamburg he boarded the liner *Deutschland* for New York, but it was not until the ship had cleared the Kiel Canal and was in the North Sea that he took a free breath. The past was behind him, the future was before him—and there was nothing in that future that promised him good. He knew in his heart that the odds were weighted against him. As he sat in his cabin, with his two battered suitcases about him, he tapped anxiously again at the purse in his breast pocket to make sure it was still there. It contained everything he had in the world, and there would be no more when it was gone.

He landed in New York on December 21, 1938. A fitful soggy snow was falling, he knew not a word of English, and he had a hundred and fifty dollars in his pocket.

On the dock to meet him was Joern Winner, brother of an actor friend in Vienna. He knew Joern Winner only slightly but clung to him grimly. Winner was his only hope in accomplishing the thing that needed to be done before seeing Risë. When Walter was established in his room at the Piccadilly Hotel in the Times Square section, he immediately got to the point. Did Winner know a man named John Smith? He produced Risë's letter with the name spelled out. Winner knew him, everybody knew John Smith in artistic circles in New York, and Winner himself belonged to that group. Would Winner look up the telephone number of Mr. John Smith and put a call through to him immediately? It was imperative that Walter talk to him.

It was Walter's idea that Winner would translate for him, but something happened after Winner began talking with Smith that threw Walter into a state of elation. Soon after the conversation began, Winner leaned toward Walter and whispered:

"He speaks German."

"*Gott Sei Dank!*" cried Walter excitedly, and reached for the phone. "Give me that!" he yelled.

It was not difficult for Walter to make himself known, for Smith had heard the name so often from Risë that he was nauseated at the very sound of it. Walter stated that he had something of extreme importance to discuss with Mr. Smith concerning Risë. Would Mr. Smith do him the honor of lunching with him? Since Mr. Smith was hopeful that he might soon make an announcement on behalf of Miss Stevens and himself, this was something he couldn't ignore.

"What restaurant had you in mind?" he asked.

"Twenty One," said Walter promptly.

Like many other Europeans, Walter had a fairly good idea of New York life from American magazines. For his purposes it was necessary to present a brave front. His pocketbook called for the Automat, but the nature of his quest demanded Chambord or the Colony. He settled on Twenty One as being the meeting place of New York's actors and writers.

Walter's first look at Mr. Smith did his mood no good: the man was far too handsome, self-possessed, and distinguished for his satisfaction. Walter covered his reaction with charm and heartiness. Mr. Smith might want to get to the matter at once, but the continental amenities must be fulfilled. There must be drinks at the bar; there must be the proper isolated table in the corner.

With exquisite tact and admirable restraint, Mr. Smith met each of Walter's moves with a polite riposte of his own. There was a meal to be ordered, and Mr. Smith went about this with a taste and thoroughness that brought a leaden feeling to Walter's midriff. On the *Deutschland,* Walter had studied American coinage with a pertinacity that must surely lead to mastery; he now saw the prices on the Twenty One menu. His heart sank, and his condition was not bettered by Mr. Smith's next words.

"And wine, of course," he said with an inquiring lift of the brow. "Have you a favorite?"

Walter smiled into his eyes.

"The choice is yours," he said, with a barely perceptible movement of the hand.

Every bite Mr. Smith ate stabbed Walter in that most sensitive of spots: the pocketbook. At first he couldn't help mentally calculating what the final damage would be, but he gave that up in despair and concentrated on playing his role as a sophisticated host. The years of theatrical drudgery made this simple; for all Mr. Smith was to know, Walter might be in the drawing room of a Noël Coward comedy. They chatted amiably, they laughed easily, they exchanged recollections of opera and theatre.

And then, with the serving of coffee, Walter leaned forward and launched into his story. More than a story: it was a challenge. He stated frankly his relations with Risë in Prague and his hope for the future. He hastened to add that conditions changed as the world was changing, and he claimed no advantage by reason of his earlier friendship with Risë.

"You are a gentleman, and I hope you will consider me a gentleman," said Walter. "I want to marry Risë, and although nobody has told me so, I have a feeling that you are about to make her an offer of marriage. I will admit that the advantages are all on your side. You have everything to give her; I can give her only myself. Perhaps I should retire from the field and give her the opportunities I can never give her, but in doing that I would be giving up my life. Let me make you a proposition: give me one week alone with Risë before she makes her final decision between us. You have been with her constantly; I have not seen her in months. If at the end of a week she has not made up her mind or has decided on you, I will return to Europe and you will not be bothered with me again."

As seen on reflection, Mr. Smith really had little choice in the matter. He could hardly turn down the proposition without putting himself in the position of distrusting his own attractiveness. The fairness of the plan might be illusory, but Risë could scarcely be expected to be proud of a man who had rejected it. Mr. Smith was not only a gentleman, but he was a person of astuteness. He was confident that his case possessed qualities not easily discounted, but he also knew that he must meet this sporting gesture head-on. He smiled with the greatest aplomb and accepted the challenge.

Walter paid the check, left a tip of such size that he still shudders when he thinks of it, and went back to his hotel. It was then that he called Risë for the first time.

"I'm coming right up," he said. "Where do you live?"

Risë told him.

"How do I get there?" asked Walter.

"Where are you?" asked Risë.

"Hotel Piccadilly, Time Square," said Walter.

"Do you know anything about the subway?" asked Risë.

"Of course, I do!" cried Walter. "*Everything.*"

He knew nothing, but what Hungarian ever admits that?

"Well, go right downstairs and take the northbound Broadway train on the IRT and get off at 103rd Street."

What Risë forgot to say in the excitement was that certain of the West Side IRT trains branched off at 96th Street and coursed away through Harlem to the Bronx. Walter followed the stations with eagerness as the trip began—50th, 59th, 66th, 72nd—then it was 96th Street, and he was getting ready to debark at the next stop when the train shrieked its way around a sharp curve and wound up at 110th Street. Walter was in a panic. By the time he recovered his wits, the train was at 145th Street in Harlem. He leaped from the train, plunged up the stairs to the daylight, and found himself in an area that, for all he knew, might be Limbo.

He knew only one word: Broadway. He tried this on a passer-by, who pointed vaguely toward the setting sun. He started to walk. Taxis passed him, and he considered them and then thought of Twenty One and reconsidered. He thought of calling Risë but refrained out of a sense of shame. He thought of taking the subway with a view to picking up the lost trail but shuddered at the very thought of braving that underground hell again. He continued to walk. His shoes were not right for walking; the fitful snow had left the sidewalks slushy and slippery; he was splashed by vehicles at crossings; the last rays of the sun were fading over the Hudson—and still he walked. He was a wet, bedraggled, and beaten character when he reached Risë's door.

"Where have you been!" she cried in pity. "You look awful. I thought you were dead."

"I *am* dead," said Walter morosely.

If Risë was astonished, Sadie and Pa were flabbergasted. Was this the suave leading man of Prague Risë was always bragging about? Was this cat-dragged-in creature the sophisticated man about town who set all feminine hearts atremble on the Ringstrasse? Sadie put the whole thing down as a grievous mistake in reporting. She saw him for what he was: a forlorn stranger wet to the knees.

"Take your shoes off," she commanded. "I'll get you a pair of Pa's socks."

This was hardly the impression Walter had hoped to make on the Steenberg household, but he subsided willingly. There were tears in his eyes from the nippy weather, his nose was running, and he knew he was in for a cold and perhaps pneumonia.

"That coat," clucked Sadie in disgust, shaking the raindrops from what Walter had considered rather an elegant sartorial item. "Did you ever see such a flimsy thing?" said Sadie to Risë, and then added indignantly: "What's so funny to you?"

Risë was leaning against the doorjamb in hysterics. The return of the prodigal lover was turning out to be hilarious farce, much like some of his better theatrical roles. She knew what he had been through, she was overjoyed to see him—and she couldn't stop laughing. The sight of the great, omnipotent, all-conquering Surovy sitting huddled in a rocking chair under the ministrations of the clucking Sadie was too much for her. She laughed till there was no breath left in her.

At the end of two weeks Risë had not only made up her mind about Mr. John Smith, but she had married Walter.

"What could I do?" she shrugs now. "He said I had to. No, that's a joke. I knew the minute he walked in the door the jig was up with me. He looked like a drowned cat, and I couldn't stop laughing, but it was Prague all over again. We belonged together, and that was all there was to it."

The marriage was set for January 6, and Risë had trouble with the preliminaries. The legal formalities had to be sandwiched in between rehearsals of *Rosenkavalier*, which had new principals and needed more work. She was particularly fearful of the blood test.

"At the sight of that needle, I'll faint," she prophesied.

"Nonsense," said Walter. "There's nothing to it. It's a flea bite."

Risë went through the ordeal with flying colors; Walter fainted.

On the morning of the wedding Walter went down by subway to the Marriage License Bureau at the Municipal Building, accompanied by Sadie and Pa and Bud. Risë was at rehearsal and would meet them there at noon. Waiting for Walter at the Municipal Building was his only New York friend, Joern Winner, who would act with Bud as a witness. Risë rushed in late; they filled out the requisite forms, Walter dutifully handed over two dollars of his rapidly dwindling hoard.

Bud had been carefully instructed in his duties. At points where Walter was supposed to say "I do," Bud was to kick him in the shins. The ceremony began in a setting as devoid of sentiment and emotion as the Sunnyside freight assembling yard of the Pennsylvania Railroad. The clerk was bored and harassed. There was a long line waiting for his services. He hurried through the solemn rite. At every pause Bud kicked and Walter piped "I do!" The pace became faster, the pauses shorter. Bud kicked; Walter piped. Finally, he couldn't wait for Bud; at every pause, Walter yelled "I do!"

"Wait a minute!" said the clerk, with exasperation. "You're gettin' married twice, and this girl ain't gettin' married at all."

It was over at last; they were married. Risë gave Walter a hasty kiss and rushed for the subway. She was already late for rehearsal. The Steenbergs, Walter, and Winner went up to the cafeteria of the Municipal Building and had a cup of coffee. They drank quietly and solemnly, as if the body were lying in the next room.

"Even Walter's friend seemed dubious about the whole thing," reports Risë. "He might have brought a flower, but he didn't. Walter or Sadie might have brought a flower, but *they* didn't. As for our friends, they were unanimously agreed that the marriage wouldn't last a month and saw no sense in wasting a wedding gift on a short-run proposition like that. After twenty years we're still waiting for our first wedding present."

When Risë got back to the Metropolitan rehearsal and was kneeling at Lotte Lehmann's feet in a scene, Madame Lehmann looked at her in astonishment.

"What's happened to you?" she asked. "You look as if you'd seen a vision."

"I've just got married," said Risë.

Madame Lehmann leaned down happily and kissed her on the cheek.

"You dear lucky child," she said.

Walter's honeymoon consisted of a return journey by subway to the Steenburg apartment, where he became established as a member of the family. Life at the Hotel Piccadilly was eating up what was left from the splendid adventure at Twenty One. He needed a heavier overcoat, and quick, before he froze to death.

His profession as an actor was closed to him, and he acquired the English language with painful slowness.

"Other people get jobs," said Walter. "I'm not proud. I can always be a waiter."

"You will *not!*" cried Risë furiously. "No husband of mine is going to be a waiter. Forget it."

This was all very nice, but it evaded the fact that Walter was a dead weight in the household. The family made no complaint and was happy having him there, but, no matter how you examined it, he was a non-producer with a hearty appetite.

During the long hours when Risë was away at her work, Walter either sat glumly in his room or walked the streets of upper Broadway in a daze. There seemed no place for him either in Risë's life or in America. One day Risë came home in a state of gloom that matched his own.

"Schoen René wants to see you," she said.

"*Me!*" cried Walter in fright. "What for?"

"I don't know," said Risë worriedly, "but do it for my sake. I owe it to her."

Schoen René wasted no charming preliminaries on him when they met. She got to the point immediately.

"I make no pretense that I like you," she said abruptly and intensely, "but it is not a personal matter. I think it was a mistake for Risë to marry, and I would have hated anybody she married. But the deed is done, and we must now see what can come out of it. I want to know exactly what you can do for Risë."

It was her way of saying that in a disaster of such magnitude, she was eager to save the little that could be salvaged. What followed was an interrogation that Walter still refers to as the "third degree." With harsh, biting questions she probed into every detail of his background and life. Walter was beaten to a pulp by the time she finished and was hardly in shape for the astonishing reversal that followed.

"Well, now," said Schoen René elatedly, "this is much better than I thought. I would still prefer Risë unmarried, but if it had to be done, I can see that you would be much better for her than John Smith."

Walter blinked in amazement.

"That surprises you, eh?" asked Madame. "The Smith money could have smothered her, and that would be fatal to her as an artist. This girl needs to be guided and driven. She is already a great singer, a great artist, but she lacks confidence. Left to herself, she might lapse into mediocrity. I can see that you are a clever man, and the marriage itself proves you are a determined man. You know the theatre and the ways of artists. You will soon learn the background of opera. Risë needs you; you can be a great help to her. I ask you a promise: will you devote your life to her?"

"I will," said Walter, and soon found himself on the sidewalk, treading on air. He knew this was a turning point in his life. From being nothing but a displaced person, he now had a purpose in life.

"Perhaps I make too much of it," says Walter, "but without Schoen René I'm afraid I couldn't have gone on. As things were, I'd have had to leave, feeling I was a burden on Risë. Madame set me on the right track."

As a matter of fact, Risë was progressing with every performance at the opera, and her success was assured. Her *Rosenkavalier*, in fact, had been a sensation. At last there was an Octavian who looked every inch the handsome hussar. The critics had refrained from stating in so many words that the Stevens legs had interested them, but the implication was plain. Newspaper photographs of the same admirable assets did Risë no harm with the public. When the critics added that her voice was opulent and was colored delicately and handled with distinction, the picture was handsomely complete.

And then in February something happened that altered Walter's status in the Steenberg household entirely. Risë had already signed for another season in Buenos Aires, and there had been worried discussion about what Walter would do during her absence. Risë's contract called for round-trip steamship passage, and there was some talk of putting the bite on the Teatro Colón for Walter's trip, but little hope was held for the idea. It was plainly beyond the Steenberg budget for Walter to go at his own expense. Out of the blue came an offer from Buenos Aires for Walter to appear with a German dramatic company just organized there. It had been formed by refugee actors, many of them former associates of Walter. They were starting on a shoestring and could not pay Walter's way down, but there would be a moderate salary and perhaps a bonus at the end of the season, if things went well.

"I'll swim," said Walter excitedly.

It was a lifesaver for him. His position in the household had been wearing on him to a point where he didn't know how much longer he could stand it; this made him again a man of importance.

"Star roles only, Sadie," he said elatedly, aiming a finger at her midriff. "It's right here in the contract; they wouldn't think of offering anything else."

"You can't make me mad," said Sadie.

As if this wasn't luck enough, Risë was offered a summer season at Glyndebourne, the enchanting English country spot where the operas of Mozart and Rossini were given in a fairyland.

"How can we do both?" asked Risë. "We're already signed for Buenos Aires."

"Glyndebourne comes early and the season is short," said Walter. "It isn't the money, but you need to make an impression on those English critics. You'll be in Buenos Aires in plenty of time."

She made an outstanding success as Cherubino, the lovesick lad in *The Marriage of Figaro.*

They sailed for South America in August on a cloud of happiness, more strictly known as an ocean liner. Walter's salary wouldn't even pay for ship passage, but he was back in the theatre, and he was with Risë.

Walter's reunion with his old friends in Buenos Aires was a joyous occasion and then came the question of what role he would appear in first. *"The Doctor's Dilemma,"* said Walter promptly. They consented, the play was given, and the theatre was almost ruined.

"That had been my first part in Prague," says Walter. "And it had been a resounding flop. But I was going to show old Bernard Shaw or die in the attempt. I died. At the end of the performance the silence could be heard far out on the Pampas."

He hastily retreated to his comedy roles, the season went on happily, and, in fact, the theatre is now an established institution in Buenos Aires. As for Risë, she was having her usual success at the Teatro Colón, where she was now an accepted favorite. With Walter on the premises her relationship with the American Embassy was of another character, but her old friends were happy to see her. The language barrier was still a handicap for Walter, but he refused to let it bother him.

"I wish to heaven you'd learn English," Risë said to him one night after a party in which he had looked a bit stupid standing in a corner.

"I know it perfectly," said Walter easily. "It's just that I can't use it."

On their return to New York, Risë found that her position with the Metropolitan had mysteriously altered. Her first season had been an acknowledged success, but in the schedule for the new season her appearances in *Rosenkavalier* and *Mignon* had been cut to a minimum—four in all. She had already agreed to do Fricka in *Die Walküre* and it was now hinted that there were other choice secondary roles that would help extend her repertory. Risë was first baffled, and then furious.

"Take it easy," said Walter soothingly, when she announced her intention of having it out with Edward Johnson. "Something's going on here, and we don't know what it is. Let's try to find out."

They found out that it was Walter himself.

"Nobody will admit it," said a knowing friend Risë appealed to, "but somebody down there is sincerely convinced that your marriage was a mistake that will eventually ruin you. They feel it can't possibly last and that the worries you'll have over it will affect you as an artist. They hired you with the thought that you'd be with the company for a long time. Now they want to build somebody else up they can be sure of."

Walter's reaction to the report was prompt.

"If I'm standing in your way," he said, "I'll go."

"If you go, I'll go," said Risë, and added furiously: "And stop talking like a half-wit."

"Well, then," said Walter, "let's sit down and figure it out."

It was at this point that Walter officially took over Risë's life. He had learned a great deal in a year around the opera house and now proceeded to put some of his ideas into practice. Risë had signed for a small salary, but it was explicitly stated in the contract that she was coming as a star, with the promise of leading roles in *Rosenkavalier* and *Mignon*. The theory that she needed to broaden her repertory could be very seductive, and Risë was not in a good position to fight it.

"*That* way you don't go," Walter said flatly. "You'll simply get lost in the mob."

"But what can I do?" wailed Risë. "They only give me a few of the good parts and keep trying to force the others on me."

"You turn them down as long as you can and then you take one, and then you turn down some others," said Walter. "Meanwhile, I'll stretch you."

This was the initial mention of the magical Surovy formula. At first hearing, it was not impressive. Risë's debut had been successful, but it had not set the Hudson River on fire, and it was hardly likely that the Metropolitan management was quaking in its boots at her disapproval of the new schedule. As a general rule, mezzo-sopranos were not indispensable. Great roles were scarce for them, and it was only rarely that a mezzo reached a top position at the opera house. Risë set down all the adverse arguments; Walter was not moved.

"If you're great, you're great," he said. "Bassos are not usually stars, but Chaliapin was."

There had been a few hopeful happenings in the first year. She had been signed by Columbia Artists Management, Inc., for two appearances at $1000 apiece. This began an association with Calvin Franklin, of Columbia, which ended with his tragic death in 1941. There had also been several guest appearances on radio at lesser fees. This was all on the good side, and if the situation at the opera house could be worked out, Risë had every right to feel encouraged. Franklin now presented a new contract for ten concerts at $750 each.

"*Hey*, now!" cried Risë, hurt and bewildered, when this document reached the house. "I'm slipping before I start."

"All right," said the sensible Surovy. "Maybe you weren't worth a thousand. We'll take this and keep mum like a mouse."

Walter made a point of meeting Franklin and working with

him. Although Columbia had an efficient publicity department, Walter provided additional material that stressed Risë's looks and personality. Risë moaned when the bills came in, but Walter was unmoved.

"You're not going to starve," he said, "and you're not going to end up singing in a choir."

From the start Walter had decided on the big gamble. Either Risë would reach the top, or she would be nothing. He knew Risë far better than she knew herself. She might convince herself that a secondary position would be all right, but from the beginning she had set her sights high. Anything less would be a defeat for her. Her great talents would get her far; it was his job to kick her along the rest of the way.

Chapter Nine

Knowing how he stood at the Metropolitan, Walter carefully stayed in the background, but Risë made no move without his advice. So far as the public knew, she stood alone. The fights with the Metropolitan were the greatest strain on her, for what she wanted to do was break up the furniture, but Walter gave her strict orders to be as sweet as treacle and as sly as the gnu. But anybody approaching her with a proposition knew that Surovy's was the hand at the tiller.

"I don't know anything about it," she would say helplessly. "Tell it to Walter."

For the past year Walter had been working closely with Calvin Franklin, who was amused by the persistence of the Hungarian. Franklin had most of the great artists on his list, but Walter always approached him as if he were handling Risë alone. Walter was full of fertile ideas for the advancement of Risë's career. Franklin would laugh and throw up his hands defensively.

"Now wait a minute, buddy," he would say. "We've got to give this girl a chance to get her breath."

He meant that the Stevens Special was going too fast, and with possibly not enough substance behind it, but this never stopped Walter. For a long time he had kept his eye on Nelson

Eddy, who was not only a Hollywood star but the hottest thing on Franklin's concert list. There was a report that the famous Hollywood team of Eddy and Jeanette MacDonald was being broken up, and Walter went quietly to work on the matter. If Eddy needed a new partner, what better than Risë?

When it came time to place the yearly advertisement in *Musical America*, Walter turned up with a beautiful photograph of Risë and suggested that they purchase a full page.

"You're not modest, are you?" said Franklin.

"Oh, you wouldn't want to spoil a good picture like that," said Walter.

When the magazine appeared with the advertisement, Walter was again at Franklin's office.

"Why don't you send this out to Nelson Eddy and just drop a light hint that Risë would be available for pictures?" suggested Walter. "You might as well be getting two commissions," he added, guilefully.

Nelson Eddy was impressed by the photograph and inquired if Risë might be on the Coast soon. By a lucky break, which Risë always seems to get at crucial moments, she was to appear with the San Francisco Opera Company. Various M-G-M big shots viewed her in those performances, and a date was set for her to take a screen test in Hollywood.

Risë picked this moment to be difficult. For some unaccountable reason she had been against the project from the start and became more hardheaded as the discussion raged.

"How do I know I won't fall on my face?" she demanded. "I'm not an actor."

"You're a *great* actor!" cried Walter.

"Oh, Walter, be sensible," she said heatedly. "Just because I can get around the stage without knocking somebody down doesn't mean I'm an actor."

Walter has since figured out that Risë was afraid that the millions of Jeanette MacDonald fans might resent her taking their idol's place. Following a star of that magnitude was something to worry about, and Walter realized that he had a fight on his hands with Risë. The big argument took place in San Francisco;

unless he won it, there would be no screen test in Hollywood. What Walter produced was a thing of genius.

"When did you last see the sun?" he asked.

"What are you talking about?" asked Risë with some asperity.

"You spend the winters in New York," pointed out Walter, "and then you go down to South America and spend another winter."

"We were in England this summer," cried Risë triumphantly.

"Did you ever see the sun?" asked Walter.

"No-o-o," admitted Risë, "but it was summer."

From then on the climate of Southern California had no competition. Walter expounded on it at length, but he might have saved his breath: Risë was convinced.

Risë was in a good mood for the screen test and went through it gaily. Walter could tell from the reaction of the crew that she was doing well, but that meant nothing in those mysterious precincts where Louis B. Mayer and his cohorts gathered. There were many things to be considered. Risë was comparatively unknown; her experience as an actress was nil. She would have to buck the prejudices of a public that had become accustomed to Jeanette MacDonald.

For two days after the test there was no reaction. Now it was Risë's turn to hold Walter's hand. He paced their hotel room like a caged lion, hitting the walls with his fist in rage and impotence. They were strangers in Hollywood; he had nobody to turn to who might help them. In desperation he called Calvin Franklin in New York. Perhaps he had heard something.

"Well, this takes the cake," said Franklin. "You're there and I'm here, and you're asking *me*."

"Call Nelson Eddy and see if he's heard anything," pleaded Walter.

"All right, but it's crazy," said Franklin. "You could go around the block and ask him."

He called back an hour later with a report that was more tantalizing than encouraging.

"Nelson likes the test all right," said Franklin, "but he's not the boss. Old Louie B. has to make up his mind. Nelson is staying strictly out of it. He doesn't want them blaming him if something goes wrong."

On the third day there was a call from Mayer's office. Could Mr. and Mrs. Surovy come to a small party in Mr. Mayer's office that afternoon? Just a few producers and directors.

"A small party to look me over," said Risë bitterly.

This was wrong. It was a large party, the annual holiday binge Mayer gave for his top executives. Not only were the producers and directors failing to look Risë over, but she had a difficult time getting a place to stand in the crowded room. In due course she found herself before the great man himself. His eyes lighted up with interest when he heard her name.

"Ah!" he said, "you're the one I wanted to see."

He looked around uncertainly, as if seeking for an open space away from the bedlam. Suddenly, he seemed to make up his mind.

"Follow me," he said, starting to make his way through the mob. Their progress was slow, but they finally reached their destination. Mayer threw open a door and gestured to her to proceed him. She found herself in the bathroom. He waved an elegant hand to the only seat. It was the toilet seat, and she took it. It was then that she learned she was to be Nelson Eddy's partner in a new version of *The Chocolate Soldier*. They would use the plot of Molnar's *The Guardsman* and keep the old music.

Risë's first shooting day at M-G-M brought on all her old indecision. At the gate she was met by a Cerberus who might as well have been a border guard. When she gave her name, he looked at her with his own special combination of superciliousness and disdain.

"Sit down over there," he said.

She waited for half an hour, seething beautifully the while. At the end of that period an inner door opened, and an irritated gentleman emerged.

"Where have you been!" he cried testily.

"Here," said Risë. "He wouldn't let me in."

"Good heavens!" said the man with exasperation. "All you had to do was say you were playing with Nelson Eddy."

Thus bolstered in her confidence, Risë went forward with trepidation to her first day of shooting. This turned out to be a period of introduction that would give her a feel of the new medium. Before the cameras could start turning on the great opus, there were painful days of wardrobe fittings, photographs, and make-up. Every trace of character was removed from Risë's face, and she was made to look like a sixteen-year-old angel, but with the great wheels of M-G-M turning there was little she could do about it.

Nelson Eddy proved to be an amiable individual—and a practical joker. In this he was merely following Hollywood tradition, in that a newcomer must be hazed like a freshman in a tank-town college. In Risë's case this took the form of a distinguished gentleman, introduced as a noted critic from New Zealand.

"Your training?" he said to Risë after hearing a number. "Rather limited, would you say?"

Risë gave him a haughty look.

"If I might suggest," he put in later, "you stand rather awkwardly. Restricts the diaphragm, you might say. If you placed the left foot rather well forward, I think you would notice a difference."

Risë scowled and kept her feet where they were.

"No, no!" cried the gentleman at a later point. "You must NOT screech on the high notes. It is *very* unbecoming."

The man, of course, was a professional ribber, and even the grips far up in the flies were holding their sides in ecstasy, but Risë's aplomb in the end was too much for him. In a quiet moment amid the turmoil, Risë uttered an aside to Mr. Eddy, quite audible for all purposes.

"Quaint little fellow, isn't he?" she said.

The audience was rather put out, the remark not being the sort of thing a victim should produce.

"Too dumb to know she was being ribbed," said one disgruntled stagehand.

"Don't you believe it," said Walter quietly.

Hollywood provided the sun Risë had been promised, and she soon began wishing she had never heard the word. It was what the loyal Hollywoodites referred to as an "exceptional" summer. More than that, it was deadly. For ten straight days the concrete desert known as the Metro lot registered temperatures of one hundred and over. On Sound Stage #5, under the murderous production lights, no one dared estimate the heat, out of fear of front-office retaliation. Suggestions that shooting might be confined to the nighttime were rebuffed by the same authorities, who knew to the penny what union overtime would be. It would have helped little in any case, since the temperature was still ninety at midnight. Minor players slept on cots on the sets rather than buck the searing traffic home and a tossing night in their own beds.

Walter had rented a small house on a crag overlooking Hollywood, with the thought that they would sit at their picture window at night and view the magical scene below, but they only rarely took advantage of the privilege. What Risë did when she reached home at night was fall in bed in a stupor. As one who has been known to sleep twenty hours without turning over in bed, and customarily regards a ten-hour stretch as a snooze, she was finding the Hollywood hours murderous. In order to be on the set at nine o'clock for shooting, it was necessary to be out of bed at five-thirty in the morning. By the time she was dressed, had breakfast, and drove to the studio, it would be seven o'clock. What followed were two interminable and infernal hours with the hairdresser, the make-up man, and the wardrobe mistress. She particularly resented the make-up man.

"They gave me a wig that made me look like Hedy Lamarr," says Risë. "I'd look at myself in the mirror and say: 'Who's that?' The first thing they did was put a card over one side of my face to see which side was better. Then they made up the other side to match exactly. The face was symmetrical, all right, and as blank as a puppet. My hair made me look like a vamp; my face made me look like a juvenile moron taking lessons to be an idiot."

Her costumes were heavy to begin with; by late afternoon they felt like armor. Shooting quit at six. By the time she got her make-up off, drove home, had a bath and dinner, it was often nine o'clock. "*You* look at downtown Los Angeles," she would say to Walter, and fall into bed. During their first weeks in town they had met some old friends and made some new ones, but now they had no time to see them. On Saturday shooting often went on till midnight. This meant a good twenty-two-hour work

day by the time she got to bed. Their weekend—meaning Sunday
—pleasures were governed by this circumstance.

"Drop in around four," Walter would say. "Risë should be up
by that time."

"Be *up?*" said their friends in amazement.

"Well, five, then," Walter would say, just to be on the safe side.

It was nerve-racking, back-breaking work, and Risë was worn
out by the time it was over.

"When do they get time for all that sin I hear about around
here?" she asked Walter one day.

"Don't look at me," said Walter, backing away defensively.

Risë was never pleased with her work in the picture, but *The
Chocolate Soldier* turned out to be a rattling success. Overnight
Risë became a national celebrity. In time, it would make her
known internationally. The first practical reaction came from
Calvin Franklin.

"I've just seen it!" he shouted excitedly into the phone from
New York. "It's great. The kid's hot. Her price goes up to $2500."

"$1500," said Walter coolly.

"Oh, come on, now, Walter, cut it out," cried Franklin. "Since
when have *you* started a campaign against money? This is the
time to get it."

"Yes, *one* time," said Walter, "but that isn't enough. We want
to keep going back into those towns. I want every local manager
to feel ashamed for making so much money out of Risë. I want
him to be happy as a lark."

This has resulted in almost twenty years of smash concert tours.
The Hungarian boy knew what he was doing.

But this is getting ahead of the story. When Risë finished *The
Chocolate Soldier* and went east to fill her concert and opera
dates, Walter stayed behind in Hollywood. Despite the hard
work, Risë had fallen in love with the place. They would make it
their home thereafter.

Risë was in her hotel room one night in Racine, Wisconsin,
when the phone rang. It was Walter on the wire.

"They've got me," he said.

"Who's got you?" demanded Risë.

"Drafted," said Walter succinctly.

Risë began to laugh.

"What a soldier *you'll* make," she said.

"I was raised as a soldier, damn it!" shouted Walter.

This was true, since Walter's only real education had been in a private military academy, but Risë was thinking about his language difficulties. When at home, they always spoke in German, and Walter had made little progress with his English. He could get along haltingly in a conversation, but he had no confidence in his abilities and would lapse at the first opportunity.

Risë was back in Hollywood in time to drive Walter to the draft board, where she deposited him in a mass of bemuscled Californians who quite overshadowed her Hungarian hero. He waved her a forlorn farewell, and she went back home to await the verdict of his physical examination. This proved all too satisfactory, and next heard from Walter was ensconced in a barracks at Fort MacArthur, where further tests would be made to establish his proper position in the Army. During the first test in arithmetic he had arisen from his seat in the middle of the assemblage and requested to be heard.

"I do not understand it," he had said in fractured English.

"Don't understand *what?*" asked the sergeant with a glower. "The words?"

"Not the words," said Walter, "the terms. You mention feet, and I know only meters. You say pounds, and I know only kilos. It is not a fair test."

The sergeant took some time to think this over.

"All right, buddy," he finally said, with a dismissing wave of the hand. "Outside, then."

Other tests were equally unsatisfactory for both Walter and Army. He kept taking them, and assorted sergeants kept saying, "Outside, then." His last test was taken at two o'clock in the morning, and Walter was half asleep. It was of the "true" or "false" variety, and Walter understood not a word of it. However, he realized that something was expected of him and did his best to please. If the look in the sergeant's eye seemed to show that he would appreciate "yes" as an answer, Walter gave him "yes." At the end of the session the sergeant shook Walter heartily by the hand.

In the morning Walter found that he had passed the test with the highest mark: he was now a radio repair man.

Before he had time to savor the full importance of this achievement, he found himself in the van of an army truck, headed north. The journey seemed interminable and in fact was over five hundred miles. They left at midnight and arrived the next midnight. Meals en route were sketchy, and Walter slept in the truck with his pack as a pillow. The camp was near Sacramento; the men were in a state of collapse when they arrived, and in no mood for humor.

"Watch the grass," said the burly sergeant who greeted them. "Just planted."

They leaped lightly from the truck—and fell up to their hips in mud. This was Camp Kohler, and a hell hole. Even the International Red Cross at Geneva had said so. It had been an internment camp for Japanese after the attack on Pearl Harbor had thrown California into a panic. Camp Kohler, an army installation abandoned after the First World War, had been quickly put into shape for the internees. Conditions had been so bad that the Red Cross had intervened. The Japanese were transferred to a better camp; the Army took back Camp Kohler. The walls of the barracks leaned wearily against the wind; the parade ground was a morass; the camp looked as if one good gust would blow it away. Walter was given a cot with a lumpy mattress, and a place in the repair room. After two days a private first class appeared with a radio.

"For Captain Twilling," he said. "Busted tube or something. I'll be back in an hour."

At the end of an hour he returned to find Walter looking helplessly at a mess of radio parts.

"Wassa matter?" asked Private First Class indignantly.

"I never fixed a radio in my life," said Walter.

This was duly reported to Captain Twilling or perhaps to the Pentagon, and Walter found himself outside again. This time he was marching with a squad. Here he was in his element, as the astonished sergeant immediately discovered.

"Hey, Fritz," he cried, "where'd you learn that stuff?"

Walter told him.

"Well, hell, you don't need me," said the sergeant. "You oughta be runnin' one of these goon squads yourself."

Walter became a squad leader with a new title: private first class. This presented difficulties. He knew how it should be done, but he didn't know how to tell the men. His first attempts in English brought nothing but guffaws and vulgar slapping of the thighs.

"*Achtung!*" cried Walter sharply.

The men sprang to attention. Walter became the only German drill sergeant in the American Army. Since the men didn't know what the commands meant in the first place, they were just as happy to have them in German. At the first general parade Walter's well-drilled outfit stood out like a jewel.

His men called him affectionately Fritz or the Kraut, and when the recreation room was finally put in shape and ping-pong tables were installed, his fame spread to larger areas.

"You know this game, Fritz?" they asked him.

"A little," said Walter.

In the tournament that followed, he blasted his way to the championship without losing a game. What they didn't know, and what he never told them, was that he had been captain of the Hungarian table-tennis team in the international championships at Stockholm. He had been eliminated in that competition by a gangling Englishman named Fred Perry, who was later to be the tennis champion of the world.

When conditions at camp had settled down to a point where the brass could look over the records of the men, something else was discovered about Walter. He received a summons to Captain Twilling's office.

"I see here that you're an actor," said the captain.

"Yes, sir," said Walter.

"Does that mean you could do something with an American show?"

"I think so," said Walter.

The captain explained that morale conditions at camp were not of the best, and the commanding general had suggested rather tartly that something be done about it. The bad day was Sunday. The men were given a day off, but no passes were being issued, and there were rumbles in the ranks that suggested either mutiny or boredom. Church services were really not filling the need, and the captain asked if Walter might possibly get up an entertainment to fill the void.

"I'm afraid you'll not find it among the men," said Walter.

"Of course not," said the captain. "I thought you might find it in Sacramento."

Sacramento, Walter found, was not a show town. There were a few scrubby night clubs that had begun hiring acts in the hope that the Army would relax its ban on passes and permit the boys to come in and spend a few quid, but the only thing in addition was a burlesque show. Even as burlesque shows go, it was not a good burlesque show. Furthermore, it was starving. It needed no patriotic approach to interest the burlesque show management in playing at the camp gratis; anything that would get the log jam broken and spring the GIs from camp was their meat.

The first performance took place the next Sunday in the recreation hall immediately after the last church service. The juxtaposition was unfortunate in any event; it was brutal in view of the show. It was not, strictly speaking, a sacred concert. The GIs hanging from the rafters whooped and hollered at the appearance of each new strip-teaser. From the audience reaction the show was a roaring success; backstage Captain Twilling alternately boiled with fury and held his head in pain. Walter kept carefully out of his way, concentrating on the general, who sat in the front row with his staff. The general had an unexpressive countenance. He kept his eye fixed grimly on the action before him, but nothing showed on his face. A young lieutenant sought out Captain Twilling backstage after the performance.

"The General wants to see you, sir," he said.

"Court martial, probably," muttered Captain Twilling.

Walter followed him out front, but at a safe distance.

"Captain Twilling!" bellowed the general, as the unfortunate man neared. Captain Twilling froze at attention, waiting for the blow to fall. Walter cringed behind him.

"Greatest show I've seen in years!" boomed the general. "Got to have more of them right away. Best thing that ever happened for the men. Keep 'em going steady, right along."

Walter was made a corporal on the basis of his triumph, and now there were further conferences with Captain Twilling.

"There may be more of them," said the captain, biting his words off bitterly, "but they're not going to be any damn shows like *that!* Where else do they have actors?"

"Hollywood," said Walter promptly.

"*Hollywood!*" cried the captain unbelievingly. "For a dump like this?"

Walter filled the captain in rapidly on the patriotic fervor of the film colony and daintily let fall the tidings about Risë and *The Chocolate Soldier.*

Nelson Eddy!" cried the captain worshipfully. "Well, *now . . .* !"

Risë almost died laughing when Walter turned up two days later on the doorstep of their modest home on the Hollywood crags.

"The Good Soldier Schweik!" she cried.

This was a reference to the famous fictional Czechoslovakian private who had driven the whole German Army out of its mind in the First World War.

"Schweik or no Schweik," said Walter, "you have to help me get some big names to go up there."

This was the simplest thing in the world in a Hollywood surcharged with emotion and the spirit of sacrifice. As if that wasn't enough, Risë enlisted the support of Ida Koverman, secretary of the all-powerful L. B. Mayer at Metro-Goldwyn-Mayer. Nobody sat nearer the throne than Miss Koverman, and a nod from her was next to a royal command. She was also a sympathetic character, who had smoothed the way for many stars who faced the great man with trepidation. The first show at Camp Kohler was headed by Eleanor Powell and included other good names, such as Lena Horne and Al Jolson.

Captain Twilling was in a state of ecstasy and hinted that the rank of sergeant was not beyond the reach of Surovy. Walter said that corporal was all right. All he wanted was to do his duty, said Walter, and honors were as nothing when a man has had the satisfaction of doing his part. He would now go back to Hollywood and prepare the next show.

But his fame was spreading despite himself, and now the authorities looked again into his dossier and uncovered his German-language background. What better than that such talents be employed to lecture German prisoners in American camps and show them the light? The Hollywood idyll would have ended in any event, because Risë was due back in New York for her opening at the Metropolitan, but Walter now took up a task that kept him coursing about the country for a year in a hopeless venture.

"They didn't want to see the light," he says morosely of the German prisoners. "They wanted to get back home."

Risë's connection with the war had its hilarious side. When Walter reported that he was freezing in camp, Risë knitted him a sweater. It was baby blue in color and too small; Walter never had the nerve to wear it in the barracks. The Army conscientiously extracted $18 a month from Walter's pay and sent it to Risë as her family allowance. She used it to buy herself a ring. After a meal of sowbelly and grits Walter would receive a letter from Risë. "Had lunch at the Colony. Bad food today, really bad." When he once wrote that he would divorce her if she didn't visit him, she arrived to find him so sick that he couldn't lift his head. The only move he could make in the three-day visit was a fifty-yard walk in the icy cold to an outside latrine.

But the separation was generally a torture for Risë, and she once broke a trip in Ohio for a single day with Walter in Seattle. It was in the dead of winter, the weather was atrocious, and on two occasions her plane was grounded. Between planes and trains, it took her four days to reach Seattle, and most of the time was spent in airports or railroad stations. She had gone because something in Walter's letters told her he was not well, and she found this was true. A subsequent army examination showed that he suffered from diabetes, and after the usual red tape had been unraveled, he was discharged from service. In a paraphrase of Ludwig Bemelman's similar experience, his war with the United States Army was over. He had converted no German prisoners, but he had enjoyed a complete tour of the country on a personally conducted free trip.

"But that isn't the big point," says Walter. "I learned the English language at last. I went in Fritz and came out Walt. I don't think I ever would have learned if the Army hadn't plucked me off that lotus bush in Hollywood."

Chapter Ten

In Risë's early days at the Metropolitan, Madame Schoen René had been a constant shadow at her elbow. For Madame, Risë's success was recompense for years of disappointment with other pupils. As a great singer herself, Madame was eternally exasperated at her failure to transmit her sacred fire to her protégés. Not only was Risë her greatest triumph, but she could conceivably be her last. Even with Risë a star at the Metropolitan, Madame never for an instant relaxed her regime of Prussian sternness. Risë was there at last; she must stay there.

When Walter entered the Army in 1942, Risë leaned even more heavily on Madame. She had complete confidence in Madame's judgment and voice theories. The collaboration had been a success; Risë got better by the year. But there was a cloud on the horizon: Madame had aged perceptibly in the last months. With age Madame became more testy and domineering, but Risë bore it gladly out of the knowledge that whatever Madame did was for her good. But there came a time when the situation could no longer be ignored.

"Walter, I'm worried," said Risë. "I've never seen Madame look so bad."

"Oh, she'll be all right," said Walter comfortingly. "She was a hundred years old when you met her; nothing's ever going to happen to her."

And then, several months later, had come the word of Madame's sudden death. Risë had returned for the funeral, her mind a swirl of conflicting emotions and apprehensions. In one sense, she was free of a force that had dominated her from childhood; in a more serious sense, she had been left without an anchor. Anna Amelia Schoen René had never asked for love, but she had demanded obedience and commanded respect. Risë knew how much she owed her; she realized how deeply she would miss her.

"You'll get another teacher, of course," said her New York friends.

"I don't know," said Risë doubtfully. "Not yet, anyway."

After all, she had done well in her Prague and Buenos Aires engagements without Madame; perhaps she could go it alone for a while. She knew that eventually she would need advice from a good coach and teacher, but she had a great fear of getting the wrong one. The town was full of fakes who had ruined promising youngsters. There was the further fact that she was so firmly grounded in Schoen René's method that a teacher with a new style might throw her entirely off balance.

She put the problem out of her mind. Walter was in the Army, and nobody knew how long the war would last. He was still chasing about the country, failing to convert reluctant prisoners. If she saw him once or twice a year, she was lucky. She hated the ugly hotel rooms and the lonely concert tours without him.

Walter had never for a moment relaxed his grip on her career. She refused to make a move without his approval. This meant irritating delays for managers who wanted decisions on the spot, but she refused to be rushed. Even their letters during the war were business communications. Walter had worked out a form of questionnaire, and Risë followed it faithfully. She would state the various business propositions in her flowing handwriting. Below would be a vacant space. Mark "yes" or "no." Walter ticked off the answers in the little squares. It was all very irksome for Risë, who is deeply emotional and affectionate. She finally began ending her letters with another proposition: Do you love me? Mark "yes" or "no."

But in the summer of 1943, Walter received a letter which he could see at a glance was not the usual official document. It was a love letter. She missed him desperately, she longed only for the time when they could be together again. It was a warm, sincere cry that came from the heart. And then, almost as an afterthought, she began writing of a meeting that had amused her: "Guess who called up last night and invited me out to dinner—Leo McCarey. We met him in Hollywood, you know, but I didn't think he remembered us that well, so I wondered what it was all about. He didn't say anything until the dinner was almost over, and then he asked if I'd like to be in a new picture he was doing with Bing Crosby. I said it sounded good, but what was the picture about. He was pretty vague about it. Bing is going to be a young priest, and I'm to be an opera singer, but the script isn't done yet, and he wasn't sure of the story line. It all seemed long off and pretty faraway to me, but I may be wrong. What do you think?"

Walter was in the barracks with his shoes off, after an exasperating day of lecturing before a group of German prisoners who did nothing but snicker behind their hands and shuffle their feet. When he reached this point in Risë's letter, he leaped up as if he had been stung. He quickly got on his shoes, ran down the corridor, and hunted up a telegraph office.

"Don't be silly," he wired. "Sign any paper McCarey hands you. Love."

This was how Risë got her contract for *Going My Way*, one of the classics of the motion-picture industry. M.C.A. had paved the way for her, but there were no tedious and acrimonious negotiations over salary and billing. There were later rumors that other singers had turned the part down, but she never knew the truth of it and wouldn't have cared in any case. Singing with Bing Crosby was a break for any actress, but the key man was McCarey. Not only did Risë like him personally, but in Hollywood he was regarded as a great director and a genius at telling a screen story. He wrote his own scripts and directed them with the special interest a man gives to his brain children. She called McCarey at his hotel when the telegram from Walter arrived.

"Walter says he'll divorce me if I don't make the picture," she reported, exaggerating a bit for poetic effect. "When do we start?"

"Oh, I don't know," said McCarey vaguely. "August, probably . . . How about your other commitments?"

"Don't worry about them," said Risë.

"Don't you want to know what we're going to pay you?"

"Don't worry about that," said Risë.

"We don't even have a script," laughed McCarey.

"That's *your* worry," said Risë.

Risë soon found that she had been slightly overoptimistic about her opera commitments and concert dates. Calvin Franklin's death had been a great blow to Risë, who had depended on his judgment and expert handling. He would have known the value of making the McCarey picture; Franklin's successors emitted a loud bellow at the thought of canceling five fall dates. Edward Johnson at the Metropolitan was even less pleased at the thought of her succumbing again to the movies.

"*Chocolate Soldier* probably did you good in a general way," he said, "but aren't you afraid another picture might hurt your opera career?"

"Maybe so," admitted Risë, "but I have to do it."

"Why?" asked Mr. Johnson, a bit tartly, lifting an interested brow.

"Walter says I have to," said Risë.

"Oh," said Mr. Johnson.

Risë went off to Hollywood in late July. Walter was already there, in the process of getting discharged from the Army. He met her at the airport and began driving home in a direction that seemed strange to her.

"Where are we going?" she asked.

"Just keep out of it," said Walter. "Enjoy the scenery."

He wound up a canyon and finally stopped in a driveway. Above was a large house on a precipitous crag.

"Yours," said Walter, waving a nonchalant hand.

A cook and a maid met Risë at the door. Risë looked at Walter with a touch of irritation, mingled with fear.

"Have you gone nuts?" she said. "This'll break us."

"Relax," said Walter. "I've seen Leo. It's all right."

Put on his honor by Risë's negligent treatment of the contract, McCarey had been almost lavish in the terms. Even the cautious Risë could see that the move wasn't going to hurt them. In truth, she had no time to worry about it; the picture was about to start, and she was in the usual turmoil about make-up and costumes.

One thing she had no worry about were lines: there *were* no lines. There were enough for the first few days of shooting, in which Risë had no part, and after that McCarey would have some more. Risë looked at Mr. McCarey with apprehension, sure that the strain must be unbearable. There was not a trace of concern on the McCarey visage. There was even less on the countenance of Mr. Bing Crosby. The first day's shooting was set for nine o'clock; Mr. Crosby arrived at ten-thirty in a great wave of lassitude. He hailed a few old friends among the grips and stagehands, looked with interest at the set, and waved a dangling hand at McCarey.

"Leo, old thing," he said with magnificent lack of eagerness, "when is this derailment set to leave the track?"

"Right now," said McCarey, seemingly in no more hurry than his star.

When Risë reached a point where she was on a level of warm personal association with the company, she once diplomatically inquired of Mr. Crosby the philosophy behind his actions.

"My dear child," said Bing, crossing one leg over the other in preparation for a lengthy session, "haste not only makes waste, but it gives me a pain right here in the middle. Did you ever see men building a road? Nobody is doing anything, and pretty soon the road is built. Get some eager beaver in there working his head off for ten hours, and next day the only noise you hear is the clang of the ambulance lugging him away. Don't you worry about this picture; we've got old Leo for that."

Old Leo didn't seem to be worrying, either. When Bing looked at the sunshine in the heavens and decided it was an un-American action and a crime against nature to be shooting a picture when he might better be hitting a golf ball, production ceased until he had fulfilled his duty. Instead of pulling his hair, McCarey seemed to take this as a divine dispensation exactly conforming to his plans for the project. It gave him time to get a few lines ahead with the script.

"I still don't know how he did his writing," says Risë. "He had a couple of writers helping him, but I swear he did most of it himself on the set. We'd run through a scene, and he'd wrinkle up his brow and say, 'That's lousy.' Then he'd pencil something hastily on a sheet of paper, read it out to us, and say, 'Try that.' It was always better. The bits of stage business he invented were done in the same way. He may have thought them up before he came on the set, but it never seemed so to me. The new ideas always came out of something that had just happened, and they were so right and original that we used to shout in amazement, 'Why, that's *it!*' That picture was really shot 'off the cuff,' and I suppose that's what made it so warm and wonderful."

But Risë could do nothing about her make-up, although she kicked long and loud to McCarey. They had carefully smoothed out her face again to rob it of all character, and made her a blonde. McCarey merely shrugged his shoulders, as if to say that those esoteric matters of beauty were beyond him. He had his hands full maneuvering his cast around on the set and was certainly not going to enter battle against the Westmores or Max Factors of the universe.

Since Bing Crosby was either just coming in late for shooting or just taking off early for golf, Risë's association with him was limited. This was not the case with Barry Fitzgerald, the Irish actor who was such a sensation in the picture. Fitzgerald arrived early, stayed late, and sat during the long waiting hours on a little camp chair just off the set. He watched everything with a musing and interested air and one day explained to Risë what he felt about his new station in life. For years he had been a star with the famous Abbey Players of Dublin.

"Do you ever ask yourself what you're doing here?" he asked Risë softly.

Risë nodded in surprise; the thought had occurred to her.

"I ask myself every day," said Fitzgerald. "I get up and look out at the weather and see Hollywood, where, as a famous writer has put it, 'The same silly sun beats down each day on the same silly people.' Then I say to myself, 'What are you doing here,

Fitzgerald?' The Abbey Theatre was really an amateur theatre; a thing of love, you might say; not a profession. Most of the players in my day came from a single block in Dublin. We acted at night; we worked at our regular jobs by day. I had a nice steady job as a government clerk. If I had stayed there, by now I would have been retired on a pension. Not much, mind you, but steady. Maybe four quid a week. Enough for a little flat and a pint at the pub as the shadows of night fell. And I've thrown that all away for *this*."

In view of the fact that four quid would run to slightly less than $12 a week under the new depreciated currency, and Fitzgerald was possibly getting $50,000 for his work on *Going My Way*, Risë had a rather clear notion that the man was pulling her leg, but there was no show of it on his solemn countenance. She laughed lightly and patted him consolingly on the knee.

But as the shooting meandered along at snail's pace, Risë became increasingly nervous. An efficiency expert coming in to report on the operation would have retired tearing his hair. Hours would elapse between shots, while the crew set up a new scene and the cameramen adjusted the lights. When the time came for shooting, Crosby would be nowhere in sight. After another lengthy delay he would be located on an adjoining sound stage, cutting up old touches with one Bob Hope. Risë couldn't help showing her worry.

Crosby gave her an affectionate pat on the shoulder.

"Easy, dear child," he said. "We'll get this thing in the box before you know it. Haste makes waste, or did I say that before? Artists are at work here, my dear girl. What are you going to sing in that big number?"

"The 'Habanera' from *Carmen*," said Risë.

"Noble," said Crosby approvingly. "Lively, but noble. Not the sort of thing the old Bingeroo digs with pleasure, but noble. You wouldn't want to do 'Because' instead, would you?"

"No, 'Habanera,'" said Risë stoutly.

The choice of the number was Walter's masterstroke. He had decided on it the minute he heard the plot of the picture, and nothing could move him. Crosby had been joking about "Because," but the "Habanera" really hadn't struck him as being the sort of rotund aria the picture needed. McCarey entered the fray, and the discussions were heated. Walter refused to budge. Risë cared little one way or the other, but she knew better than to hint it with Walter around.

"This is a chance of a lifetime!" he told her heatedly. "They've been futzing around at the Met for years about letting you do *Carmen,* but they never get around to it. We'll *make* them do it."

The shooting ambled along with no apparent end in sight. Risë would never get used to the long delays, the hours spent sitting around waiting for something to happen. Like all other movie actresses, she took up knitting in self-defense. The end, when it came, was an anti-climax. McCarey threw up a hand one day at the conclusion of what seemed a particularly tame scene and said:

"That was it, children. That wraps it up."

As a matter of fact, Risë was called back for minor retakes a few months later, but for all important purposes *Going My Way* was now for the ages. Risë was freed for her concert and opera dates. She headed back east immediately.

Along about February, Risë's associates at the opera house began to lift an interested brow; things had obviously changed for Miss Stevens. In plain fact, she was pregnant. The happy news flew about backstage, but it took an amusing episode on stage to make it publicly known. The opera was *Mignon;* the conductor was Sir Thomas Beecham, the eccentric Englishman. Mignon is a sweet young thing of twenty, and Risë was properly self-conscious of her figure. Short of hiding in the wings, there was little she could do about it, but when an opportunity presented itself in the second act to take partial cover, she seized it. Instead of being in her usual spot, stage left, she sought the protection of a sofa, stage right.

"Sir Thomas is a wonderful man," says Risë, "and he has his own wonderful way of conducting. On this night he looked up suddenly at the spot where I was supposed to be—and I wasn't there! His mouth fell, his baton dropped. Sir Thomas looked around wildly and finally spotted me behind the sofa. I thought he was going to fall off the podium; he literally doubled up with laughter. He picked up the beat again, but it was a sight to see him there: his muted haw-haws were coming across the footlights, and tears of laughter were running down his cheeks."

Risë returned to Hollywood with the intention of sitting down quietly and waiting for her baby. Walter was far from quiet: he had already hired a nurse.

"Good heavens!" said Risë in disgust. "It isn't going to happen tonight. What are you trying to do—scare me?"

Walter drew himself up with all the dignity of a hotel doorman and said that nothing was too good for his son.

"Oh . . . so you're going to tell me what to do about *that*, too," cried Risë sardonically. "You'll take what you get, and like it."

Walter had other problems. Sadie and Pa were coming out, and with a maid, a cook, and the nurse living full time in the house, he might have trouble finding a bed for himself. He was also taking daily insulin shots for the diabetes and trying to talk himself into being an invalid. But, sick or well, Risë found him a comfort around the house. There was nobody better than the little fellow when things got complicated.

Nicky was born on June 30, 1944, at the Cedars of Lebanon Hospital in Hollywood. Risë had an easy time and was bubbling with good cheer and self-admiration when Walter came in to see her. He had taken a look at his heir through the glass window of the nursery, and the experience had exalted him.

"Well, what do you say now?" chortled Risë.

"You mean his being a boy?" asked Walter, with wide-eyed ingenuousness. "What other kinds are there?"

Risë's recuperation was rapid, and she was eager to get home long before the doctor would allow it. When he finally gave the signal, a small roaring crisis followed: the doctor declared flatly that she would have to go by ambulance.

"*Ambulance!*" cried Risë in horror. "Why, the way I feel now I could *walk* home."

"I've seen that house of yours," said the doctor. "Getting to the front door is like climbing the Matterhorn."

Risë couldn't deny it: Walter had really fixed them up with a secluded residence on a mountain peak. There was nothing for it but the ambulance.

"Was *that* a production!" says Risë in retrospect. "I felt like a side of beef being lugged up that cliff."

But they all settled in happily. The nurse was a jewel, Nicky was blooming, and Risë had never felt happier in her life. Walter was taking daily shots of insulin for the diabetes, but the doctors held out hope that this would be a temporary condition. The hired help made a fuss over him, and he couldn't make up his mind whether to be an interesting invalid or the Great Father of the West. It was a time of supreme happiness for them all—and then came a blow that was to affect Risë for years.

One night about eight o'clock there was a long-distance call from New York. Sadie's brother, Uncle George Mechanic, was on the wire. Sadie took up the phone in her bedroom on the second floor; Risë listened in from below.

"Bud is dead," said Uncle George.

Both Risë and Sadie fainted.

Bud had fallen in action in France. It had happened on June 9 on Omaha Beach, Normandy, on the fourth day of the Allied invasion. He had been a member of the Engineers Corps. The telegram from the War Department had been pushed under the door of the Steenberg apartment and had lain there for almost a month before Uncle George found it.

It was a crushing blow for the family. When Risë's marriage had taken her out of the house, Bud had been left as the apple of Sadie's eye. He was a calm, amiable, charming boy who had been set for a successful future. The attachment between Risë and her brother was very deep. They had been through the hard days in the Bronx together, and he possessed something of Walter's quality in being unimpressed by her fame. Even after her marriage Risë and Bud had romped about the house to shrill Indian cries, much to the disgust of Sadie.

"Will you stop it!" she would cry angrily. "You're grown-up."

When Walter had entered the household he was relieved to find Bud on his side. Whatever pleased Risë, pleased her brother; it was as simple as that. Bud had even picked up a few German words to help Walter out. They ran to *Dummkopf* and *Donnerwetter* and really helped very little, but they gave Walter the feeling that he wasn't alone. When affairs reached an impasse, Bud was a genius at getting Walter out of the line of fire.

"Come on," he would say. "We'll shoot some pool."

They would go instead to a neighborhood movie, where Bud ruined any chance Walter might have of picking up something from the screen by insisting on translating the dialogue for him.

"*Hul di mul*," Walter would mutter irritatedly.

"All right, old hat," Bud would say. "Back to your old teacher you go."

This was considered a hilarious episode in the family. In his eagerness to conquer the great English language Walter had picked up a teacher soon after he got to New York. He had been recommended by a Hungarian who had declared flatly that after a few months of instruction with this eminent pedagogue Walter would be ready for a career on the lecture platform. At the end of the third lesson Walter had come home and engaged Risë in conversation.

"What in the name of heaven is *that!*" asked Risë in astonishment.

"Eengleesh," said Walter, a bit shaken by her tone.

"It is like anything," said Risë flatly. "It's gibberish. What's that fellow teaching you, anyway?"

It turned out that the instructor had reached America only a month before Walter and was barely keeping a page ahead of him in the book. Walter lapsed rapidly into German and was sour on the English language for a long time.

It took Risë a long time to get over the shock of her brother's death. Coming as it did at the time of Nicky's birth, it left her shaken and uncertain. The feeling of good health and well-being that she had brought from the hospital now deserted her. She was so nervous at her first attempt at singing that she had given it up immediately. It had sounded all right, but she knew she must be wrong. She put thoughts of the future out of her mind and gave herself over to tending Nicky. The summer was still before them; they would enjoy Hollywood while they could. Once in a dark moment she hinted to Walter that her career might be over.

"Because why?" demanded Walter bluntly.

"The baby," said Risë.

Walter looked as if he was about to explode.

"Schumann-Heink had a dozen children," he shouted. "Louise Homer had them every six months . . . and if I *told* you to stop your career, you'd hit me!"

This was comforting in a strange perverse way, but it solved none of the problems agitating Risë's mind.

Chapter Eleven

Long before *Going My Way* was nationally released, and even when it had been seen only by persons connected with the production, its fame had permeated the Hollywood hills like a perfumed fog. No Indian drums were beaten, no smoke signals drifted into the air, no native runners set out with the news—and yet at a magical moment all of motion-picture Hollywood knew that Leo McCarey had another hit. The favorable public verdict would come later, but Hollywood didn't need it: the fact had been determined before the picture was ever shown to a paying customer.

But there was one dissenter to this otherwise unanimous acclaim: Buddy De Sylva, production head of Paramount. He became obsessed with the fear that the Catholic Church might resent the appearance of old Bingo Crosby as a priest. Crosby was known as a crooner and a light, very light, comedian. His popular successes had been in the celebrated "Road pictures," with Bob Hope and Dorothy Lamour, replete with sarong and waving torso. How would the Catholics take a picture in which the young priest solved his parish problems with song and witticisms? Risë was the love interest and the sex interest in the new film. She had been the former sweetheart of Crosby, and it was even hinted that the affair might have gone beyond hand holding.

McCarey argued heatedly that De Sylva was seeing shadows where none existed. It was a warm and winning picture, he insisted, and as a matter of fact it was no longer a Crosby film: Fitzgerald had stolen it. Since McCarey shot without a script, the canny Fitzgerald had quietly kept building his part until it finally overshadowed Crosby's. The results were so marvelous that McCarey had abetted the crime, and Crosby himself had been tickled to death.

This failed to sway De Sylva, and the film was placed on the shelf while he wrestled with his conscience and his acute financial sense. It stayed there for six months until an eminent archbishop was called in to view the picture. The nerves of the harassed group that assembled in solemn conclave with the archbishop in the projection room were not materially soothed when the archbishop arose in the middle of the showing and disappeared through a door into the sunlight. The picture was stopped, the lights went on, and the group stood in stunned silence. This, most obviously, was the end. Before anyone could gather the courage to speak, the door opened again and the archbishop reappeared.

"What happened to the picture?" he asked.

"We turned it off when you went out," De Sylva said. "What happened to you?"

"I went to the toilet," said the archbishop testily. "Start it up again; it's a wonderful picture."

The archbishop's only complaint was about the title. It was then called *Padre*, and the prelate felt that something rather more general might give a better idea of the film's contents. The usual scurrying about followed, a thousand suggestions were proposed and discarded, and finally they came to a dead end. It was then that somebody reached far off into the blue and suggested *Going My Way*. It was the title of a song number in the film. They heaved a nervous sigh and settled on it . . . thus proving the old Hollywood adage that a good title is the title on a successful film; and a bad title is a title that sounds good and draws no money at the box office.

The first reviews proved that Hollywood had been right in its verdict. Crosby and Fitzgerald were the heroes, but there was plenty of glory left over for Risë. The "Habanera" was a sensation. Her face made an indelible impression on millions of people who had never before seen an opera star close at hand. She was young, she was talented, and she photographed beautifully.

The first reaction to the picture's success came in the concert field. Ever since *The Chocolate Soldier*, Risë had been a top attraction in concerts, but now her popularity leaped to fabulous proportions. People were to see her who had never before entered a concert hall. Walter kept a tight hand on the controls, and her concert manager, Kurt Weinhold, was in agreement with Walter on how she should be handled. Her fees had been edging up gradually each season; now they could take a decided jump. She was eventually to be in the $2500-to-$4000-per-performance bracket.

The other reaction came from Louis B. Mayer and M-G-M, but this was a continuation of a contest that had been waged since *The Chocolate Soldier*. Mayer was determined to wean her from opera and make her exclusively a dramatic screen actress. He saw her as a successor to Garbo, or at least to the type of roles Garbo had been noted for. The temptation was great, for the fees at the Metropolitan were minuscule in comparison with Hollywood salaries. The financial climb at the Metropolitan had been painful. On her first three-year contract she had started at $150 a week and been raised $50 a week in each of the next two seasons. Another one-year contract brought her to $500 a week. Her next leap was to $500 a performance, a fabulous salary in a day when the opera had still not recovered from the effects of the depression.

This was chicken feed in Hollywood terms, and Mr. Mayer could never understand how Risë could resist his blandishments of a long-term contract. The doors had been opened wide, the great man was there to sponsor her personally—how could she turn down the opportunity? He worked on her through her friends, he made a point of including the Surovys in his small parties, where they met the elite of Hollywood and saw how the other half lived. This was wealth of a type that even a Caruso couldn't ignore. At this point in the history of motion pictures there seemed no more worlds to conquer. Television was merely a cloud on the horizon; even the worst pictures were making fortunes. In this kingdom of titian-haired beauties and polo-playing knights, L. B. Mayer was Czar. He was offering her the world on a platter. The Surovys smiled politely and were unmoved.

"You're great in opera," growled Walter, "and that's where you're going to stay."

He knew better than Risë herself that she would die away from it. From her days on the "Children's Hour" she had thought of nothing else. She was just coming to her peak at the opera house. She possessed a glorious voice with an amazing range, an instrument rarely equaled in the history of opera. Walter had analyzed Risë like a psychologist; he knew exactly what went on in her mind. If he insisted, she would give up opera for the movies— but the moment the contract was signed, she would begin dying inwardly.

They put the movie temptation behind them and began thinking of the future. There was still a mountain to be climbed to the top at the Metropolitan. Always at the back of his mind Walter had the memory of his promise to Madame Schoen René. Along with his own determination that she should be first among other firsts, there was the feeling that the fates had somehow ordained it. He knew the handicaps; he knew how heavy the blow of Bud's death had been; he knew that Risë was going to make it.

After Nicky was born, Walter set himself to planning their future, but he could have saved his effort, for Risë had it settled. They were keeping the home in Hollywood. She was in love with Southern California and wanted Nicky brought up there. Walter had offered a weak defense of New York, as being their natural center of operations.

"Don't tell me about New York," said Risë. "Even if we had a penthouse, it still wouldn't be any good. We put the baby out on the terrace, and in fifteen minutes he'll look as if he had just come in from the mines. I want him to have this sunshine."

This had been in the happy days after Nicky's birth and before the news of Bud's death. That blow had set her back abruptly in her recuperation, and the doctor had decided now that she needed a complete rest of three months before she could think of working again. As she sat on a deck chair in the back yard and let the sun pour down on her, it seemed to her that she never again wanted to leave the spot. But as her strength slowly returned, she knew that she would eventually take up the old trail again. That left Walter to worry about. If Nicky stayed, Walter would also have to stay. The nurse was good, the house well run, but it would mean months of separation.

Walter solved part of the problem himself. Through friends he learned that Howard Hawks was having trouble casting the part of a Frenchman for a picture to be called *To Have and Have Not*, starring Humphrey Bogart and Lauren Bacall. Hawks had already tested thirty or forty applicants without success when Walter was urged to have a try at it. After a brief period for learning the lines and an equally short appearance before the cameras, Hawks had hired him on the spot. The price was $1500 a week on a seven-year contract, with options.

"But I'm not a Frenchman," said Walter.

"You will be in this picture," said Hawks.

He reported the news to Risë almost like a schoolboy caught stealing erasers from the blackboard. He hadn't intended taking a screen test, it had turned out to be ridiculously easy, and now he had a feeling he had done the wrong thing.

"Of course, you'll take it!" said Risë flatly, before he had a chance to organize the usual contrary arguments.

"I won't be any good," said Walter.

"You'll be great!" cried Risë. "Stop talking like that."

Risë had always had a sense of guilt about Walter's career. He had been the big man in Prague and for her sake had taken a back seat in America. The deal with Hawks was a godsend. He would be content to stay behind in Hollywood with Nicky if he had a job of his own.

For the first time in America, Walter became the big man in the house. It was he who now got up early in the morning, splashed the sleep out of his eyes, and groaned at the idea of another day under the studio lights. The maid wakened him, the cook prepared his breakfast with pride, the nurse waved good-by to him as he drove down off the mountain peak in the direction of Burbank and the Warner Brothers studio. His part was good, there was fun on the set, and the picture had all the aura of being a success. Best of all, Risë began to bloom again. Walter was happily working, the baby was thriving, the household was functioning admirably—and she could leave with the secure feeling that there was happiness behind her. The matter of her voice was still very much in her mind, and she eagerly accepted an offer to appear with Leopold Stokowski in a concert version of *Carmen* with the Los Angeles Philharmonic Orchestra. She had reason to regret it when rehearsals began, for she found herself much weaker than she had imagined she would be. She went through with the performance and sang acceptably, but it was generally felt that she lacked her usual fire.

There were tears when she left for New York, and she was chagrined to find that the baby took her departure lightly. She smothered him in kisses and placed him tenderly back in the playpen, where he grasped a toe and gazed about with unconcern. The performance was repeated when she returned four months later. She arrived, frantic with excitement and affection; she found him strangely unmoved.

"Ow-wow!" she wailed. "He doesn't know me!"

Walter pointed out sensibly that Nicky hadn't sneered, hadn't given the Bronx cheer, hadn't turned his back on her. Risë rejected the solace.

Their life for the next four years operated on this level. Walter's picture appeared and was well received. However, roles of the same sort would be hard to find. After six months Warner Brothers dropped his option because they had nothing else for him to do. Walter was happy enough, thinking that this meant the end of his Hollywood exile. He ran up against an adamant Risë.

"I simply won't have Nicky living in stinky old hotels with us," she said firmly. "He's got to stay out here."

Walter shrugged helplessly and began planning ways of keeping them together in California. For a year Risë had her own weekly radio show from Hollywood. Since she also clung desperately to her Metropolitan career, it meant hasty and tiring plane trips between the two coasts. At this juncture Walter took up his running battle with the servant problem. The nurse quit, the maid quit, the cook quit. Walter valiantly hauled new ones up the cliff. They quit. Risë cooked, Walter cooked, Nicky yelled. Risë fled to New York. Walter hired an old Finnish woman who couldn't speak any other language, couldn't cook, wouldn't do housework, but was good at keeping Nicky from falling off the precipice.

For the next two years Risë was on the "Prudential Family Hour" on radio. It originated from New York, and that made it all right for her concert and opera appearances but not so good for her family life. When she couldn't stand it any longer, she flew out to see Nicky. He greeted her with a nonchalant "Hi!" and went off to climb a rock by the kitchen door. They had a swimming pool hacked out of the rocky landscape at monumental cost, and Nicky was an accomplished swimmer at three. He had never owned a pair of shoes, walked and climbed everywhere like an ape, and had feet like a Percheron. There was no doubt that Hollywood was doing him good.

Walter had formed an artists' booking agency with an old friend, Rudy Polk, and had worked up a good business. Their best client was the Hollywood Bowl, where they put on concerts with such box-office sensations as Jascha Heifetz and Grace Moore and filled the hillside with paying customers for miles in every direction. Walter's heart was not in California, but he kept mum in the face of Risë's stubborn insistence that Nicky couldn't survive without the Hollywood sunshine. On each trip home Risë seemed more irritable and upset, but she angrily shrugged away any suggestion that her career wasn't progressing favorably. Since *Going My Way* she was bigger than ever in opera and concerts and radio. She still sent Walter the urgent questionnaires, and he kept a firm hand on her business affairs, but there were problems that had to be handled on the spot, and she was getting increasingly tart with her associates. One night she called him on the phone from New York.

"I saw Blank today," she said, after the usual preliminaries.

"Yes?"

"I talked contract with him."

"Yes, what happened?" asked Walter.

"I tore it up and threw it in his face," said Risë.

There was a prolonged silence from the Hollywood end.

"Walter!" she cried. "Are you there?"

"Yes, I'm here."

"You're not mad at me, are you?"

"No, I'm just thinking," said Walter.

"What about?"

"I'm thinking how silly it is for me to be working out here for peanuts," said Walter, "and you throwing a fortune away back there . . . Also . . ."

"Also what?" Risë asked eagerly.

"Also, I think I'd better grab the first plane and get back there before it's too late."

"Oh, Walter!" she breathed. "*Would* you?"

The arrival of Walter and Nicky in New York was something of a spectacle. It was the dead of winter, and Walter was taking no chances. Nicky looked like a junior Eskimo who was about to mush off with the precious serum to save the old trapper in the mountain cabin. He wore a fur-lined jacket with a hood that resembled a subway entrance. On his feet were a pair of fur-lined boots, and his gloves were large enough for a motorman. Walter had dug up the equipment in a store catering to the Lake Arrowhead and Sun Valley trade. When they deposited Nicky in the lobby of the Essex House, the hotel that Risë had selected as their future home, they had to push him along the marble floors to the elevator. His boots were so large that when he took a step all he did was bring himself to a halt. Risë went into a laughing fit, a sure sign that everything was right in the world again.

Risë and Walter sat down to take stock. In a financial way, things had never been better. The radio program was bringing in big money, her concert dates were growing in number every year, her position with the Metropolitan was secure. But Walter could tell from Risë's attitude that something was wrong.

"Why kid ourselves?" she finally said angrily. "I'm singing lousy."

"Nobody else seems to think so," said Walter comfortingly.

"Walter, you don't know," she cried piteously. "It's been coming on ever since Madame died. I'm doing things wrong, but I don't know what they are. When I fix one thing up, something else goes wrong."

"You need a teacher," said Walter. "I've always told you that."

"Yes, but *who!*" said Risë. "I'll get one of these fakes, and he'll ruin me."

"Vera Schwarz," said Walter. "Madame told you herself to go to her if anything went wrong."

"But she's in Hollywood," wailed Risë. "What good would that do me?"

"Does she always have to be in Hollywood?" asked Walter quietly. "Maybe she hates it as much as I do."

When they returned to Hollywood to sell the house and dispose of the furniture, Walter arranged a meeting with Vera Schwarz. After fifteen minutes of friendly talk Risë practically threw herself into Miss Schwarz's arms. This was the teacher she had been looking for; this was the solid protection she needed. And, most marvelously of all, Miss Schwarz was making plans to move to New York. For three years she had been singing coach at M-G-M, a job given her through earlier friendship with L. B. Mayer. But Vera Schwarz had been the great prima donna of the Vienna Opera House. She had appeared with Gustav Mahler and Bruno Walter; the great Richard Strauss had been her friend and confidant; her fame was international. Guiding the musical destinies of Kathryn Grayson and Judy Garland was really not enough for a woman who had sung with the greatest artists of her time.

Miss Schwarz suggested that they might start some quiet work after she was settled in New York, but Risë insisted on singing for her at once. Her manner was desperate; she was obviously in need of help. She had a mystical feeling that she must somehow grapple Vera Schwarz to her; once out of sight she might never see her again. She sang, and Miss Schwarz listened quietly.

"If you think I should," said Risë tremulously, at the end of her singing, "I'd be glad to start from the beginning again."

"No, no, the voice is good," cried Miss Schwarz hastily. "There are just a few little things to fix up."

This was far from the truth, but Miss Schwarz was wise enough to see that Risë needed consolation more than instruction. This was a singer on the verge of a musical crack-up. Her confidence,

never good at best, had almost deserted her. Minor technical
faults had been magnified into disasters. Instead of concentrating
on interpretation and stage action, she was worrying about *how*
she was singing. This could eventually be fatal to a career.

"When everything is right," explains Risë, "your voice is there
as naturally as your breathing. When you get to worrying about
how you're going to do a certain note, then you're in trouble.
Before Vera came into the picture, I was worse than being in
trouble; I was an unholy mess."

The crisis was so apparent that Miss Schwarz hastily rearranged
her plans so that she could go back to New York with the Surovys.
They took the train, and for three days Risë and Miss Schwarz
did nothing but talk of singing and singers. In reminiscing of the
old days at the Vienna Opera, Miss Schwarz subtly brought in
stories of great singers who had temporarily run off the track in
their careers and been brought back to normal by a little sage
advice. It was the most ordinary experience in the world, she
said. Everybody went through it, everybody was terrified by it—
and the end result was always good. By the time they reached
New York, Risë was no further along in her cure, but she had
gained a state of faith in Miss Schwarz that persists to this day.
She knew that she was safe again; she sank back into that security
like a child who has been rescued from an overturned boat.

Walter's problems were a bit more complex. In her harassed
state Risë had succeeded in antagonizing practically all of her
professional contacts. She was in trouble at the Metropolitan,
where the management was becoming increasingly irritated by
her outbursts and rebellions. Her contract with the "Prudential
Family Hour" had ended, and the directors uttered a great sigh
of relief. A talk with Risë's concert accompanist showed Walter
that a great deal of fence-fixing was needed in that department.

"Oh, I was doing it up *good*," says Risë bitterly, in retrospect.
"That old inferiority complex of mine was working full time. The
more unsure of myself I became, the higher line I took. It's a
wonder somebody didn't crown me along the way."

Now that Vera Schwarz was working the kinks out of her voice,
Risë was very content to have Walter take the business worries
off her mind. She admitted frankly that she had been a bust at

handling her own affairs and furthermore stated that she would never handle another as long as she lived. What the lady was finally getting was protection, and she took it in great gulps.

As for Walter, he was again in his element. The next assault would be against the old "yellow brewery on Broadway"—the name given to the Metropolitan by its early rivals. The weapon used for this would be *Carmen*. Risë's great need was for big starring roles, which were always scarce for mezzo-sopranos. The "Habanera" in *Going My Way* had been the first shot in the campaign. What followed was a masterpiece of promotion. Before she ever sang a note of the opera at the Metropolitan, Risë was an internationally known Carmen. It had started with the release of the picture, and Walter never let up on it for a moment. When she appeared in a Chesterfield advertisement, she was in the costume of Carmen. Other testimonials showed her with a flamenco costume, a flower in her teeth, and her hand thrown aloft in ecstasy. This gave rise to a quip by Geraldine Farrar.

"In my day," she was quoted as having said, "artists became Carmen by *singing Carmen*."

Columbia Records attended to that by producing a Risë Stevens album of *Carmen*. It was the sensation of the season, outselling every other operatic record. When Risë appeared as a guest artist on radio, something from *Carmen* was always on the program. A concert performance without the "Habanera" or the "Seguidilla" was unthinkable; audiences simply refused to leave the hall unless they were included. Sounds of the avalanche finally reached the Metropolitan. The matter came up when she discussed her next contract.

The Metropolitan people took great care to show that they were not responding to pressure. They merely said rather solemnly that it seemed to them it was time Risë began singing *Carmen*. With equal solemnity, Risë agreed.

She would probably have got the role anyhow in time; this gave it to her ready-made for success. There was no question of whether she could do it; she had already done it in foreign parts to acclaim.

In fact, not only had she done it in Prague and Buenos Aires with marked success, but in Prague she had introduced a bit of "business" that had been copied everywhere. As she prepared for her dance in the second act, she found that her stocking was falling down. Dancing with that handicap could be a fiasco. Putting her foot up on a chair, she calmly pulled up her stocking and fastened it, revealing at the same time a flash of flesh above the knee. The house broke into an uproar of delight. Hardly a Carmen since has omitted the gesture.

Not only was opera the medium in which Risë functioned most happily, but she had fallen in love with the old opera house at 39th Street and Broadway. As Frederick Gutheim was later to say in an article in *Harper's Magazine* (October 1958): "The Metropolitan occupies a wholly inadequate site at the southern end of the Broadway theatrical district. Its dingy brick building, dating from the 1880s, is completely obsolete. The acoustics are tolerable only in about half the seats—the expensive ones. The stage cannot even be seen from one sixth of the seats, especially those on the sides in the balcony. Because there is no space for storing stage sets, the opera has to pay $200,000 a year just to haul them from its warehouse in the Bronx—to say nothing of damage from doing it in snow and rain. Backstage is a theatrical slum of over-crowded dressing-rooms, inadequate lavatories, and other inconveniences. The masonry building cannot be remodeled, and the impossibility of air-conditioning condemns it to a short winter season which, last year, amounted to only 167 performances. Despite these handicaps, the Metropolitan is the world's leading opera company, and Carrère and Hastings endowed its interior with a magnificence unlikely to be duplicated today."

Behind the scenes the house was filled with the ghosts of the great singers of other generations, and Risë was highly susceptible to the influence. On these boards had trod the fabulous Caruso and the De Reszkes. At the cluttered wooden table where she made up for her performances, there had sat such idols as Marcella Sembrich, Emma Eames, Nellie Melba, Lillian Nordica, Olive Fremstad, Geraldine Farrar, and Louise Homer. That had been the Golden Age of Opera, when artists had been worshiped as divinities. There were no movie and television stars to share the limelight. Although they held themselves regally aloof, opera stars were the focus of concentrated attention. Their feuds, their peccadilloes, their marriages and divorces were the meat upon which newspaper circulations fed.

This had now changed, but the magic of the house remained. Risë had her mind fixed on opera with a ferocious intensity. Eventually she was to have a repertory of forty roles—from *Hansel and Gretel* to Laura in *La Gioconda*. With the Opera-Comique and at the Juilliard she had specialized in French roles. At Prague she had been forced to relearn everything in German. In her second season at Teatro Colón in Buenos Aires, the war had cut off the supply of German singers, and the German operas were dropped. Risë had returned to her French roles and had acquired a new repertory in Italian. She had sung Wagner in South America and in her early years with the Metropolitan. Risë's great roles were eventually to be *Rosenkavalier* (German); *Mignon, Samson et Dalila,* and *Carmen* (French); and *Orfeo* (Italian).

Walter left the Metropolitan discreetly alone. This policy was to change, but the time was not yet ripe for it. In the meantime, Walter confined his activities to lugging Risë's heavy equipment downtown on opera nights. One huge suitcase contained decorations to lighten the solemnity of her dressing room. In the old days Geraldine Farrar had kept her own tiny dressing room, with decorations that made it a small jewel box. Lily Pons still had her dressing room decorated to her own taste. Risë, of course, occupied number eleven, which looked very much like a prize fighter's cubicle at the old Stillman's Gymnasium. Along one wall was an old battered upright piano. Along another wall was a long counter, resembling something found in a village grocery store. This was the dressing table. Two large glaring lights hung from the ceiling by long cords. Three kitchen chairs and a wobbly upholstered chair completed the picture.

But what irked Walter exceedingly was another heavy suitcase in which he carried Risë's good-luck charms. On a fair count it was determined that she had upward of 712 superstitions. To be on the safe side, she had a defense for each of them.

"For a levelheaded dame," Walter said, "I can't understand what you want with all these silly gadgets."

"Never mind," said Risë easily. "They've got me this far."

At a much later time the good-luck suitcase was lost and never recovered. Risë swore that Walter had dropped it out of a window; Walter denied the accusation stoutly. But she soon forgot about it, and the loss of the charms seemed to make no appreciable difference to her career.

Since there was nothing to be done at the opera, Walter turned his attention to Risë's concert tours. She was in grave trouble in that sector. Toward the end of her bad period even the critics in the smaller towns were beginning to hint that there was a falling off in the quality of her singing. This was bad enough, and she was becoming increasingly fed up with the hardships of travel. Wartime travel had been sheer torture. For anyone who traveled on a fixed schedule like Risë, it had been a nightmare. Airplane accommodations were reserved for military personnel, and only rarely could a civilian wangle a seat. Civilian priorities were confined to businessmen whose work was helping the war effort; a mere opera singer didn't come under that heading.

What was left was passenger trains jammed to the roof and running on schedules often ten and twelve hours late. Getting a Pullman reservation was a monumental task; passengers stood in the aisles for hours waiting for a place in the dining car. Risë had the help of Brooks Smith, her accompanist, and, at different times, two exceptionally talented and loyal secretaries, Melanie Romero and Doris Hellman. Even so, they faced each journey with a sense of helplessness.

The situation after the war was little better. The boom was on, and the planes were now filled with industrial moguls flitting about like bees from one lush contract to another. They also seemed to have magical entry to the high places of airline management where reservations were made. It was a constant struggle for Risë to make her engagements on time; she was in a state of nerves when Walter took over.

An immediate emergency arose which tested his capacity. The illness of another singer had threatened the cancellation of a lucrative date at Purdue University, Lafayette, Indiana. Risë's concert management had prevailed on her to fill the gap. The move had to be made in two days, and Walter set out to get the reservations. The clerk at the airplane ticket office shook her head sadly: all filled up. Walter persisted and ran into a stone wall. He continued to insist, demanding to be put in touch with somebody in the higher echelons.

"Well, it won't do you any good," they said finally, "but Colonel Brown is the man for you to see."

Walter perked up at the sound of the title. If there was any one thing in the world he could do, it was handle high military brass. Colonel Brown had evidently returned to civilian life with a marked reluctance to giving up his rank. By a devious route which nobody but another Hungarian could follow, Walter found his way to the presence of this august gentleman. By the time Walter got through inoculating him with the virus of art, it was plain that the postwar health of the state of Indiana depended on the presence of Miss Risë Stevens in Lafayette. Walter came away with a priority for the trip from New York to Indianapolis. He also left an admirer behind him.

"Mr. Surovy, if you'll pardon the expression," said the colonel, "you're a bloody wonder. How do you do it?"

"If I told you," said Walter, "that I had gone into the Army with $300 and come out with $300, would that mean anything to you?"

The colonel said it would.

Aside from the financial rewards, Walter has never particularly liked concerts. This is a personal feeling, having nothing to do with the merits of the medium or Risë's performance in it. It is simply that Walter is bored on a concert tour. A train trip bores him; a plane trip scares him to death. Once arrived in the town of the concert, he has nothing to do. This was less true in the early days, when he kept his eyes open. Since he couldn't help Risë on the platform, and indeed drove her to distraction by his restlessness, he watched her concerts like a hawk.

"There's something wrong with them," he finally said to Risë.

"*What's* wrong!" she cried, flaring up instantly.

"It's not the singing," said Walter. "It's something else . . . Look, you're up there on that big stage with nothing but the piano and the accompanist."

"What's wrong with that?" demanded Risë.

"It's not theatrical enough," said Walter. "You're not giving the audience a break."

"What do you want?" asked Risë sardonically. "Dancing girls and a string combo in the background?"

"No, but there's something," persisted Walter. "The way it is now, you might as well be singing in the street. The house lights are all on, and you can't tell where the audience stops and you start. It has all the glamour of a clambake."

"Well, think of something," said Risë, a bit annoyed.

"No, don't toss it off, now!" protested Walter. "This is serious. Do you know something else I've found out by watching you: the audience really doesn't like a number unless they can see the articulation of the words. They have to see your mouth working before they really understand the song and enjoy it."

"Why don't we use a spotlight?" asked Risë.

Walter leaped up excitedly.

"That's it!" he cried elatedly. "Why didn't I think of it?"

"You know who has the brains in this family," said Risë, with what has come to be known, repulsively, as a twinkle in the eye.

This was the job Walter had been waiting for, and it almost proved to be more than he could handle. The local auditoriums either lacked spotlights and were reluctant to buy them or rent them; or they had them and were chary about hiring a union operator to run them. Walter's Hungarian blarney was not always successful with the local committees. They had provided the hall and the newly tuned grand piano; they felt they had done enough.

"And we've even given you the white strip," they would invariably add, testily.

The white strip was a piece of canvas placed on the stage to prevent the train of the singer's gown from being soiled. Long education had been needed to get local committees to provide the strip, and now that they had given in on the point, they considered their obligations ended. They took great pride in the strip, laid it with religious care before every concert, and felt that this easily placed them on a par with other cosmopolitan centers. But Walter persisted, somehow the spotlight was managed, and the results were highly edifying.

"Well, it *is* better," the local chairman would admit, "but I still don't like that twenty bucks for the electrician."

Refunding the money would not have harmed Risë, but Walter carefully refrained out of a sense of professional loyalty. If local managers got used to the idea of a spotlight, they would soon accept it as standard procedure. It would help young artists who came along later for modest fees and needed all the help they could get. Also, it saved twenty bucks.

But Walter kept his eye fixed on the Metropolitan. That was where the battle had to be won. Risë was inside; Walter still had the ramparts to climb. On the next spring tour Risë's performances were sensational. Risë's appearances in *Rosenkavalier* and *Carmen* had been the only sellouts. The reception given her was tumultuous, and the critics, less reserved than their eastern colleagues, had thrown their caps in the air. As the train bore the weary troupe eastward, Walter went to visit Mr. Johnson in his drawing room.

"Mr. Johnson," he began, "I needn't remind you of Risë's grosses on tour."

"Indeed, not!" agreed Mr. Johnson heartily. "They were wonderful."

"Then I think it's time she received the fee of the other top stars of the opera house," said Walter steadily.

"Oh, come now," said Mr. Johnson, starting up. "She's young, she's a mezzo, she has plenty of time. The taxes will get it, anyway. What does she want it for?"

"She doesn't want it," said Walter. "*I* want it."

"*You!*" cried Mr. Johnson.

"Risë has already made good," said Walter. "Now I want to make good."

Mr. Johnson was an astute man and knew exactly what the words meant. This was official notice that Walter was no longer on probation; the cold war was over. He looked at Walter for a long moment and broke into a smile. He reached over and touched Walter on the knee, a gesture of surrender, reconciliation, and friendship.

"I get it," he said. "I'll take care of it."

At one leap Risë's fee at the opera went to $1000 a performance. The money was significant only for what it meant: Risë was at last at the top; she was a *prima donna assoluta,* the goal of all opera singers. For Walter the event was even more important. He moved into the opera house as a force. It could no longer be ignored that he was the power behind the Stevens throne.

Risë turned the reins over to him with a happy sigh of relief; Walter quickly consolidated his position at the opera house. He reinforced the situation during the declining years of the Johnson regime. He was in a good state to welcome the beginning of the reign of Good King Bing.

Chapter Twelve

Risë had met Rudolf Bing during her first engagement at Glyndebourne, a beautiful estate outside London which Sir John Christie had turned into an international musical haven. In a small jewel-like theatre set among the trees, the Glyndebourne Opera Company had established a reputation for performances of delicacy and charm. Assisting him was the continental triumvirate of Bing, Fritz Busch, and Carl Ebert. Each performance was an elegant as well as a musical event. Formal dress was obligatory for the audience; at the end of the second act a full dinner with champagne was served the customers on the terrace.

In his native Vienna, Mr. Bing had studied art and music. At twenty, abandoning the idea of a singing career, he had entered the concert management field. This had led to posts with the Darmstadt State Theatre and the Charlottenberg Municipal Opera in Berlin. In 1935 he had come to Glyndebourne as an assistant to Carl Ebert. When Glyndebourne reopened after the war, in 1946, it was under Mr. Bing's direction. His greatest triumph was to come next when he founded the Edinburgh Festival in 1947 and put it on such a sound footing that it is still regarded as the premier musical festival in the world. His Metropolitan engagement had come as a result of that success.

Mr. Bing came to New York in 1949 to spend a year in analyzing the problems of the Metropolitan; he was to take charge of the company in 1950. Risë had heard that Mr. Bing was also staying in the Essex House, and one day in 1949 she ran into him in the lobby. With her usual openhearted exuberance, she rushed toward him happily.

"Darling!" she cried, enfolding him in her arms and giving him the customary light peck on the cheek.

Mr. Bing froze into a small gelid statuesque mass. With formal care, he disengaged himself; with a cold bow, he withdrew.

"Oh, oh!" said Risë to herself. "That tears it."

She had every right to fear that her re-entrance into Mr. Bing's life had been less than propitious. Others in the company were soon to have the same apprehension about the slim, self-reserved gentleman. From the beginning it was plain that Bing was to be boss of the opera house. The Lauritz Melchior affair has never been satisfactorily explained, but in February 1950, Mr. Melchior departed the company with the declaration that he would never sing there as long as Mr. Bing was general manager. Since Melchior had for years been the bulwark of the Wagnerian forces at the opera, his defection was a heavy blow.

A second stunner followed with the later departure of Helen Traubel, the great Wagnerian soprano, who had so well filled the gap of Madame Flagstad's absence during the war. Miss Traubel had achieved great general fame in her amusing television appearances with Jimmy Durante and other popular buffoons. She now added appearances in night clubs to her program. Mr. Bing held this to be a reflection on the honor of the opera company; Miss Traubel answered that she got great satisfaction from such endeavors and intended to continue them. She continued them, but she no longer sang at the opera house.

At a later date Robert Merrill, popular baritone with the company, announced his intention of dropping the spring tour with the opera to take a Hollywood contract. Mr. Bing announced just as firmly that if Mr. Merrill canceled the tour, he might consider himself no longer a member of the Metropolitan. When Mimi Benzell continued to bill herself as a "Metropolitan Opera soprano" when she was no longer on the roster of the company,

Mr. Bing went into court and secured an injunction ending the practice.

Mention must also be made of the celebrated Maria Callas-Bing imbroglio, which occurred only last year with reverberations heard round the world. Her engagement at the Metropolitan had been acclaimed with hosannas. Her first appearances were sensations, compounded of the cheers, boos, and hectic encounters that make opera managements happy. But when Miss Callas refused to do performances of *Traviata*, which she signed for in her 1958–59 contract, Bing discharged her on the spot. He added insult to injury by a statement which read like the fourth satire of Juvenal.

In short, the thin man was tough. After the Essex House episode Risë considered herself in the Bing doghouse. Because of his solid position inside the opera house Walter was not long in hearing of Bing's amazement at finding a mezzo-soprano among the top names in the company. The hubbub over the Melchior incident hardly added to Walter's comfort. The first meeting with Bing would be crucial, and Walter worked to prepare Risë for it.

"He's big and you're big, but that doesn't mean you have to start a battle royal," he warned her. "Be on your dignity, but let's hear what he has to say."

When word came that Mr. Bing felt the time was ripe for a discussion of her next season's plans, Walter gave Risë a final pep talk. They arrived at his office a positive picture of confidence and good will. His reception of them was warm and friendly, and they took new heart. Perhaps they had been wrong in thinking he still held the Essex House incident against Risë. His next words disabused them of the notion.

"I'm afraid I have bad news for you, Miss Stevens," he began. "We'll not be doing *Carmen* or *Dalila* next year."

"Why not?" asked Walter, sharply.

"You've seen the scenery?" asked Mr. Bing. "Disgraceful. It wouldn't be tolerated by a small company in Albania. I'm sure you never sang in anything as bad in your beginning days."

Walter nodded glumly; the facts were all too true.

"We need new productions for both those operas, but that can't be done this season," said Mr. Bing.

"And that leaves me *Rosenkavalier?*" said Risë. "Or must *that* be done over, too?"

"No, that's yours," said Mr. Bing, and paused. "Now I must ask you a great favor. Would you do *Fledermaus?*"

Walter could see Risë's jaw begin to harden. He had seen it before and knew what it meant. Unless something happened quick, there would be an explosion. He kicked her under the table.

"We'll think it over," said Walter hastily.

He hustled Risë away with a minimum of ceremony. Once outside, she was in a towering rage.

"I'll have a black and blue mark on my shin for months," she cried irately. "I know what you were trying to do, but you didn't have to break my leg, did you?"

"It was better than breaking the contract," said Walter.

"Well, I'm still not going to do it," fumed Risë. "It's a silly light opera, and I'd look like a fool in it."

"We'll talk about it," said Walter soothingly. "Maybe it'll turn out better than you think."

Here was a situation where Walter could be of real help to her. Since it was a part in which nobody could win laurels as a singer, the emphasis must be on the acting.

"What's that American saying of yours: there's more than one way of skinning a dog?" asked Walter. "Well, maybe we can do something with this Count Orlofsky of yours."

Walter sat down to analyze the problem. In this he had the assistance of Edgar Vincent, Risë's press agent and an opera buff of the first water. Count Orlofsky had to be entirely new in conception; the question was how to do it. It was the old thing of Risë's playing a man's part. She would look stunning, as she always did in roles like *Rosenkavalier*, but something else was needed.

"How about putting a mustache on her?" suggested Ed Vincent.

"Eh?" said Walter, starting up. "Why, *of course*," he shouted. "If she's going to be a man, let's make her a man that'll knock their eyes out."

The cigarette holder was Walter's idea. He produced from

somewhere a holder about two feet long, which Risë soon learned to use like a rapier. It was a hilarious satire on every aristocratic young twig ever known. As Risë waved it about nonchalantly, it was a complete distillation of an effete and slightly warmed-over decadent civilization.

As an old stage expert who knew every turn of creating a memorable character, Walter worked on Risë for days before the opening. He concocted a trick of quick laughter that would bring roars of mirth from the staid Metropolitan pewholders. Her Russian accent was an amalgam of one part Russian (picked up from a coach) and three parts of Middle European gibberish (furnished by Walter) that could pass for anything. Risë might not be an Orlofsky that anyone had ever seen before, but when she stepped out on the stage on opening night, nobody had eyes for anybody else.

The New York critics, always reserved to a fault, showed a few faint signs of life. Virgil Thomson, of the *Herald Tribune,* said: "As actor, only Risë Stevens seemed to this observer to be distinguished. Playing the role of an adolescent and fabulously wealthy Russian prince, she had style, elegance, and carried conviction." Olin Downes wrote in the *Times:* "Risë Stevens was very comical as the foppish Orlofsky, with his monocle and yard-long cigarette holder and rapid laughter."

The monocle had also been Walter's idea, and Risë had fought it to the end.

"The first time I open my mouth," she said, "it'll fall out."

"No, it won't," said Walter. "I always used one when I played *Doctor's Dilemma.*"

Risë began to laugh.

"That wasn't why I was bad," said Walter angrily. "If it hadn't been for the monocle, I'd have been worse."

Risë had no luck with the monocle at first but finally conquered it. It became as much a part of her as if it were imbedded in concrete.

The *Fledermaus* was Bing's first great New York success, and opening night was a triumph. By means of a stunning production and a sprightly group of singers, he had forced the Metropolitan on the attention of the general public. The production was done with Broadway bounce and precision; the opera rivaled anything to be seen on West 45th Street. There were ancient boxholders who complained about the lowered standards of the opera house, but their grumbles were lost in the swirl of acclaim. Bing had no intention of making the Metropolitan the home of light opera; he merely wanted the town to know that the Metropolitan and a man named Bing were around.

When he entered Risë's dressing room after the performance, she knew from a glance that the Bing-Stevens feud, if it ever existed, was at an end. He grasped her hand and held it.

"You *did* it," he said. "I knew you would do it. I thank you from the bottom of my heart!"

She would have liked a small kiss on the cheek to make everything even, but she realized that Bing was not the sentimental type. She pressed his hand in return, and let it go at that.

Their treaty of peace received approval from both sides during a New Year's Eve performance of *Die Fledermaus* when Risë sang new lyrics by Howard Dietz to her number *"Chacun à son Goût."* The new words really shattered the audience.

> If he is in a Wagnerian mood
> We're forced to strain a lung
> And serve the ponderous musical food
>   of *Goetterdaemmerung.*
> But if he feels the surge of an urge
> To charm the Op'ry house
> With Viennesy tunes that emerge
> As light as the *Fledermaus*
> The spring in Bing can turn off a dirge
> And turn on Johann Strauss.

Risë nonchalantly turned her lengthy cigarette holder in the direction of Bing, sitting in his box. He could hardly be insensitive to the gesture or to the ovation that followed it.

Bing had taken a great gamble with the *Fledermaus* production and was entitled to his triumph. The direction had been placed in the hands of Garson Kanin, Broadway and Hollywood director; Howard Dietz, the Broadway lyricist, had been entrusted with a new English version of the German text; and Jack Gilford, the Broadway and night-club comedian, had been brought in for what turned out to be a hilarious depiction of the role of the jailer. A failure in the venture would have badly shaken Bing's position with the company. He had gambled, and he had won. The Metropolitan suddenly became a topic of conversation. By one daring gesture it regained a pre-eminent position in New York theatrical life.

There was happiness backstage, and there was also conflict. A running fight had started about curtain calls. The audience was cheering the cast to the echo; the curtains were parting endlessly for bows and curtsies. In this contest Risë and Patrice Munsel were on one side; on the other was Ljuba Welitsch, the Viennese singer who had won such acclaim in *Salome*. In operatic circles the Vienna Opera is thought of as the jungle. Singers will fight feverishly at La Scala for a favorable position before the curtain; at Vienna matters reach the stage of war. Ljuba Welitsch had come through that ordeal by fire and had at her finger tips every device for stealing the limelight. She began practicing them during *Fledermaus*.

Risë and Miss Munsel were at first unconcerned about the matter. They were happy enough that the opera was liked; there was plenty of praise to go around. As a matter of pure fact, Miss Munsel's singing and acting had taken the town by storm. Both she and Risë were given ovations when they appeared before the curtain. It was when the cast gripped hands and swept regally toward the footlights that the fun began. After two or three instances, when she found herself far out in left field, Risë felt the thing had gone far enough.

The episode was essentially hilarious, for Ljuba and Risë were devoted friends and not rivals in any real sense. Welitsch was going entirely by Viennese rules, which she had learned so painfully. There was nothing personal about it; she had almost a duty to steal the limelight; it was how the game was played. Risë had also been through the operatic wars; she had even sung at the Vienna State Opera House. What Ljuba needed was a small innocuous lesson in stage manners. From their friendship she knew that Ljuba was extremely shortsighted. This suggested an idea. When next the cast swept forward, Risë whispered advice in the Welitsch ear.

"You're nowhere near the center of the stage," she said under her breath. "Keep moving to the right."

When the line finally came to a halt, Welitsch was indeed on the right; Risë was smack in front of the prompter's box in the middle of the stage.

On another occasion Risë winked significantly at Patrice Munsel as they prepared to make the rush forward. As the curtains parted and the procession started, Risë and Munsel seemed to be deferring to Ljuba. They bowed daintily before her, they seemed to press her forward, as if the roaring applause from the audience was meant exclusively for Welitsch. They also edged her rapidly away from the center of the stage and occupied it themselves. Welitsch got the point. When she came off, she looked at them with a gaze compounded of exasperation and amusement.

"Oh, you two," she said disgustedly, and broke into a laugh. It ended with the three in a small bubbling huddle, laughing fit to kill.

But Risë had been tortured several years before by a singer who persistently "covered" her on stage. While Risë sang, this individual stood off to the side twitching convulsively, as if stung by a gnat. She lifted her arms and fixed her hair. Occasionally she turned an ecstatic gaze on Risë as though overcome by her brilliance, looking as if she might break into applause in the middle of the aria. At other moments she either looked off stage, as if seeing a vision, or gave a small start to indicate that a fire had broken out in the wings and would soon reduce the audience to an ash. The result was that Risë was singing her head off— and might as well have been yelling down a mine shaft.

"I would have handled it very simply," says Walter. "I'd have walked off after the scene and strangled her. Risë had a much better plan. She gave her the well-known treacle treatment; she smiled in most friendly spirit. 'My dear,' said Risë amiably, 'you went a little far tonight. You really shouldn't do that again.' The words were pleasant, but the meaning was plain. The singer was scared to death and was a good little girl from then on."

Risë is the most even-tempered of opera singers, but her friends and associates do not concur on the salient characteristics of her personality. They are agreed, however, on one point: there is more to the lady than meets the eye. Walter, who knows her best of all, merely smiles when the subject arises. Ed Vincent, her press agent, considers her "enigmatic—no one knows her completely." James Shomate, her concert accompanist, who travels alone with her for months at a time, holds her to be a paragon of kindness and frankness.

"Even if she tried," says Shomate, "she couldn't be devious or calculating. She's all out here."

He accompanies this with a gesture of the hand held off from the forehead. This means that Risë's emotions are honest and out where they can be viewed by the world. There are no hidden places in her character, no reservations that contradict her public actions, no secret thoughts that would make a mockery of her obvious open-mindedness and sincerity. But he hastens to add that she can sometimes surprise you.

"We were doing a concert in Pennsylvania and had stayed overnight at a hotel in a nearby town," Shomate reports. "The chauffeur who was driving us over next day turned out to be drunk as an owl. Half of the time he was on the left-hand side of the road, and *all* of the time he was gabbing away like a maniac. Finally Risë couldn't stand any more of it. 'Stop at the next road-side stand and get me a hamburger,' she said, leaning toward the driver. 'I'm starving.' When the chauffeur went in for the hamburger, Risë simply moved around to the driver's seat and took off. 'You know what you're doing, don't you?' I said. 'You're stealing a car.' She shrugged and said, 'Well, then, we're stealing it.' I didn't like that suggestion of plural guilt, but by this time she was banging along so fast I had all I could do to hang on. For a mild-mannered lady who wouldn't say boo to a goose, she's the damn wildest driver I've ever seen. She always drives as if she were two laps behind at the Indianapolis Speedway race and will make it up the third time around. She parked the car in the lot by the hall, and we went in to start the concert. Everything went fine until we got to the last group of numbers. Then we could hear the sirens. Every member of the Pennsylvania State Constabulary was evidently on the job. I paled and looked up. Risë was finishing a number, and I could see that if she didn't get through it quick, she'd burst out laughing before that whole crowd. Under cover of the applause that followed the number, she leaned over to me, and whispered, 'Why, Jimmy Shomate; how could you *do* such a thing!' When the concert was over, the chauffeur and the cops were waiting out front for us, but Risë fixed that. When she came out, she had around her the most distinguished citizens of the city—the mayor, the head of a world-famed company, the ministers of three churches. The chauffeur took one look and faded away. I suppose he thought he was lucky to get his car back."

But this is an isolated instance and proves merely that Risë can take action when she feels action is needed. Otherwise, she lets the world very much alone. Natures of this kind, however, can be contradictory. She will take a week and go miles out of her way to avoid making an enemy, but when she gets an enemy, she treasures him. The operatic life is not for tender souls. If she ever needed instruction on the point, she got it early in the Opéra-Comique. It is not a question of marching over dead bodies to the top, but a star must be prepared to demand her rights. Risë had been lucky in her early years in being treated well by her elders, but she had learned from her experiences in Europe and South America that there comes a point in a singer's career when justice can be obtained only by a loud bloody shriek of defiance.

The opera house was full of tales of famous feuds between singers, and there were many still present who had been on hand for the performances when Grace Moore and Jan Kiepura had fought it out to a finish. On high notes Jan pinched Grace, and what came forth was not a thing of beauty but an anguished yelp. When Jan raised his arm at the conclusion of a stirring passage, what he got from Grace was a jab in the ribs that caused him to emit a startled "glub."

And there had been the celebrated vendetta between Olszewska and Jeritza at the Vienna State Opera House. It had ended with Madame Olszewska spitting in Madame Jeritza's face as they came off after a lovely and spiritual duet. Risë had this firsthand from Vera Schwarz, who had also conducted a running battle with Jeritza at the same bear pit. Miss Schwarz had refrained from physical action, but she never ceased rejoicing in the memory of having seen Jeritza fall off her horse during a performance of *The Girl Of The Golden West*.

"Not slipped off, mind you," she would tell Risë, "but *fell* off, right on her most interesting rear. Oh, it was wonderful!"

The fact that the gentle Miss Schwarz would cherish to this day such a recollection of her esteemed colleague is enough to establish the point about operatic rivalries. Old-timers at the opera house still recall the famous "battle of the flowers" between Madame Gadski and Madame Fremstad. It was customary at that time for admirers to pile the stage high with floral offerings for their idols at curtain calls. When two great names and two bitter rivals were in the same cast, the result could be ludicrous. This proved to be the case on that celebrated evening when the opposing camps decided on a showdown. When the curtain fell on the first act, the Gadski cohorts dashed from the left aisle looking like a portion of Great Birnham wood brought to high Dunsinane. The other aisle was filled with a cheering horde of Fremstad devotees looking like the daisy chain at Vassar. Between them, they seemed to have the full annual output of the Bronx Botanical Gardens.

At the left, Madame Gadski was curtsying to the floor at such a well-deserved tribute to her art. At the right, Madame Fremstad was peeping out from behind a bower of roses, entirely overcome by such adulation. As they bowed, the flowers continued to come. Within a few moments there was noted a frenzied commotion in the Gadski sector: there were so many flowers that Madame could no longer be seen by the audience; she was fighting her way bravely to freedom. As her regal countenance gleamed again through the poppies, Madame Fremstad's lovely visage disappeared, after a desperate struggle which had touched the hearts of all observers. The roses had finally got her.

Such exhibitions are no longer countenanced at the opera house, and, indeed, it is generally agreed that the Metropolitan has less intrigue than any opera company in the world. However, so long as prima donnas exist, there will always be rivalries and jealousies; the Metropolitan merely insists that the more vulgar manifestations of the illness be kept from the public. The *cognoscenti* may be well aware of the tactical maneuvers on stage; the general public will see only a shining picture of sweetness and light.

With *Fledermaus* such a success, Risë was reconciled to her short season at the opera house. *Fledermaus* would never be her favorite opera, and in time she acquired the habit of backing away hastily when the subject of reappearing in it was broached, but it had temporarily served a good purpose. She awaited now with eagerness the new productions of *Carmen* and *Samson*. Conditions had improved immeasurably under Bing's direction. At her debut there had been only the suspicion of a rehearsal; for *Fledermaus* the cast was rehearsed in Broadway fashion. There had been weeks of preliminary preparation on stage business and text. That had been followed by repeated rehearsals with the full orchestra. What had resulted was a finished performance that would have done credit to a leading dramatic company.

In her usual way of taking time by the forelock, Risë was already making plans for the new *Carmen*. She had been encouraged in this by Vera Schwarz, who had brought Risë to such a comfortable state of mind that she could now make a few pointed remarks about her failings.

"Would you mind," asked Miss Schwarz, "if I gave you a few extra notes at the top of your range?"

"Would I *mind!*" said Risë excitedly. "Do you mean you could?"

"Oh, I think so," said Miss Schwarz easily. "You'll lose a bit at the bottom, but there'll be plenty left."

This was accomplished without difficulty and gave Risë a feeling of confidence she hadn't enjoyed in years. She had been doing well before; she now felt she had climbed a peak. Whatever Bing did, he wouldn't change the music of *Carmen*. But what *would* he do?

"It'll be *something*," said Miss Schwarz, nodding her head sagely. "I know that boy from Vienna."

Chapter Thirteen

When it was announced that Tyrone Guthrie, the English director, was being brought in to do *Carmen*, it was plain that things were about to happen. Mr. Guthrie's distinguished reputation had been made on novelty. He was a forceful and imaginative man; it was unthinkable that he would be on hand for a little tinkering on the original Paris Opéra-Comique production. Interpretations had varied through the years, but the pattern set in Paris had been generally adhered to. The characterization of the famous Emma Calvé had established a tradition followed by all succeeding Carmens. The carnation clinched firmly in her teeth had been her trademark; all Carmens chewed grimly on a flower.

The first Carmen was Maria Celéstine Galli-Marié, who sang the part on opening night, March 3, 1875. There has been great dispute on how well it was received. The traditional story is that it was a complete fiasco, was roundly berated by the Paris critics, and caused the death of Bizet of a broken heart three months later. Further research reveals that Bizet was already a sick man, who died of natural causes. He was only thirty-six at his death but had been ailing seriously for years. As for the opera, it ran for twenty-three performances at its first showing, and Vienna and Brussels immediately tried to get it. This seems to prove that it was at least a modest success from the start.

Bizet wrote the part of Carmen for a mezzo-soprano, but it has been sung in its time by everybody from coloraturas to contraltos. After the success of the opera had been established, Adelina Patti, the most famous coloratura of all time, essayed the part and achieved a disaster. It is said to have been her only failure in opera. Ernestine Schumann-Heink, equally celebrated contralto, was much admired as Carmen in Germany but never tried the part in this country. The role calls for a voice of high top and a rich, dark lower register. It tempts most great singers; it defeats most of them.

"It's a killer," Risë was to say later, with a touch of grimness.

Minnie Hauk did the first American Carmen, October 23, 1878. The first performance at the Metropolitan was by Zelia Trebelli, who sang it in Italian in 1884. Lilli Lehmann, the great Wagnerian soprano, sang it at the Metropolitan in German. The greatest of all Carmens was Emma Calvé, who sang it first at the Metropolitan on December 20, 1893. She was called a "creature of unbridled passion." She is the Carmen who is always remembered, and the one that all other Carmens are compared to, but the evidence seems to show that she was small, plump, and possessed of an ordinary voice. This makes no difference; she is still talked about enthusiastically by people who couldn't possibly have seen her on the stage.

The box score on other Carmens goes much like this:

Mary Garden (Chicago Opera, 1920): "Hoydenish."
Geraldine Farrar (1914): "Lacked elemental force."
Rosa Ponselle (1935): "Artificial."
Gladys Swarthout (1940): "Too much the perfect lady."
Risë Stevens (1945, old version): "Always has the trace of a
    well-bred sorority girl."

When Maria Jeritza tried it at the Metropolitan in 1928, she got the roasting of her life. She was reproached for singing the fourth act like a "screaming, scrapping fishwife." Her second-act dance was held to be a "genuine Coney Island hoochy-coochy. It was all sound and fury signifying—exactly nothing."

Ponselle's experience was the worst of all, and many people

feel that it finished her career. Olin Downes in the New York *Times* wrote: "We have never heard Miss Ponselle sing so badly, and we have seldom seen the part acted in such an artificial manner. Her dancing need not be dwelt on, although in the inn scene it raised the question whether the Spanish gypsies preferred the Charleston or the Black Bottom as models for their evolutions." Ponselle had been wavering between career and marriage. Friends believe that the fiasco of *Carmen* tipped the scales; she retired during the next season.

This was the situation when Tyrone Guthrie arrived for the first rehearsal. Risë had achieved a real success in the old version; she awaited the impact of the new dynamo with trepidation. He had done several opera productions in England, but he was essentially a stage director. It was all very well to say that the two mediums had everything in common, but Risë was not convinced of the fact. If the acting was of such strenuous and original nature that she had no time for singing, she might find herself in trouble with the audience and the critics.

Risë's first meeting with Guthrie was at a luncheon given for the express purpose of getting them acquainted. In preparation for it she had talked herself into a nervous fit. She was too tall for Carmen, she was too Norwegian, the color of her skin was wrong, she lacked the Latin physique. She was five feet eight; she was blond. Guthrie held her hand as they were introduced and looked at her quietly.

"Perfect!" he finally said with conviction.

"But I'm too tall," cried the honest Risë before Walter could get to her with a kick.

"You don't know Spanish women," said Guthrie. "They're all taller than the men. I want you to play this with a straight back, I want you to wear your highest heels, I want you to forget that the opera is in French. This is a Spanish story; we're going to play it Spanish."

They sat down to discuss the opera. Risë had been pleased about her Spanish figure, but Guthrie's next words were hardly reassuring.

"I don't know how you've been playing Carmen, but I know

how I want you to play her," he said. "She's a tramp. She's a bum. Play her like that."

As one who had been accused of playing her like a well-bred sorority girl, this was strong meat, but Risë took a firm grip on herself and bade him lead on. Girls reared in the Bronx had a very good conception of tramps; she had known them; she thought she could play them. She still retained a fixed determination to keep Mr. Guthrie on a straight line when it came to the music.

She was joined in the struggle by Fritz Reiner, the conductor, who was as much concerned as Risë in preserving his position. For Reiner it was a difficult situation. He had conducted *Carmen* hundreds of times in the old version. The signposts were well marked on that well-traveled road. He was now being asked to take an unknown route through a strange forest. Matters were complicated by the fact that Reiner didn't like Guthrie on sight. This was only part of Guthrie's troubles: he was carrying on guerrilla warfare over a wide area. He has since written in sympathy to a young director who was doing a later Metropolitan production: "I don't envy you. Those high C's will drive you nuts."

The Metropolitan was successful in keeping reports of the battle out of the newspapers, but it was known that a titanic struggle was going on behind scenes. Guthrie was bucking traditions of a hundred years; every step he took was on the toes of a wounded associate. The miracle was that a great production should have come out of it. There is no certainty that Reiner liked the final result; there are many people who still don't like it. Risë herself feels it is unfair to criticize singers who have followed her in the role because they have strayed from her interpretation. She created the part for her own special talents; that version may die with her.

The Guthrie idea was not only new; it was revolutionary. Everybody connected with the production had to put his mind in a new gear. He had to forget everything he had ever known about *Carmen* and look at it afresh. For almost a century haughty sopranos had played Carmen, the tobacco-factory girl, in garments that might have been designed by Dior. Guthrie swept that away with one indignant wave of the arm.

"These are working stiffs," he said heatedly. "Did you ever

see girls coming out of a cotton mill? Put them in rough grays and blacks—and let the hems hang down."

Risë also wore a drab creation looking like a burlap sack, but an exception was made in her case by providing a strikingly low-cut neckline. Guthrie had insisted on it, and Risë refrained from saying him nay. Guthrie explained that Carmen was an unmoral little wench who had no objection to giving the boys a view of her physical charms. Risë thought it might help in getting her appeal across to the back rows.

Guthrie was a souped-up hot rod; there was no doubt of it. Some of the things he did to the beloved old opera are still considered sacrileges by the *aficionados*. When the traditional ballet in the fourth act got in the way of his plans, he threw it out. Instead of playing the death scene in the same act in front of the bull ring, it was now to be played in Escamillo's tawdry hotel room.

"Now, wa-a-a-it a minute!" said some of the more cautious at the opera house. "We'll get killed if we start fooling around like that."

He bore them down with argument, belligerence, and pure stubbornness. But behind Guthrie was Bing, backing him to the hilt. His theory was simple: Guthrie had been brought over to do a new *Carmen;* let him do it. Guthrie had done brilliant productions at Old Vic, Stratford-on-Avon, and in the London theatre. If you didn't have faith in a director, why hire him in the first place? Friends of Bing felt that Rudolf might be whistling through a graveyard. The impact of the new *Carmen* had to be so great that it would overwhelm the old-timers and their memories of Calvé. Anything less could be a disaster—musically and dramatically.

Singing *Carmen* had always been strenuous; Risë now felt she was part of a six-day bike race. Guthrie did nothing by halves. If there was to be a dance, it must be the most vigorous dance ever conceived. If Carmen climbed a staircase, she must climb it like a panther. If Carmen was to be killed, she must be killed dead, dead, dead—with the point of the knife sticking out the other side. Guthrie didn't appreciate it at the beginning, but Risë was just the girl for him. She had the agility of a cat, the voice of an angel, and the strength of an ox. At the end of the day, it was Guthrie who fell heavily into a chair, dead with fatigue; Risë was shadow-boxing with an assistant conductor. In the scene on the stairs, a man at a table below was to throw her a tambourine. He always tossed it tenderly; a miss at this point would look ridiculous.

"Come on; throw it!" Risë exhorted him. "I'll get it. I was the best softball player in the Bronx."

It is a matter of record that Risë has never had a failure in this scene. The throw may be wobbly; it may be short or it may be long; but she always gets it. Other honors may be denied her, but Risë Stevens is without doubt the Willie Mays of the operatic world.

But there was one particular in which Guthrie failed her completely: the interpretation of the role. He was concerned with action on stage, with the effective moving about of the players, with the dramatic impact of the scenes. Risë needed a definite point of view for Carmen to fit the new all-over conception. Guthrie seemed to have no time to work with her on this.

"You know how you want it," he said. "You've done it before."

The job was left to Risë. Night after night in the apartment, after a day of slogging rehearsal on stage action, Risë labored by herself. She could see that it would be a travesty to superimpose the old interpretation on the new production. She restudied the role to see how Halévy's words and Bizet's music could be fitted into what Guthrie was doing. Carmen could be a tramp, but she must also be the vibrant personality that accounted for Don José's infatuation. Bizet had written Carmen as a human being with virtues and failings. Being a villainess was not enough. She was alluring and irresponsible, but she was strong. Unless sympathy was built up for Carmen, the story line had no meaning, the death scene would be a ludicrous anti-climax.

Never had the bulldog quality in Risë's make-up been so pronounced as in this period. She knew exactly the position she was in. Guthrie's sensational new production was bound to attract the attention of the critics; a weak or old-fashioned or unimaginative Carmen would be fatal against that background. Almost literally, she had to top Guthrie. All day long she worked on the rehearsal stage with the company; night was the time for her private warfare with the part. Insiders knew what was happening, but the world only heard of the new Guthrie *Carmen*.

Tension mounted as the opening neared, and tempers were not always seraphic. Many in the company were secretly resentful of Guthrie; they were not at all sure he wasn't violently wrenching the successful old opera out of shape and ruining it. When opera managements talked of a new production, it generally meant new scenery and new costumes. Guthrie seemed to be creating a new opera. Bing must have had serious doubts along the way, but he held his peace. His previous moves had not always been successful. New productions of the operatic twins, *Cavalleria Rusticana* and *Pagliacci*, had been openly laughed at by audience and critics. The very thing that observers feared with *Carmen* had happened in this case: the productions were so modern and stylized that the operas themselves had been smothered.

The business of fitting music to action had been a troublesome problem for Guthrie from the start, and he deferred to Reiner in all debatable questions.

"I understand what you're doing here dramatically, Mr. Guthrie," complained one of the artists, "but I really can't sing standing on my head."

Reiner and Guthrie went into conference. From it came a new treatment of the scene. It gave the singer his chance, and it didn't take away from the forcefulness of the action.

"This is a *tragedy*," Guthrie would say tensely. "It's not just a few happy Spanish girls and soldiers romping through a charade. It's a matter of life and death!"

Guthrie religiously refrained from tampering with the music, but he insisted on an emphasis that conveyed the essence of the tragedy. This was ticklish business, and it can't really be said that Guthrie ever achieved his ideal. Musical phrases have a life of their own; they can be tempered, they can be shaded, but the notes are there in all their rigidity and must be sung.

Great composers may approach a perfect union of thought and music, but singers are human and subject to human failings. They are permitted great latitude in interpretation, but out front is

A complete costume and
wig change within fifty seconds
is nothing new on TV.
Walter wears extra wig.

Ed Sullivan with Risë as
he plans to introduce her to
Russian audiences in Moscow
in summer of 1959.

Risë and Richard Tucker made the new production of *Carmen* Met Opera history.

Risë as Orfeo at the theatre of Herodes Atticus in Athens.

SEDGE LE BLANG

Stage door, after a Met performance.

LADIES' HOME JOURNAL—JOE DI PIETRO

Risë as the Rosenkavalier at the Met in famous silver-rose presentation scene, with Thelma Votipka and Hilde Gueden.

Jennie, the beloved dresser, helps Risë with final costume touch for Hansel in *Hansel and Gretel.*

Risë as Delilah at the Met.

With Mario Del Monaco
recording *Samson
and Delilah* for RCA
Victor at Symphony
Hall in Boston.

Heavy concentration for playbacks during the
same recording. Left to right: Erich Leinsdorf,
Del Monaco, Risë, Vera Schwarz,
Fausto Cleva, Mrs. Del Monaco.

Pierre Monteux, Risë, and Richard Tucker go
over score for new *Tales of Hoffmann* production.

Risë and Bing Crosby in a scene from *Going My Way*,
a scene which has haunted her to this day, because many
expect her to sing *Carmen* with a rose between her teeth.

Below, from same movie, with Barry Fitzgerald stealing the
limelight from Bing, Risë, and Frank McHugh.

Visited by Lotte Lehmann,
the famous soprano, on the MGM
lot of *The Chocolate Soldier*.

Risë checks score with conductor
Fritz Reiner a few minutes
before curtain time
of new *Carmen* production.

Risë and Rudolf Bing,
who made *Carmen* one of his
greatest productions.

Risë as Cherubino in
The Marriage of Figaro,
with the late Edward Johnson.

Risë as Orfeo, her favorite role, before the Parthenon in Athens.

The President congratulates Leonard Bernstein, Leonard Warren,
Risë, and is followed by John D. Rockefeller III at the
ground-breaking of the tremendous Lincoln Center
in New York, May 1959, which includes the new Met and
the new Juilliard School of Music.

that great beast known as the public, which also insists on lovely sounds issuing from the human voice. It is a dilemma; the artist generally solves it by singing as well as he can.

But from the moment the curtains parted on opening night, a mood of triumph was in the air. There was a gasp of delight at the new settings and costumes by Rolf Gérard and a burst of excited applause at the entrance of the factory workers in their sack cloth. Gérard had the feeling of *Carmen* in his bones; his mother was Mafalda Salvatini, a famous European Carmen. At the outset the bubbling enthusiasm was confined to the orchestra and balcony; the box holders were reserving judgment. They admitted that the music was being sung in the traditional manner, but they awaited the entrance of Carmen and the beginning of her great arias. That would tell whether Bizet had been thrown out the window and Guthrie installed in his place.

Risë's entrance as Carmen stirred a hubbub in the house, when it was seen that she was no better dressed than her fellow workers. It was a break with tradition, and it was a shock, but it seemed right. The daring of the low-cut dress caused lifted brows in the Diamond Horseshoe, but it was received well elsewhere. It was when Risë sang the "Seguidilla" that the box holders succumbed. It was lively and passionate, but it was done with every care for the lovely music. The house came down with the thunderous ovation at its close. Mixed in the wild applause was elation— and relief. It was a new *Carmen*, but it was Bizet's *Carmen*.

The performance progressed from triumph to triumph—and from shock to shock. Risë was producing a Carmen never seen before on land or sea. She was light and seductive; she was brooding and vicious; she acted with a passionate intensity that caused the walls to shake. In the famous scene where she urges José to take up smuggling, she was at a peak of rage. When he refused, she slammed the table so hard it seemed it must shatter and collapse. Her fury contained disdain and menace. This was not play-acting; it was life.

If there was regret at losing the fourth-act ballet, it was lost in the swirl of the tragedy. Gérard's setting for the toreador's hotel room was a masterpiece of ugliness, false pretension, and decay. It was a scene of almost unbearable intensity. Murder was in the air, the feverishness of the music mounted, the spectators were frozen in their seats in horror. A down-to-earth report in a tabloid next day gave the essence of the event.

"José pins Carmen to the wall, a knife blade flashes, she screams, the audience shudders—and she really gets it in the belly . . . As she dies, she pulls down a huge red window drape in her fall. It had the spectacular effect of the whole theatre caving in."

Pandemonium followed the closing of the final curtain. The new *Carmen* was that most welcome of all theatrical events: a newspaper sensation. Opera lovers might carp at the few liberties taken with Bizet's work, but the show was a Broadway smash hit. Tickets for any Risë Stevens performance in *Carmen* would be at a premium in the theatre ticket offices for years to come. The first-night audience was wildly enthusiastic; the curtain calls were endless.

Through the years that have followed, *Carmen* has been a steady source of newspaper copy. In such a strenuous performance, somebody is always getting hurt. The papers made a great to-do about an incident in March 1952, when Mario del Monaco, playing Don José, assertedly threw Risë against the staircase with such force that she fell with a thud and almost broke her arm. Signor del Monaco protested heatedly that the story was a fake: Risë had caught her heel in her dress and stumbled. Which was probably true, but who wants *that* in a newspaper story?

The most sensational of all *Carmen* happenings took place in the same season at the opening of the new production. At the height of the stirring events in the last act, one of Risë's breasts popped out of her low-cut dress—and stayed popped out! In the excitement of getting herself killed and remembering to take the draperies with her when she fell, Risë had no time to pop it back in again. Even the most cynical observer could hardly expect her to lift an embarrassed hand to her ex-lover and present-murderer and say, "Pardon me, old boy, while I readjust myself here a bit." Getting back in the mood to die would have been difficult after the interruption. It was pure accident, and Risë was careful to see it never happened again, but accidents are what newspaper columnists thrive on.

In the spring tour of the same year, Washington witnessed a performance of *Carmen* which is still talked of with awe in the capital. Everything went wrong from the start. The curtain stuck, and it seemed hours before they got it up. In the light of what followed, it was the measured opinion of many viewers that it might have been better if they had never succeeded. Risë was her usual wild self in the scene where she urges Don José to take up smuggling. When Richard Tucker, the Don José in this instance, politely refused, Risë seemed to take it as a personal affront. The Washington *Post* commented on the situation next day:

"Miss Stevens got so mad she slammed over the table with a bang and kicked a small stool into the orchestra pit, missing a cellist by the width of an 'E' string . . . At another point, when the captain of the guard hurried in to arrest Don José, he tripped over a wire and entered the scene on his face. It was a great night for Washington."

Atlanta seemed to cower under the impact of the new *Carmen*. One headline read:

STEVENS' CARMEN
WILD, TERRIFIC
Carmen a Gripping Study of Animal Fury

Boston was impressed and not reticent in stating the fact. Harold Ross wrote in the *Christian Science Monitor*: "Miss Stevens is beyond all cavil today's leading singing actress. Her voice has a lush opulence that pours forth with ease in all registers. It is projected in the same manner as her acting: without effort or strain."

Everything about the new *Carmen* seemed to lend itself to publicity. In one of the early broadcasts of the opera from the stage of the Metropolitan, a particularly rough Don José was working on Risë. In the midst of a tumultuous scene, the listeners got a shock.

"Leggo my arm!" yelled Risë indignantly.

Millions heard it; millions more were informed of it next day in the newspapers.

On another occasion a tenor who feared being known as a

171

roughneck and mistrusted his ferocity in the death scene, came armed with a rubber dagger. It would have bent if it had struck her, but, worse than that, it split in two as he approached her.

"I died that night, all right," said Risë. "I died laughing."

What happened in 1955 in *Carmen* was really serious, and Risë suffers from it to this day. She was singing with Guiseppi Di Stefano. In one scene she is supposed to stumble and fall. She did in this case—and dislocated her right shoulder. It was in the third act, and she managed to finish the scene, but she was in agony. There was a great scurrying about backstage between acts. Dr. Adrian W. Zorgniotte appeared with a rush, prepared to strap up the shoulder. Risë refused, knowing that she couldn't appear in the vigorous fourth act trussed up in this manner. The shoulder was out of its socket; Dr. Zorgniotte popped it back in again. The pain was almost unbearable, but she finished the opera.

However, she was uncertain of herself, and in the fourth act, just before the stabbing, she fell again and threw the shoulder out of place. Dr. Zorgniotte was waiting for her when she came off, taping the shoulder up and rushing her off to the hospital without waiting either for curtain calls or taking off her make-up. She was in the hospital ten days and spent weeks recuperating at home. Not even the columnists ventured to call it a publicity stunt. The shoulder is still weak, and she has to watch it constantly. It is impossible for her to get into her formal gowns without help, and if she slouches in an easy chair the shoulder tends to get out of whack again. It is Walter's job to keep an eye on her.

"Sit over here!" he will say sharply, and people will be amazed to see Risë docilely transferring from a comfortable chair to a straight chair. She hates it, and gives him a hard look, but she does it for her own good.

Among the humorous *Carmen* incidents was the cover on *Newsweek* magazine in February 1952. Risë was lying in a reclining position, with plenty of the upper rigging showing. It got a big reaction from the public, some of it shocked. A lady in Saginaw, Michigan, wrote in indignation: "I don't like naked dames. There are other things in life besides dames and bosoms."

Nobody thought to ask her what they were. The incident died.

On the day of the first performance of the new *Carmen*, Risë
wandered about her new apartment in the East Sixties in a state
of happy abandon. The dress rehearsal had gone off well; she
looked forward to the night with confidence. She buffed her
nails, sang snatches of the opera in a muted voice, and hummed
merrily. Walter was terrified. This was exactly the wrong state
to be in for a bitchy part. He began the subtle needling which
can always be counted on to arouse Risë. She knows what he is
doing, but his insults are so pointed and wounding that she finds
herself forced to react. There are light mentions of family in-
eptitudes; there are backhanded reflections on Sadie and Pa;
there is the hint that she has never looked worse. She starts by
laughing off these obvious ploys, and she ends in a rage. Everything he says contains a great deal of truth, but is slightly off-
center: this must be corrected. As she corrects the suave gentleman, she finds herself becoming increasingly annoyed. It ends
with her throwing anything handy at him, going into her room,
and slamming the door.

By the time she reached the opera house, she was as evil-
tempered as a shrew. She either snarled at people who greeted
her or sat in a corner in a surly huff. Ed Vincent was worried
by his reception and came to Walter for an explanation.

"Leave her alone," said Walter. "She's just right. She's as mean
as a snake."

When it was over, she was bubbling with joy. She kissed
everybody in sight backstage and repeated the performance when
her friends crowded in with congratulations. It required physical
force on Walter's part to get the mob out of her dressing room
and allow her to get rid of her costume. Since Risë always makes
up all over for a part, although only her arms and shoulders may
be showing, this was a job for the shower bath at home. He
bundled her up in coat and scarves and hustled her out to the
Carey car waiting by the door. There was to be a party at the
apartment, just for the family and her intimate friends.

Amid the scene of happy satisfaction Risë sat in a corner and
smiled and sipped at a glass of hot milk. They were waiting
up for the newspaper reviews, just as is done with a Broadway
first night. When they read them along about two in the morning,

their elation reached a new point. There was no doubt about it: the new *Carmen* was a smash hit, and Risë was the toast of the town. As the New York *Post* was to say in an afternoon review: "Let's forget about Calvé from now on." *Time* magazine was later to say: "The whole thing was a personal triumph for Miss Stevens." Emily Coleman in *Newsweek* wrote: "Since Miss Stevens's Octavian in *Der Rosenkavalier* is generally accepted to be the finest delineation of that role on any operatic stage, it was clear that her Carmen now gave her two for the record."

When they went to bed about four o'clock, Risë and Walter were a happy couple. Walter was shaken awake at noon.

"Walter," said Risë in agitation. "The cook's left. Who's going to get breakfast?"

"You are, of course," said Walter.

"*Hey,* now!" shouted Risë indignantly.

"And, for heaven sakes," said Walter, preparing to turn over, "put a little coffee in the pot for a change. Dont' be so chinche about it."

He turned over with a thump and was asleep again almost immediately.

And this was how the famous prima donna whose picture was in hundreds of newspapers and whose name was on the lips of millions tiptoed downstairs to get her own breakfast on the morning after her greatest triumph.

Chapter Fourteen

The move from the hotel to the apartment had been Sadie's doing. She was outraged at the thought of Nicky's being raised in an atmosphere of bellhops, assistant managers with white carnations in their lapels, and meals on bridge tables.

"What a life for a boy!" she snorted indignantly. "When anything comes up he can't handle, he calls room service."

Risë and Walter could scarcely deny the indictment. Hotel life was comfortable enough for them, but it wasn't ideal for Nicky. The fact that he came through it unharmed is a testimonial to his soundness; he could just have easily emerged a spoiled brat. Strangers fawned on him, he had the run of the hotel, and when he went out he was guarded like a foreign prince. Nobody particularly desired this, but it was obviously impossible for a boy of six to be running about the streets of New York alone. Central Park was directly across the street, and the view of it from their windows was one of the comforting sights of the town, but it might have been the Swiss Alps for all the good it did Nicky. Boys from Harlem might run wild in the northern end of the park; in the southern end, they strolled sedately with their nurses.

When it came time for him to start school, the school bus either met him in front of the door or Walter drove him up in a cab. It was even worse after school. He was redeposited at three o'clock and for the rest of the day was on his own. He was as isolated as if he lived on a remote farm in the Berkshires. And there was the insoluble problem of meal hours. Growing boys had to be fed regularly. Nine o'clock dinner after a delightful cocktail hour was fine for the elders; it was torture for Nicky. This meant that meals had to be conducted in relays. There was a never-ending procession of waiters bringing in trays and taking out dirty dishes. At the hotel, no matter how late he had been out the night before, Walter made a point of being up for breakfast with Nicky. He has always considered this his high mark in bravery. His head might be bursting, his eyes might be leaden, he might speak with the blubbery tones of a seal, but he sat staunchly across from Nicky every morning and commanded him to finish his oatmeal.

Inevitably, Walter became both father and mother to Nicky. Risë was away for months on concert tours; at home during the opera season, she lived like a princess in a tower. There must be no noise in the suite while Mama was resting; nobody must speak to her on the day of a performance. The only exception was Nicky himself, and he rarely exercised the privilege. It finally got too much for Risë herself.

"Sadie's right!" she burst out one day. "It's a dog's life. We've simply got to get a place where we can start acting like a family."

Walter had seen it coming and had been looking around for apartments, but he knew it wouldn't appreciably better his own situation. Instead of the hotel taking the burden of running their household, he would have it himself again. He remembered Hollywood all too well. Nicky was older and easier to handle, but there would still be the help problem to contend with. But the change was needed both for Nicky and Risë. When they rented the duplex in the East Sixties, Risë threw herself into housekeeping with fury. She had always liked to cook; she now made a nuisance of herself in the kitchen. At dinner parties at the homes of friends she invariably took the hostess aside after the meal and asked her the ingredients of that wonderful meat sauce or the contents of the salad dressing.

And it was well that she learned to cook, for otherwise they would have starved to death. Walter was maintaining his impeccable record of never keeping a maid. He hired them with the greatest hope and began hating them on the second day. The truth is that he couldn't bear anybody in the house but Risë and Nicky. It was both his home and his office, he spent most of his life between its walls, and his irritation soon reached a point where it could only be relieved by the slam of the front door and the departure of another maid. He could handle anything else for Risë, but he was a dud with the help.

"It's not only that they're always quitting," said Risë irritatedly, "but they always quit just when they shouldn't. Next time, let me do the hiring."

She employed a handsome Negro maid whose first essays in the kitchen produced meals of such superior elegance and succulence that the Surovys hugged each other with joy.

"I don't think I caught it right when you came in," said Risë to the new paragon. "What is your name?"

"The Flowering Field of Justice," said the cook.

Risë took a step backward.

"It's very pretty but rather long," she said. "Don't you have a shorter name we could call you?"

"The Flowering Field of Justice," repeated the lady stoutly. "That's the name."

She was a follower of Father Divine, and everybody agreed that there was no better domestic help to be found in New York, but Risë had to let her go.

"She was wonderful, but I could see it would never do," she says sadly. "If I had to keep calling her that on the day of a performance, I wouldn't have had any voice by night."

The experience was to be repeated with variations to the present day. Risë quickly abdicated her power of choice, and the duty fell to Walter again by default. In time he acquired an admirable proficiency in hiring new maids and cooks; he had never lacked decisiveness in firing them. Generally, there was no need of it: they left under their own power. This almost invariably happened on the eve of a big dinner party. On one occasion Risë came home around four o'clock after a hard day of rehearsal to find that her cook had flown the coop at noon.

"Oh, *NO!*" she said disgustedly.

"I told her we were having eight guests," explained Walter, "and she said she had made a compact with the Lord never to cook for more than six people. She was afraid if she broke her word, He'd hit her with a thunderbolt or something."

"Why didn't *you* hit her?" asked Risë tartly.

"And get the Lord sore at me, too!" cried Walter in alarm. "I'm on thin enough ice as it is."

"Oh, nuts; come on," said Risë, heading for the kitchen. "I'll see what we can dig up. It'll be a mess."

She dug up her old specialty: Hungarian goulash, and it turned out all right. She does something good, too, with broiled chicken, which has been remarked upon favorably by her acquaintances, and in some circles she is regarded as a first-rate operator. The one certain thing is that she is devoted to the profession. During the summer, when she might better be doing her scales or working on her new concert program, she is spending hours in the kitchen putting up peach preserves and strawberry jam. However, there are critical observers who feel that, as a cook, Risë is much like the third-string quarterback who comes in for the last ten minutes and holds the team's lead. Good in an emergency but not particularly effective for a whole game. Risë regards such gentry with disdain.

But the maid troubles in the new apartment couldn't hide the fact that the move had done Nicky a world of good. Their sector of Lexington Avenue was not exactly a small-town green, but Nicky was now cruising about the neighborhood with a gang of his own age. He was still going to Browning, his only school in New York, but he either got there by bus or he walked. Before his first departure alone into the world Risë had given him a tearful lecture on trucks, drunken accosters, and red lights.

"For heaven's sakes, Mom," he said disgustedly, "I've lived in New York all my life."

From Walter he had picked up the conviction that, for her own good, Risë's feet must be kept on solid ground. She might be Risë Stevens, the opera star, to the world: at home she was the third member of a trio. One night when she set out for the opera house looking a vision of loveliness, Nicky brought her down with a thump.

"The triumph of Max Factor," he said.

This was amusing, but it worried Risë, quite aside from the fact that it pricked her vanity.

"He's too sophisticated," she said worriedly.

"Of course, he is; how could he help it?" answered Walter. "We're lucky he hasn't turned out to be a monster."

As a matter of fact, he was a sensible and normal boy, with an amiable disposition much like Risë's brother, Bud. What he had picked up was not so much sophistication as a light touch, inherited from both his parents. Without ever stating the proposition formally, Risë and Walter were agreed that if they ever became solemn bores, they were to be kicked for their pains, mutually, individually and en masse. Nicky could expect the same fate if he came around acting like a pursy-faced dolt. The men of the family would spoil Risë to a point; after that they would bring her down with poisoned darts. Walter could strut about as the big business success, but Risë could deflate him with a phrase. "You look like somebody in *Doctor's Dilemma*," she would say. Walter subsided immediately.

One night there was a row when Nicky asked permission to go to a weekend basketball game at Madison Square Garden with some of his schoolmates. Risë said he could go; Walter said he couldn't go. He added it was ridiculous to think of a boy of nine traipsing all over Manhattan Island at midnight with a bunch of nitwits not dry behind the ears. Risë said *Bah-midnight;* they'd be home in bed by eleven and what difference did it make, anyway? They'd go by taxi and come home by taxi. What could happen to them? Walter said, *plenty!* Risë said, *Bah!* again, repeating herself. The date was two days off, and Nicky wondered what all the excitement was about. The argument waxed, and soon both Risë and Walter were yelling. It then suddenly occurred to them that Nicky was taking it all in.

"What are *you* standing there for!" howled Walter. "Go on to bed!"

Nicky left, and the argument continued in the living room. It simmered down after a while, and Risë and Walter went to bed. They were just nicely snuggled down when the door opened and Nicky could be seen in the doorway, with the light shining behind him. He advanced toward Walter, pointed an accusing finger, and said:

"Next time you're mad at me, don't take it out on Risë."

He turned, walked slowly to the door, and slammed it behind him.

That was their boy, all right! They stuck their heads under the pillows and laughed till they were weak.

Their chief fear was that Nicky would either be overwhelmed by his mother's reputation or that he would try to capitalize on it. They had seen other children of operatic and theatrical families who were either dragged helplessly along in the wake of their famous parent or treated with such soft-headed concern that they were ruined. The temptation was great for a star to dodge her responsibility as a mother by turning her children over to nurses or maids. When a sense of guilt overcame her, she appeased it by lavishing gifts on them.

The presence of Sadie and Pa in New York was a great help for Nicky. It gave him the assurance that there was more in life than the strange routine Risë was forced to follow. Their battered old apartment uptown struck Nicky as just about right. When the atmosphere became tense on the day of a performance, Sadie would take him uptown or to the Central Park Zoo or to a movie. The only drawback in Sadie's case was that she was the original and most fanatic of all Risë Stevens fans. She did her best to keep a level head on the subject, but she couldn't help hinting that Nicky was a lucky boy to have such a mother. Nicky agreed dutifully but seemed unimpressed. Grandma could say what she liked, but Walter and he knew Risë: she was just a big, jolly, friendly girl who was a positive menace in a pillow fight.

But before a performance at the Metropolitan, it was tough. Risë would sleep late, which was no novelty since she always slept as late as Walter would let her.

"Ten or twelve hours is normal for her," says Walter, "and she'd do twenty if I didn't yank her out."

She would have a solitary breakfast, which consisted of a three-and-a-half-minute boiled egg, toast, jam, and lots of coffee. She would then run through the score of the night's opera, glance at the newspapers, and sit down to a good book. "Or, more preferably, a bad book," says Walter sourly. "Like all presidents, field marshals and great atomic scientists with weak minds, she likes mysteries."

At one-thirty or two she went back to bed again. Not for a snooze, but a full sleep. All clothes off, plugs for the ears, and a bandage for the eyes. At four she was up. She would then have a big dinner, again eating alone. A big thick steak, baked potatoes, sliced tomatoes, rye bread and butter, and a piece of chocolate cake for energy. But why the solitary meal?

"I like to let her stew in her juice," says Walter. "At this point she's generally as smug as a tabby cat; I want her to get worrying about being a flop."

At four-thirty she would start vocalizing, very softly at first, running up and down the scales. She would fool with her costumes and wigs, walk upstairs, walk downstairs, look out the window. The telephone would be silent; anybody coming to the door would be shunted away as if they had inadvertently broken in on a service of the Black Mass. Nobody would be allowed to speak to her, except with a message about Nicky.

"And then only if Nicky has been hit by a car," says Walter sardonically.

At about five she would go to her private dressing room in the apartment, which is far superior to anything provided by the Metropolitan. There is a dressing table and the best of modern lighting equipment. She would work on her hair and make-up. She would meticulously check the costumes, embellishments, and props she needed for the night's performance.

Somewhere in the midst of the routine would come the moment when the cook and maid left, generally never to return. It would be Walter's duty to get them out of the house. Often they objected to leaving the house; they had nowhere to go. When they did leave, it was with packed suitcases and an angry glint in the eye.

It was also the time when Walter kept close watch of Risë to see how she was behaving. If she was smug and relaxed and sure of herself, he picked a fight. This would end in a loud row, with things being thrown—and she would be in fine fighting trim for the night.

At six o'clock they would leave for the opera house. They would stand on the corner of 67th and Lexington Avenue and hail a cab. Once in the taxi, Risë would say to the driver, "Put down that window at your side; put down that window on the other side; put out that cigar." The reactions of the drivers varied. They may be listed generally as follows:

(a) "Why don't you drive the hack yourself?"

(b) "All right, if you want the Black Hole of Calcutta."

(c) "The customer is always right . . . sometimes."

(d) "If you don't like it, get out and walk."

Once Walter felt called on to explain.

"She's a singer at the Metropolitan," he said apologetically.

"What's she playin'—*Traviata?*" asked the driver, sourly. "Got T.B. or somethin'?"

The taxi route has been set by tradition and superstition. The cab was to go across 67th to Fifth, and then down to Central Park South. Along Central Park South to Seventh Avenue. Down Seventh Avenue to Times Square, where it becomes Broadway. Down Broadway to 41st Street, turn right to Seventh Avenue again, and then left to the stage-door entrance on 40th Street. By the stage door is the fruit stand of Jacob Toppel. Risë is always hungry. She buys a pretzel; Walter takes the pretzel away from her. If there had been any break in the cab routine, they would stop the driver, get out and take another taxi.

The doorman at the Metropolitan would meet Risë with bows and smiles, lead her to her dressing room with care. For nineteen years he has been performing this rite, and for nineteen years he has been taking her to the wrong room. At number ten, the star's dressing room, he would halt and make a wide sweep of the arm.

"Your room, Madame," he would say proudly.

"I'm sorry, Tony," she would invariably say, "but I'll just keep eleven, as usual."

Risë and Walter would unpack the bags and set up for business in number eleven. Jennie, the celebrated wardrobe mistress of the Metropolitan, would be there to handle the costumes and would lay out the make-up on the wooden counter, Walter would be tacking up the bits of adornment calculated to dispel the notion that the room was a hen coop.

At seven o'clock Vera Schwarz would appear, and they would go over the entire score. Parts of it would be done in half voice; the different passages would be done with all stops out. The audience filing reverently into the opera house could have no knowledge of the turmoil back stage. Like baseball pitchers warming up for a game, the singers would be getting limbered up for the performance. On one side of the house, the bellows of a basso would be mingled with a tenor doing snatches of an aria, ending on a high C that shook the rafters. La-la-la-la-LAH . . . LAH-la-la-la-lah. On the other side, the women would be running up and down the scales like magpies. It was Sunday afternoon in Bedlam; it was feeding time at the zoo.

If Risë was in a good mood, she would be sipping tea; if she needed perking up, it would be coffee. At the proper time she would go down on stage to check on the setting, the position of the furniture, and the props. Back in her dressing room, there would be last-minute dabs at her make-up and a last careful accounting of everything she needed with her on stage. A handkerchief, a scarf, a dagger. Just before the performance she would go to the door and speak to the friends or fans who were gathered there.

As she left the dressing room, Walter would embrace her and spit three times over her left shoulder, an old Hungarian custom to bring luck. John Stephen, publicity associate of Ed Vincent and an opera fanatic, would pat her on the arm and say: "Have fun, now." An American superstition. And down the warped steps she would go to the stage. Precisely at eight o'clock a bell would ring loudly backstage. The punctuality of the opera was amazing to anybody who knew the casualness of Broadway. Theatre curtains seemed to rise by impulse and never on time. The opera kept to a strict routine, perhaps on the theory that the box holders would be late in any case. A few moments after the ringing of the bell promptly at eight, the first strains of the overture could be heard from the pit. Then the curtains would part, and the opera would begin.

After the performance Risë would take off her costume, clean the make-up from her face, change into street clothes, get bundled into heavy coat and scarf, and prepare to go home. First she would talk with the friends and admirers who had come backstage to congratulate her. At the stage door there would be autographs to sign. Then into the hired limousine, and home.

The first thing Risë would do when they got to the apartment was run the water in her tub; the next thing she would do was rush out in a rage.

"No hot water again, damn it!" she would howl. "I'll kill that superintendent in the morning."

Risë would somehow get cleaned (an onerous task with the full body make-up of Dalila or Carmen), wrap herself in a dressing gown, and come down for a quiet party with her friends. She would talk in a low voice, laugh at the jokes, and sip a little hot milk.

Next day she would sleep till noon, and a small amount of normal life would return to the household.

But nobody could pretend that a singer's routine was anything but extraordinary. Risë had her choice between being a dutiful housewife or a top-flight prima donna. She hates the word and never uses it, but she can't escape it. The regimen she follows is not new; it has been used by divas since opera was born. The opera is a hard taskmaster; it can't be operated as a side line. Anybody sustaining the lead role of an opera has to be in good health and in superb physical condition. Singing and acting at full force for three or four hours is grueling work. Only a singer dedicated to her art can accomplish it. Risë brings to it what Martin Mayer has called "single-track ferocity." That is the only way it can be done.

This would seem to leave the problem of Nicky and Walter unresolved, but this is not the case. They handle it quite simply by ignoring opera. This strange creature who wanders silently around the house for days like a Trappist monk is merely a freak who happens to be their beloved relative. If she wants to preserve her voice for the Great Beast Public, it is all right with them. They whistle, they shout, they talk their heads off. Walter is not an opera lover; Nicky merely shrugs it off. Just to keep Risë in her place, he maintains stoutly that Patrice Munsel is his favorite opera star. If he has any say in the matter, he stays carefully away from the opera house.

"Don't you want to see the new *Carmen?*" Risë once asked him wistfully.

"No, *sir!*" he said emphatically, preparing to run. "I saw the old one."

Later, when he was attending prep school at Choate in Connecticut, Risë and Walter went up to see him. Earlier in the week she had appeared in a television production of *Little Women*.

"Did you have a chance to see it?" Risë asked, tentatively.

"The last part," said Nicky. "It was good."

He explained that he had been assigned to the library that night and couldn't get away any sooner. Walter considers the incident a complete compendium of the virtues that keeps the Surovy household happy and intact.

"It never occurred to Nicky to ask permission to get off to hear his mother on the show," he says. "Risë was not the slightest bit upset by his answer. It never occurred to her that she was important enough to have Nicky break a school rule to see her."

From this it can be held that the Surovys have worked out a difficult problem with success. This happens to be the truth. When Risë is a mother and a housewife, they accept her gladly; when she departs on a cloud for the Metropolitan Opera House, they wait patiently for her return.

Chapter Fifteen

As a relief from the opera performances, Risë's appearances in radio and television were considered a blessing by Walter and Nicky. Things at home were much pleasanter when the shadow of the Metropolitan didn't hang over them. Risë agreed to radio and television dates but generally only after a fight. She was convinced that each new appearance was going to ruin her.

"What am I doing on with Milton Berle?" she would ask heatedly. "I'm not fast enough for that company."

Walter first worked on her with patient argument. If that failed, he turned to guile.

"All right, we'll turn Berle down," he said. "I'll simply tell him you're too dumb for it."

That did it. Risë might be painfully unsure of herself, but nobody was going to accuse her of stupidity. Her indignation mounted as the argument progressed. Poor Mr. Berle was merely waiting to hear if she would sign the contract; she turned him into an opponent who was trying to keep her off the air.

"Who does he think he is, anyway!" she cried hotly. "I'll show him, if he thinks he can walk over *me*."

This is an exaggeration of her general attitude; for she has one of the most logical minds extant. Walter might propose, but Risë insisted on good sound reasons why. When Walter cooked up a scheme he knew would meet with resistance, he worked hard at preparing a complete analysis of its merits. Risë is malleable as soap, but she can spot a fake proposition a block away. Once she gets her back up, no force on earth can move her. Walter is a very fast thinker, and a wit. His barbs are pointed, and his gags come fast and furious. In a discussion about a contract he can be outrageous and insulting. Risë can be annoyingly calm, for the simple reason that her thoughts are miles away, and things go in one ear and out the other. But there will come a point where her attention is engaged, and she finds that Walter has been belaboring her with a mental bludgeon. Her mind seems to halt; a steely glint comes in her eye.

"*Hör' auf!*" she says quietly but pointedly.

Walter backs hastily away. He knows he has gone too far; he is aware that he is up against the stone wall that nothing can move. The public knows only the engagements Risë has appeared in; they know nothing of the others she has refused. Walter presses on with his campaign to broaden Risë's audience; Risë fights back. In most cases, she gives in to his judgment; in the few other cases, he wishes she had fought harder.

The Milton Berle appearance teetered on the brink of disaster. During rehearsals Risë sang an aria from one of her operas. Berle followed with a broad burlesque of it. Risë stopped him in the middle of it.

"If you do that during the show, I'll walk out," she said.

Berle looked at her in amazement.

"What did *I* do!" he cried in a hurt voice. "*Everybody* kids opera."

"You can do it one way, and it's funny," said Risë. "You can do it the way you're doing it, and it makes opera a fake. Well, I'm an opera singer, and I think opera's the finest thing in the world. You can make a fool of it if you want to, but don't ask me to help you do it."

This small oration helped to clear the air, but it didn't convince Berle. He pointed out that Risë had appeared several years before in a burlesque of *Carmen* with Fred Allen. If Allen could do it, why couldn't he? Risë explained the matter at length and finally resorted to a review by Harriet Van Horne in the New York *World-Telegram and Sun,* which had said: "Allen takes enormous liberties with the original libretto, but he never descends to the shoddy level of most lampoons."

"All right," said the irrepressible Berle promptly, "I'll climb right up there with old Fred. We'll do a lampoon, too, whatever the hell *that* is."

They worked on a treatment suggested by Risë, and it was the hit of the show. Berle came off beaming.

"Hey!" he cried unbelievingly to Risë. "The thing was *funny.* Yocks all the way through. I'm gonna lampoon 'em to death from now on."

Walter kept Risë supplied with a steady procession of radio and television dates. She did parodies with Eddie Cantor; she did skits with Fred Allen; she did turns with Jack Haley and Bing Crosby and Jack Benny. She did duets with Frank Sinatra at a time when it was felt he was a national menace. The bobby-soxers were mobbing him on the street; the police were out in force when he appeared at a New York theatre. It was held in some circles that juvenile delinquency was directly connected with the little fellow from New Jersey. The presence of an opera star in his program was thought to be an insult to the profession. Risë was unmoved.

"Even if I didn't know he was a fine singer and a nice fellow," she said, "the holler those kids put up would convince me. You never fool the young fry. Was it publicity and advertising that got them interested in Frankie? You just bet it wasn't. It was the other way around. They discovered him, and the publicity came afterwards."

Through the years she has had a warm spot in her heart for Sinatra. She sang with him when he was a sensation; she sang with him later when everybody said he was finished. Their big-city backgrounds were similar; they had both fought up from the streets. If their rehearsals could have been put on the air, they would have been sensational. Sinatra had a New Jersey routine; Risë matched him at that and lapsed into a Bronx accent that shattered him. The Stevens-Sinatra shows were a romp, and great successes.

"Those were the shows she would have done for nothing—if I had let her," says Walter.

But it wasn't all beer and skittles. There was the Liberace bit on the "Ed Sullivan Show," about which both Risë and Walter still cringe. It sounded good in conception; it turned out to be a horror. Liberace had become a national byword. No comedian would dare appear without a burlesque of a Liberace show, with mention of brother George, Liberace's flamboyant costumes, and the candelabra on the piano. It seemed to be the perfect showcase for Risë. Liberace would play; Risë would sing.

"Liberace played, Risë sang, and it was something awful about a concrete mixer," reports Walter wryly. "We were afraid to appear on the streets for a month after."

Risë couldn't charge Walter with this mishap, for she had been strong for the idea when it was first broached. But on another occasion she met the news of an engagement with the steely quietness that has always disconcerted Walter. When he casually let drop the information that he had signed her for a television show with Ray Bolger, she merely looked at him silently for a long time.

"What am *I* going to do on the show?" she asked, holding his eye firmly.

"Dance," said Walter, beginning to squirm.

She continued to look at him without speaking, a form of torture he doesn't enjoy.

"Do you happen to know that Ray Bolger is one of the finest dancers in the world?" she asked with deadly calm.

"You're a good dancer yourself," he protested hastily.

"I'm a good dancer in the same sense that Bolger is a good soprano," Risë pointed out. "Is there any way we can break the contract?"

Walter said there wasn't, and added quickly that she was making a mountain out of a molehill, or whatever the silly phrase was. This was her chance for a completely new character. People who thought of her as a cold and majestic opera singer would get a different notion of her warm humanity.

"Humanity-schumanity," answered Risë, with inelegant disgust. "I'll look like a jackass up there with a dancer like that."

But the deed was done, and Risë was piqued by the thought that she might somehow pull it off. It was true that she was a very good ballroom dancer and did the rumba with a hip-tossing abandon that brought small cries of delight even from the wall-flowers. Dancing with Bolger would be a different matter, but she was somewhat reassured after meeting him. He said it would be the easiest thing in the world; just a question of learning a few simple steps.

"A few simple steps that almost killed me," Risë now says sourly. "Before I was through I was doing the rumba, waltz, Charleston, black bottom, and soft shoe. I rehearsed till I was blue; every bone in my body ached; it was months before I got over it. Did Surovy care? Not a bit of it; he danced right along with me. It turned out that among his other loathsome early achievements, he had also been a hoofer."

This was one television show that Nicky enjoyed. Not content with the long hours of rehearsal at a studio, Walter worked out on Risë at home. As a phonograph ground out the corny old tunes for the black bottom, Risë groaned and wept and danced.

"Just one more time!" Walter would cry. "You've almost got it."

"I've not only got it, but I've *had* it," Risë would answer furiously, throwing herself on a divan in a decisive way that showed she would be there till the cock crew. "If I had any sense, I'd shoot you dead right now and get out of the contract."

"That's the only way you'll get out," Walter assured her easily. "You've almost got this thing licked. You'll be a riot."

Nicky regarded the performance at home as the finest tableau ever enacted for an audience of one. He chirped with glee; he capered about like a goat. When Risë shuffled grimly through the soft-shoe routine, he doubled up with laughter. Risë gave him a sour hard look.

It was great fun for everybody but Risë, and there were reefs still ahead. In the excitement about their dancing they had forgotten about Risë's costume. She had been wearing a gown in the early rehearsals, but Bolger felt this was merely a practice outfit. When he discovered the truth at dress rehearsal, two hours before the show was to go on the air, he threw up his hands.

"We don't need another rehearsal," he lied. "It'll just get us balled up. We're set now."

He went in search of Walter. That gentleman was a picture of aplomb.

"What's the matter with the costume?" he asked quietly belligerent.

"Nothing, if you want her to look like one of the witches in *Macbeth*," said Bolger heatedly. "Where'd she get it, anyway?"

Walter suavely mentioned the name of a famous *couturière*, where Risë had most assuredly *not* bought it.

"Well, send it back to her," shouted Bolger, "and get something in gingham. Denim, even. But not *that* monstrosity."

The astute Risë had caught on to the truth the moment Bolger called off the rehearsal. She looked at herself in a mirror and started back in fright. What in the name of heaven had she been thinking about? Well, she had been thinking about those blasted dance steps and had allowed Walter to pick the dress. She now approached him in a rush.

"Come on, you!" she said fiercely. "*Home.* We'll dig up something there."

She berated him all the way back in the cab, he answered with humility, and inside he was laughing fit to kill. This is the diet upon which the mighty Surovy thrived. What was the fun in a performance if there couldn't be excitement? For years he had practiced the trick of holding things off till the last minute. It put Risë on edge, it drove the director to suicide, it made Walter feel just right.

Risë rushed into the apartment and started going through her wardrobe closets. In a minute gowns were flying in all directions. She would yank out a dress, look at it eagerly, give a small despairing cry, and throw it to the floor.

"There's not a thing here I can wear!" she wailed. "Call Bolger up and tell him it's all off."

"You've got a hundred dresses," pointed out Walter, for the first time experiencing a touch of anxiety.

"*Concert* gowns!" exploded Risë. "Heavy as armor and dragging all over the ground. Could I dance in one of *them?*"

Walter admitted sadly that she couldn't. He took a hand at

looking through the closets. He was becoming more than slightly panicky when Sadie came to the rescue. She was there looking after Nicky. She drew out a dress, stroked it down gently with her hand, and smiled.

"I can fix this one," she said.

Risë rushed off with her to the sewing room, after bestowing a murderous look intended to annihilate Walter on the spot. Walter received it with humility and in fact used it as a counterforce to abate his inner trembling. He would be the first to admit that at last he had gone too far. The dress was altered, it was far from being spectacular, but it would serve. The trip downtown was made in icy silence. Risë sat in a far corner of the cab and refused to look at her lord and master. Walter opened his mouth two or three times—and then thought better of it. At the studio Bolger looked at the new gown, made a smiling upward gesture of the hands which might mean anything, and the show went on. It was the hit of the season. The New York *Times* said: "This is one show that should be repeated annually."

When she came off the stage, Risë was suffused with two dominant feelings: (a) fatigue and (b) rage. She looked around for Walter; Walter was nowhere to be seen. She was swarmed upon by directors, assistant directors, sound engineers, account representatives, actors, secretaries, and stagehands. She found that she had been wonderful, stupendous, out of this world. Hugs, kisses, pats on the back, heartfelt wringings of the hand. Walter re-appeared at the psychological moment, and they started home. Nothing was said until they neared their door.

"You and your dress," she said bitterly.

Walter looked at her with fake amazement.

"Good heavens," he cried, with open-eyed innocence. "Were you worried about *that?* You'd have wowed them in a Mother Hubbard."

This served to get him off the hook temporarily, but there is no doubt that the Bolger experience shook Walter. He was a chastened man . . . and stayed chastened for the better part of a week.

As Risë's career in television progressed, her rows with Walter marched along a parallel highway. He was forever pressing her into things she didn't want to do. She would swear on a Bible that this was one time she was absolutely not going to follow Walter's crackbrained plan for her. Just as inevitably, she did the program, it turned out well, and she had to admit that he had been right. There was a great battle over a *Hansel and Gretel* show. It was the part of the mother, it called for an important singer, and every singer in town had turned it down. Walter thought it would be fine for Risë.

"Now, be sensible, Walter," she said. "Jeanette MacDonald knows her way around show business, and she wouldn't touch it. Why should I?"

Walter advanced twenty-five thousand well-considered reasons for believing that the enterprise would advance her artistic career immeasurably. Risë suggested that they have a look at the script. The script turned out to have only a few scenes for the mother's part.

"You'll build it up," said Walter.

Risë pointed out with asperity that there was only one song in the show for her.

"They'll find you another one," promised Walter.

Risë still doesn't know why she let him talk her into the venture. Hollywood stars in their sixties run like thieves from the suggestion of a father's role. Actresses continue to play ingénues to an age when even their grandchildren get weary of them. Risë was a glamorous operatic star; what was the advantage of playing an older part? Walter could never explain it properly; he had a hunch. The hunch turned into one of Risë's most popular television shows.

As always happens when she appears on a show, she was so well prepared in rehearsals and dominated the scene so thoroughly that the director inevitably found himself building up her part. When a scene they had banked on proved to be weak, they strengthened it by transferring the lines of other actors to Risë. Midway through rehearsals the director was struck by a magic thought. He clapped his brow exultantly.

"Why, *I* know what's wrong here," he cried. "We need a song by Risë in this spot."

Hurried negotiations were launched, and they paid $5000 for

the television rights of Humperdinck's "Children's Prayer." Every critic picked it as the high point of the show. By the time the cameras began whirring on the actual performance, Risë's share in the proceedings had been built into a fat part. Red Buttons worked mightily, the other players acted with fervor and devotion —and Risë got all the notices. When it was over, Risë kissed Walter lightly on the forehead.

"Oh, don't look so smug," she laughed.

Next morning she had less cause for elation. She was to open the spring tour of the Metropolitan that night in Washington. As she got out of bed, she found she couldn't speak. Fumes had been used in *Hansel and Gretel* to represent magical forest clouds. Risë had a bad case of chemical poisoning. Walter hastily called Dr. Leo Reckford; the doctor said it was impossible to think of Risë singing that night.

"I must," whispered Risë, with a croak.

The doctor continued to work on her, shaking his head dolefully the while.

"You might start," he said finally, "but you'll never finish."

Walter bundled Risë up, and they rushed out to La Guardia Field for the one o'clock flight to Washington. The field was shrouded in fog; all flights had been temporarily canceled; it was hoped that the fog might lift. After a forty-five minute wait the fog showed no sign of being so obliging. They rushed to Pennsylvania Station and missed the two-thirty to Washington. There was no drawing room available on the three-thirty; they were lucky to get parlor-car seats. They wired Mr. Bing about their plight, assuring him that they would arrive at seven-thirty. By luck they might even be able to get the curtain up on time at eight.

They settled into their seats on the three-thirty, the train slid quietly out of the station, ran into the tunnel for a few hundred yards—and stopped with a jolt that threw passengers out of their seats. They found later they had killed a trackwalker in the tunnel. The train backed into the station, and there was a great scurrying of men with lanterns and litters. After an hour the train started again. Walter bit his nails and looked repeatedly at his watch and the timetable. The best they could do now was eight-thirty in Washington. Fortunately, Risë was too worried about her voice to be concerned about making the opera. She closed her eyes and leaned back against the parlor-car seat.

Walter conferred with the Pullman conductor. It was absolutely necessary that a telephone call be put through to Mr. Bing at Philadelphia. How could it be arranged? The conductor shrugged his shoulders helplessly.

"We only stop two or three minutes," he said. "You wouldn't possibly have time for it."

Walter considered dropping off at Philadelphia and letting Risë go on alone, but in her present state it was unthinkable. She was under great tension; her few attempts at speech had brought nothing but a gravelly rasp; she relapsed into silent misery. When the train neared North Philadelphia, Walter was first in the vestibule to get off. He eyed the descending passengers anxiously. He finally fixed on a young man third in the line. When the passengers issued onto the platform, he pressed a five-dollar bill into the man's hand and told him his predicament.

"Risë Stevens!" cried the young man with amazement. "Now, you'll never believe this, but I knew her brother Bud very well; he was one of my best friends. Don't worry about it; I'll take care of it."

Walter repeated the information about Mr. Bing.

"Oh, I know who Bing is," said the young man. "I've been following Risë's career for years. I'll get him, all right."

He handed back the five-dollar bill.

"Let me do this just for the fun of it," he said. The train had begun to move; Walter rushed to get on; he had time only for a final hasty wave of the hand. To this day he doesn't know who the man was.

Risë had begun to show signs of life. She looked up at their bags in the rack above; she pushed small bags into a pile about her with her feet.

"What are you doing now?" asked Walter worriedly.

"Well, if I'm going to sing, I have to get ready for it," said Risë, with a return of spirit that elated Walter. "We'll be lucky to get the curtain up at nine. I've got to be made up when we get there."

The passengers were then treated to the peculiar sight of Mr. Surovy lugging bags into the ladies' washroom. Risë entered the room and locked the door. She did her hair, she did her elaborate make-up—and then she began to vocalize. Lah-la-la-la-LAH . . . LAH-la-la-la-lah. It was heavenly music to Walter's ears; the Pennsylvania Railroad customers were shocked by the cacophony of sound. They were even more startled when they saw her emerge from her cave. Operatic make-up is done on the broad principle of a circus poster. The artist is appearing on a huge stage; there will be no intimate close-up scenes on the stage apron; the singer must be easily distinguished from the most remote perch in the top balcony, a city block away. Hence, the eyelashes that stick out like talons; the face coloring laid on with a trowel; the elaborate wig that seems to take on a life of its own.

If Risë was aware of the sensation she was causing, she gave no sign of it. She was too happy about her voice. As she sat in her seat, looking like something seen through a window on Halloween night, she gave joyous little trills in the back of her throat. Her voice was there; it felt good.

At the station to meet them was Mr. Bing at the head of a Washington delegation of big shots. A motorcade of cars stood panting at the door. Policemen on motorcycles led a siren-shrieking procession uptown to the theatre. The train had arrived at eight-thirty; the curtain went up promptly at nine. Risë began with the determination to go as far as she could; to her delight, her voice grew stronger as she went along. The opera was a triumph; the newspaper publicity on her hegira was icing on the cake.

Risë still makes a pretense that each television engagement is her last, but in truth she has fallen in love with the medium. She will have a dozen arguments ready to prove that the new show will be wrong for her, but there is never any chance she will turn it down. Despite the mechanical limitations of television—restricted space, the need to have every move worked out geometrically—she feels great freedom when working before the cameras.

"I must be queer, but the cameras don't bother me at all," says Risë. "Other actors tell me they're scared to death of those cold-looking machines, but I never think of them like that. I see a lot of friendly people sitting in their living rooms before their sets. If they're there at all, it seems to me they must be pulling for the actors to make good. If you do your best, they're going to like you."

The intimacy of television appeals to Risë. Her career has heretofore been confined to the large concert hall, the movie screen, and the huge opera house, where the singer exists in a geographical vacuum, cut off from the audience by space and the beautiful din of a large orchestra. With television the artist is virtually knee to knee with his audience. This brings a warmth and friendliness to a television program that is not possible in any other form of entertainment.

"She makes a fuss about doing a television show, and then she positively basks in it," Walter explains. "It's the ham in her. When she's once on, she has the time of her life."

Chapter Sixteen

From the beginning of her Metropolitan engagement, Risë had made a point of keeping up with music abroad. This was one case where Walter had no need to stretch her. She had enjoyed the days in Prague and Buenos Aires and felt that a singer should be known everywhere. Walter agreed with her, without yielding his conviction that she might be wasting her time. In his view, the Metropolitan was the pinnacle; anything else was little stuff down there below.

But it was impossible to turn down a contract for three performances at the Paris Opéra in the summer of 1948. She was to appear in *Rosenkavalier* and was the first foreign artist to be invited after the war. It was an honor. They were to travel with their friends, Bill and Suzanne Weintraub, and Risë was excited about the expedition until they got on the ship. Then she immediately became ill.

"Damn it, we're still tied to the dock," cried Walter, annoyed.

This made no difference; Risë could get sick looking at a ship. No matter what the comparative merits might be in comfort and rest, Risë was one who welcomed international flights by air. The planes could dip and bump and lurch, and Risë never had a twinge of sickness; the mere sight of the *Queen Elizabeth* as they drove down the West Side Highway was enough to ruin her day.

By a quirk she always got better when the ship put out to sea. At the point where the others would be hastily gulping Dramamine and retiring to their cabins, she would be absorbing a seven-course meal in the dining salon.

On the boat train from Cherbourg to Paris they found that the gentlemen had neglected to arrange for seats in the dining car. Walter is eternally baffled by this problem. From somewhere the other passengers got tickets for the dining car; Walter never gets them. Do they get them in advance? Well, some of them do, but the others get them from a man coming around on the train. Why doesn't the man ever come around to *them?* Risë asks this question, and Walter never has an answer. He had no answer on the Cherbourg-Paris journey; and neither had Weintraub.

They were repulsed on attempting to get in on the first sitting; they were repulsed at the second sitting; when they did get in, the dining car steward informed them the kitchen was closed for the trip. They were starving and had nothing for sustenance but a half-filled box of chocolates. They soon got very sick of chocolates. Walter spotted a little boy coming through the corridor with a hunk of bread in his hand. He snatched the bread out of the boy's hand, gouged out a hunk, and stuffed it in his mouth. Weintraub grabbed for it and got himself a handful. Between them, the bread disappeared as if by magic. The boy ran screaming back down the corridor. In a few minutes his mother appeared, with blood in her eye. Walter had the box of chocolates waiting for her.

"With our compliments, Madame," he bowed sauvely.

The woman went away smiling.

Risë went smiling to the first rehearsal at the Paris Opéra and came away muttering. It was a great and famous opera house; she expected great things from it. The orchestra had disappointed her.

"They're playing something," she growled to Walter, "but it certainly isn't Richard Strauss."

Walter assured her that things would get better as she went along; they got worse. The Paris Opéra was state-controlled; the manager and director and conductor were artistic gentlemen with the right political coloration; the orchestra was made up of seething individuals who kept up a running fight with the conductor and had never lost a battle. They played what they saw before them; it was just too bad if they didn't see it the conductor's way.

Walter tried solacing Risë with the news that Verdi himself had found this orchestra insufferable and had torn his hair. He added that Hector Berlioz, the famous French composer, had considered suicide during a performance of his symphony, when half of the players had left before the end for their jobs in a nearby theatre. Risë replied that it was all very interesting but had really little to do with the case. She was worried about her own performance.

This was a success, surprisingly enough, and probably stems from the fact that Risë ignored the orchestra and sang the notes Strauss had written for her. Walter was intrigued by the whole business and particularly by the scene backstage. Everybody seemed to be in uniform, including the stagehands. With the first act of Risë's first performance well launched, Walter was approached by two small dignified gentlemen in uniform, who bowed politely and inquired if he was Madame Stevens' representative. Walter admitted the soft indictment. One gentleman then dug into a huge reticule that hung about his neck and presented Walter with one hundred 1000-franc notes, each as big as a towel.

"Madame's *cachet*," said the gentleman, and bowed again and departed. It was Risë's fee, which in European theatres is always paid in cash before the singer finishes the opera. Walter hefted the bale of money and looked about wonderingly. He was in evening clothes. It was plain that he wouldn't be able to hide the wad in his pockets. He loosened his cummerbund and shirt and stuffed the bale in at his belt line. He knew immediately it was a mistake.

"I looked about eight months gone," says Walter.

He went out through the stage door and took a taxi back to their hotel, where he placed the pile in a bureau drawer and carefully locked it. It was still safely there next morning. He returned to the opera house in plenty of time to find that Risë was doing well. From the acclaim at the final curtain it was easy to see that she had beaten the orchestra to the wire by a nose. The critics next day were enthusiastic. The three engagements were well spaced in time, and the Surovys and Weintraubs spent the intervening period touring the country. When they once hit the Riviera, Nicky saw that they never left again. He swam like a seal; the Mediterranean was the place for him.

Walter was awakened in their hotel room in Paris on the morning after the final engagement by Risë banging their suitcases around.

"Wassa matter?" he asked sleepily.

"My wrist watch," she said. "I can't find it. I must have left it in the dressing room."

Walter rolled out with a grumble. If it wasn't the watch, it was the good-luck ring or some of her superstition gadgets: she always lost them.

"All right," he said grudgingly. "When I get some breakfast, I'll go back over there."

When he approached the opera house, it occurred to him that he might have trouble with his French, of which he had none. The elegant uniformed man at the stage door greeted him with a smile. Walter pointed to the watch on his wrist and made stabbing gestures at it with his forefinger.

"Ah-h-h!" cried the gentleman elatedly, and swung the door wide open.

He met another dignitary at the top of the stairs and repeated the gesture with the watch.

"Ah-h-h!" cried that worthy, and passed him on to a third ambassador, with gilt stripes and suggestion of epaulets. This dignified figure received Walter's exposition with sheer exultance.

"*Ah-h-h!*" he cried and, with a bow and a light wave of the hand, ushered Walter through a slight opening to his right. He found himself on the cavernous stage of the opera house! Out in the auditorium he could see masses of people tiered to the roof. On stage a ceremony of some distinction was being enacted. There was a plump white-haired man of distinction standing on a small platform, with his face half turned to the audience. Supporting him as a background on stage was a solid phalanx of field marshals, assorted generals, and important dignitaries in full evening dress. Walter found himself a part of this group, being edged forward eagerly by his mentor from the wings. In a steady stream the participants went forward and were presented with a ribbon. Walter went forward in his turn and received a ribbon and a kiss on either cheek from the master of ceremonies.

He returned to the hotel without Risë's watch but with a large round shining medal on his chest.

The Paris experience had scarcely been calculated to stir Risë's love for foreign opera houses, but the passage of time softened that recollection, and she began dreaming again of European appearances. One Sunday night driving in from Westhampton, the Surovys got trapped in a traffic jam that gave them plenty of time for talk.

"You know," began Risë musingly, "I'd like to sing abroad again."

"I thought you had enough of that," said Walter caustically.

"No, when it's done right, it's different," protested Risë. "I mean a big house with a big reputation."

"Such as what?" asked Walter warily.

"La Scala," said Risë. "I don't know whether it's the best or not, but it's the one everybody talks about."

"What good will it do you?" asked Walter with exasperation. "You're known all over the world now."

"I've never sung in Italy," said Risë. "It's the home of opera, isn't it?"

"Yes, and what difference does it make?" growled Walter. "Every Italian singer is breaking his neck to get over here, and you want to go there. It's a bum trade."

"Anyhow, I want to do it," said Risë.

"And how are you *going* to do it?" asked Walter testily. "You can't just walk into La Scala, you know. If you show them you want to come in, they'll think you're washed up here and are just looking for a job."

"You'll fix it," said Risë, tapping him on the knee.

They reached the apartment, turned the car over to the doorman, and rode up in the elevator to their floor. Among the mail pushed under the door was a letter from Dr. Antonio Ghiringhelli,

manager of the La Scala Opera House in Milan! They wanted
Risë to create the leading role in a new opera by Mortari.

"Nobody believes me when I tell the story," says Walter, "but
it is the absolute truth. It was uncanny. We'd been hashing over
the La Scala thing for the last hour—and there was the letter
waiting for us. Risë had to drag me away from the phone to keep
from cabling acceptance on the spot. That's the sort of break that
comes from Heaven; you don't monkey with it."

The score of the opera arrived two weeks later, and Risë began
studying it with Victor Truco, an assistant conductor with the
Metropolitan. At the end of ten days they were still working on it.
Risë wasn't at all sure she wanted to do it. What she didn't know
till later was that the indomitable Surovy had cabled La Scala
on the fourth day that she was delighted to do it.

"It was in the cards," he explained to his irate wife. "You got
a sign. You don't fool around with things like that."

It might have been a case of celestial prompting, but it stirred
a monumental rumpus when it was announced. Her concert
manager Kurt Weinhold came on the run.

"What are you doing to us!" he exclaimed. "It'll mean canceling
five or six concerts."

"Oh, more than that," said Walter easily. "You know how Risë
prepares for a new opera."

In the end it was estimated that Risë's month in Milan was to
cost $40,000 in canceled concert dates. A few of them were
salvaged by clever shifting of the dates on Weinhold's part, but
the net loss was high. The Surovys left New York for Milan on
February 27, 1954; they returned to New York on April 3. A solid
month before she left for La Scala, Risë put everything else aside
to work on the new opera. It meant that two months were taken
from her schedule for the Italian venture. La Scala was furnishing travel expenses for two people and was paying $1000 a per-
formance for five appearances. In addition, the Surovys were paying the expenses of Vera Schwarz and Ed Vincent out of their
own pockets. It was not exactly a financial coup. John Stephen
paid his own way, refusing to miss it.

The Weintraubs were accompanying the Surovys on the trip,
and Suzanne Weintraub had made the sacrifice of going by boat

to handle the mass of luggage that would have cost a fortune to transport by plane. As the TWA plane carrying the Surovy group neared mid-ocean, there was a break in the clouds, and the stewardess pointed excitedly to a ship below which was slowly coursing upon a glassy sea.

"The *Andrea Doria*," she said.

Walter was at that point in his air travels when he thinks he is about to die.

"The lucky stiff," he moaned, referring to Suzanne, who was obviously having a smooth crossing.

This was a mistake. Mrs. Weintraub considers it the worst voyage she has ever experienced on the North Atlantic. During a storm, in which the *Andrea Doria* was tossed about like a toy in a bathtub, the mound of luggage did flying nip-ups and finally lodged firmly against the door of her cabin. She was trapped but kept her head. All she needed to do was phone for help. But if the luggage was stuck so hard that she couldn't budge it from within, the same situation existed for those attempting to get in from without. It took hours before she was released, and she had to do most of the rescue work herself.

Walter was having little better luck on the plane. When he crawled from his berth on the morning after their departure, his appearance frightened even his friends.

"Good heavens," cried Ed Vincent, "you've actually turned green!"

Risë laughed unfeelingly.

"Green, nothing," she said. "That's yellow."

They landed in Paris and took the train for Milan. They were established at the Hotel Duomo in Milan, where Risë insisted as usual on room eleven and, for her pains, was given a closet under the eaves, where she bumped her head if she stood up straight. She was so eager to get started with the opera that she could hardly wait to get unpacked. Since Ed Vincent was of Italian parentage, he was along both as press agent and interpreter.

"Get them on the phone, and let's get started," said Risë.

The first meeting with the management turned out to be a special affair. Nobody seemed in the least excited about the new opera. The tenor hadn't been cast, the dancer hadn't been cast, nothing had been done. But they were charming in their own way and evidently quite surprised and elated at seeing Risë.

"We had your photographs, of course," said Ghiringhelli, "but we had no idea you were so beautiful."

All very pleasant, Risë agreed silently, but when do we get started?

After a lapse of two days, in which Risë began biting her nails, there was a first rehearsal. Sanzogno, the conductor, was evidently seeing the score for the first time. His approach to it was highly tentative. Risë's aside to her interpreter, Vincent, was tart.

"Tell him to stop groping," she said. "I know it cold."

The Italians were never done exclaiming over this phenomenon. Prima donnas were evidently not expected to know their roles. Risë knew hers because she always knows everything perfectly she is doing, but in this case there was also the matter of time. They might prefer to dawdle along, but she had to be back in New York on April 3. At the rate they were now going, she would be lucky to get away by Christmas. She decided that *being* a prima donna was the only thing that would impress them: she started to holler. The pace picked up imperceptibly, and they did manage to get a tenor, but the *première danseuse* they had counted on turned the job down flat.

The task of Risë's entourage was to keep her sane during this leisurely period. She pushed for action; the directors and cast moved at a snail's pace. At the end of two weeks the director had to leave the production for an engagement previously arranged at Palermo. The work was turned over to three directors, who handled it exactly as had been done by the cooks of legend. Risë thought of Mr. Rudolf Bing and repented of the La Scala venture. He had warned her what would happen—and it was happening.

"You're crazy," Mr. Bing had told her. "That's a state opera house; they don't care anything about time. You've got the best thing here in the world; why do you want to go over there and be messed around?"

She knew that Bing had been right, but there was no way now of getting out of the engagement.

Signor Virgilio Mortari, the composer, appeared on the scene.

He was filled with exultation at seeing this beautiful woman who was to bring his creation to life. He insisted on hugging and kissing his beloved prima donna. He had a very bad cold. His nose ran, he sneezed. She fled.

"She couldn't have been more scared if he had been a crocodile," says Ed Vincent.

Things are also going badly at the Hotel Duomo. The marble floors of their suites were elegant, but they were freezing. Sunny Italy was proving to be as cold as Goose Bay, Labrador. They requested electric heaters for their rooms.

"No, no!" cried the shocked management. "There is no such thing here. Nobody has ever complained before."

"Then we will buy our own heaters," said Walter.

The heaters were immediately provided by the management. It was the same with rugs. There were no rugs; the Surovys would buy rugs; the management produced rugs. It was the same with an extra wardrobe for Risë's clothes. There was no wardrobe. Walter was walking through the corridor; the door was open on an unoccupied apartment; there was a wardrobe plainly to be seen. A five-thousand lire note to a porter—and the deed was done.

The routine was set for the Surovy group.

Breakfast in Vera Schwarz's room. Risë had her breakfast in bed.

Lunch at the famous Savini's restaurant.

Cocktails in Risë's cubbyhole.

Dinner in John Stephen's room.

Risë and Vera Schwarz were rehearsing at the hotel. There was a piano in Risë's room, but they needed another for Mme. Schwarz's room. Walter was sent on this errand. His Italian was sketchy; his determination was great.

"I want another piano," he told the manager.

That gentleman threw up his hands in horror.

"You've got a whole *piano* now!" he cried.

The Italian word for floor is *piano*, first *piano*, second *piano*, etc. Ed Vincent came rushing to the rescue. What Walter wanted was a *pianoforte*.

One day they asked the concierge to order them a car to take them to the theatre. They waited patiently, and no car appeared. Vincent interceded with this man of great power.

"Why, it's sitting out there waiting for you," said the concierge. He pointed to a huge hotel bus that stood before the entrance. It was used for meeting the trains and held about fifty people. Four lonely Americans climbed in and arrived at La Scala in state. The Italians shook their heads resignedly.

"That's the crazy Americans for you," they said. "Do everything brown."

By this time crisis was piling on crisis. The famous painter, Usellini, had done the sketches for the costumes. When Risë saw them, she uttered a wild cry of pain. They were awful. There wouldn't be a spectator left in the auditorium ten minutes after she came on stage. The Italians calmed her down: there would be new sketches *domani* (tomorrow). *Domani* dutifully arrived, but there were no new sketches. Risë blew up. This was the end, and she was burned up. She proceeded to Ghiringhelli's office, pushed his secretary out of the way (a cardinal offense in these sacred precincts), and stormed into the great man's presence.

"The *domani* I'm talking about is tomorrow," she said tensely. "If the sketches aren't ready then, I leave."

The sketches were ready next day, and they were sensational. Usellini explained what had happened.

"I was mistaken about the lady," he said. "When I saw how handsomely and gracefully she moved and what a compelling stature her figure lends to her stunning voice, it was another matter entirely."

With that solved, Risë had nothing to worry about but the opera itself. At this juncture it might be well to give a hint of the operatic story. It was called *La Figlia del Diavolo* (*The Devil's Daughter*), based on the old story of Salome and John the Baptist. The Mortari version was done with the emphasis on the grotesque. Risë played Herodias, the mother of Salome. It was the only woman's part, Salome confining herself to dancing. Herodias appeared not only as diabolical but as actually possessed by the Devil, who through her destroys the Apostle. Salome helps destroy John by her dancing, but in reality she is trying to help him.

She ends by receiving a divine pardon. Mama is the bad one.

The opera was done as a "sacra rappresentazione," with three choruses. One chorus was on stage with a realistic function; the second chorus was in the orchestra pit, employed in an instrumental manner; the third chorus was out of sight behind the scenes, for abstract passages. The scheme presented manifold chances for confusion; La Scala seized upon every one of them.

At the first orchestra rehearsal the musicians stood and applauded Risë at the end, which is said to be a rare event at La Scala. This was an encouraging sign, but everything else pointed to failure. Everything depended on Risë; the opera was a tour de force built around the role of Herodias. Unless she put it across with tremendous power, the opera would sink at her feet and expire.

The dress rehearsal was on a Friday. It was an utter disaster. There was a trap door through which Risë was to fade at a crucial moment. Red fire played on her as she descended; she descended only part way, and stuck. The chorus off stage couldn't see the conductor through the scenery; they sang very effectively, but always at the wrong time. Spotlights failed to appear on cue; singers tumbled over the elaborate scenery; the orchestra chased the singers frantically, and lost.

"Never, never in the history of La Scala has there been such chaos," elatedly cried the *espresso* drinkers in the Galleria, near the theatre. They liked events to be historically important.

There was a council of war after the dress rehearsal. Monday would be the important performance for the critics. The formal opening would be Wednesday night, but the opera's fate lay in what happened on Monday. Risë was sunk; she could see disaster looming straight ahead. The management was strangely calm.

"There's nothing to worry about," said Signor Ghiringhelli. "We'll simply get new scenery."

"But you can't!" cried Risë. "There isn't time."

Ghiringhelli bestowed on her a light confident smile.

"La Scala can do anything," he said.

Risë refrained from asking why they hadn't done it in the first place. She returned to the hotel and lay on her bed in mute despair.

At three o'clock on Monday morning John Stephen was building a new hairdo for Risë. The old one was impossible and made her look like a hag. As he worked along, a thought suddenly occurred to Stephen: "What am I doing here? Why isn't La Scala doing it?" There was no answer. When he returned to his room at five o'clock, he found a note on his bed from Walter: "Risë has a bad cold, can't sleep, is a wreck."

The management had insisted on a half-hour rehearsal on Monday. Risë had a firm policy of resting on the day of a performance, but this was an emergency. They were amazed on reaching the theatre to find that the new scenery was all in place. Most importantly, the scenery was painted on a scrim, so the offstage chorus could see the conductor. Instead of a short rehearsal, Risë worked at full speed from two till seven. There was no time for rest or dinner. Savini's produced a dinner, with thick steak, potatoes, and coffee, brought across town in a hot boiler. Risë began vocalizing with Vera Schwarz. What came forth was a strange gurgling sound.

"She's lost her voice!" cried Walter in horror.

Ed Vincent's mother had been an opera singer. He listened closely.

"I know what it is," he said. "She's holding her tongue between her lips with her fingers."

"What!" said Walter unbelievingly.

"I'll bet you," said Ed. "It's the best discipline for the vocal cords. When the tongue is like that, the cords must absolutely close without any trick."

This proved to be true, and things had taken on a calmer air when Risë stood in the wings ten minutes before the curtains parted. An assistant manager of La Scala approached.

"Oh, we forgot to tell you," he said amiably. "There's a new place for the trap door."

"*Where!*" shouted Risë in panic. "Show me!"

"I can't," said the gentleman. "The first act scenery covers it. There'll be a flashlight from the wings; just follow it."

Risë threw her arms aloft in a tragic gesture.

They settled down to wait for the formal opening on Wednesday. There were just a few matters to thrash out with the manage-

ment. The curtain at the end of the second scene, for instance.
Risë is holding Salome in her arms as the curtain descends, after
a twenty-minute scene in which Risë both danced and sang. The
director had insisted on having a blackout at this point, thus
ruining any chance for applause. Risë had complained, and they
promised her a spotlight for the scene. At the dress rehearsal,
there was no spotlight. At the performance for the critics, there
was no spotlight. At the opening, there was no spotlight. An in-
vestigation was made. The man who was supposed to work the
spotlight from a place high in the house had never been notified.
At this juncture he invariably went out for a sandwich.

Opening night proved to be historical in a way nobody had
figured on. The bill consisted of three one-act operas. It opened
to applause with Gian-Carlo Menotti's *Amelia Goes to the Ball.*
What followed was Mario Peragallo's *La Gita in Campagna* (*A
Trip in the Country*). It is a modern work, based on dissonance
and fury. The audience was first restless and then furious. There
were catcalls and whistles. This was followed by angry shouts
and general pandemonium. As the singers and orchestra plowed
desperately on, the excitement in the auditorium mounted.
Elegant women stood up in their boxes and howled in rage. A
man in the orchestra seats took off his shoe and hurled it on the
stage in fury. Fights broke out all over the opera house. The opera
ended in a perfect bedlam of imprecations and denunciations.

That Risë could follow this outrageous scene with a striking
performance was a testimonial to her determination and talent.
She achieved a tremendous personal success, although the opera
itself was not generally liked.

There were eleven critics and eleven enthusiastic reviews. For
Risë the *Corriere della séra* (the Italian equivalent of the New
York *Times*) said: "On stage sparkled the quicksilvery and fiery
Risë Stevens, with a beautiful voice and outstanding histrionic
abilities. In fact a superb singing actress."

The critic of *L'Italia* wrote: "Even though there were no real
emotions in the opera, emotions nevertheless were projected
through the dynamism and through the admirable interpretative
powers of Risë Stevens, an evil and seductive Herodias. In her
incarnation, the devil certainly was victorious. However, despite

her stunning craft, the opera cannot be saved for the future. It remains a tour de force for Mme. Stevens in the present presentation."

From the other members of the La Scala company she received nothing but cold looks. After years at the Metropolitan she had almost forgotten how bitter competition was in foreign opera houses. The audience might throw flowers on the stage, but even the most moth-eaten old basso could think of nothing better for her than a broken leg. She sang five performances at La Scala, and each was worse than the one before. Either gremlins were at work or the backstage crew was determined to ruin her. The trap door stuck with regularity, the spotlight never appeared, curtains closed while she was still singing, cues were missed like magic.

"The last performance was low comedy," says Risë grimly. "I thought the whole thing was going to collapse around me."

She sang for the last time on Thursday night; she was due in New York for the matinee on Saturday. They sat up with friends until two o'clock Friday morning, packed, and raced to the airport. Bad weather had canceled the direct flight to Paris; they were being rerouted by way of Zurich. At the mention of Switzerland, Walter began turning yellow again; he could think of nothing but mountain peaks. Switzerland was also having bad weather; there was a long delay in Zurich.

"I forgot about the mountains," says Walter. "All I could see now was the face of Rudolf Bing. He had been sore as a boil about Risë's going off to La Scala; if she balled up that broadcast matinee for him, it might be the end of her at the Met."

The Swiss weather suddenly decided to be friendly; the plane took off for Paris. Paris was beautiful in the sunshine; their connection for New York was waiting for them; they soared off into the blue as happy as larks. Three hours away from France they ran into a storm that buffeted the plane with rough murderous jolts. The passengers strained desperately against their seat belts as the plane swooped, twisted, and shook convulsively in an attempt to throw off the shock. Walter prayed. It was only later that he found time to analyze the prayers.

"I first prayed we'd get back to Paris, and then I saw Bing's face and that scared the idea right out of me. I prayed then we'd keep right on going, and the storm answered by giving us such a whack that the plane practically turned over. I don't know what I did after that, except to hang on grimly and moan."

They were lucky to get down safely in Iceland. Their gratification soon turned to worry. The weather had closed in again, the clocks ticked away, they saw nothing but the angry countenance of Mr. Bing before them. Just when it seemed they would be in Iceland forever, the clouds parted, the pilot revved up his plane —and they were off. They arrived in New York three hours before curtain time, it made a fine newspaper story, and it left Mr. Bing grinding his teeth. He would get more of this in the future, but it could never be said that he enjoyed it.

The only pleasant memory Risë retains from Milan is her first meeting with Maria Callas. Risë was rehearsing in her opera; Callas was rehearsing for another. They found themselves on stage together, with their backs to one another. Each was aware of what was happening, and Risë, with her eagle vision, could even see Callas out of the corner of her eye, but both carried on an animated conversation with people in front of them. An amused assistant conductor came to the rescue.

"You are both Americans," he said ironically. "You should meet."

Risë and Callas turned at the same time, astonished beyond measure.

"*Darling!*" they caroled in unison, and rushed into each other's arms.

Aside from this happy scene, Risë is sometimes dubious about the whole La Scala incident.

Chapter Seventeen

As they waited helplessly in Iceland on the way back from Milan, Risë had raised her hand aloft and said solemnly: "Never again!" Walter snorted derisively, knowing her far better than she knows herself. The pain of La Scala wore off after two years, and now came an invitation to sing again at Glyndebourne in England. Risë leaped at the chance. Her appearance there in 1939 had been one of the pleasantest experiences of her career.

The second coming was a mistake. Conditions had changed, and Glyndebourne was no longer the theatre she remembered. Fritz Busch was dead; Rudolf Bing was in New York.

"What's happened to this place?" Risë asked Walter after the first day. "Everything seems so small. The theatre is a doll's play-house, and I swear nobody over there today was more than two feet tall."

She was doing Mozart's *The Marriage of Figaro* and after each rehearsal reported back to Walter.

"The voices are small, too," she said. "I let out once today, and you'd have thought I yelled a dirty word."

The next day she was even more worried.

"You'd better come over and have a look at this thing," she told Walter, uneasily. "It's beginning to get silly."

Walter turned up at a point in the rehearsal when Risë was called upon to crawl through a window. The window was the approximate size of a small picture frame. Risë could only manage it by putting one arm through first, inserting her head, dragging the other arm behind, and wiggling her torso forward in convulsive jumps.

"For comedy, it'll be great," said Walter sardonically. "You looked like an elephant going through a hoop."

He took up battle with the management and got a few of the more glaring deficiencies corrected, but they could feel that this wasn't going to be one of Risë's more memorable moments. She had either got beyond Glyndebourne, or their memories were playing them false. She could swear this wasn't the Glyndebourne of 1939, but the evidence refuted her. No change had been made in the size of Glyndebourne; the change must be in herself. More exactly, it must be a change in the approach of the management. They preferred the small and precious production of opera in a bandbox; in that setting Risë looked like Gulliver among the Lilliputians.

Risë never ceased shaking her head in befuddlement. This was the way it was, and yet it couldn't be true. She buckled down grimly to the rehearsals. She hoped that some miracle would intervene to save the performance, but it wasn't forthcoming. With the other members of the cast singing in polite well-modulated tones suitable for afternoon tea at the manse, Risë had to keep her own voice down. She was glad when it was over; they left town as fast as decency permitted.

"I was a great big soggy flop," says Risë, with a wry twist of the lip.

In her more self-pitying moments Risë would like Walter to give her an argument on the point, but he refrains. He recognizes a defeat when he sees one.

Risë retreated to America and happily took up the concert trail again. Opera might be in her bones, but there was no denying the warmth and affection of audiences in towns far off the operatic path. She even enjoyed the hardships of the tours, taking pride in making connections by an eyelash and never missing a date from carelessness. As a good driver herself, she made an excruciatingly annoying back-seat driver and would harass her accompanist, James Shomate, with directions, reproaches, and suggestions until he would lose his temper and yell in his loudest voice, "For heaven sakes, Risë; SHUT UP!" This always set her laughing, and silenced her for the better part of fifteen minutes.

"She sincerely believes that every town she's in is her favorite town," says Shomate, "but Atlanta and San Francisco actually are."

From constant traveling over the country Risë has met thousands of people. She never forgets a face or remembers a name. A meeting with an old acquaintance would be a production—hugs, kisses, warm words. Thinking it was one of her dearest friends, Shomate would hang in the background. Risë would be furious.

"Why didn't you do something?" she would demand furiously.

Now Shomate waltzes right up, shakes the hand of the unknown with a firm grip, looks him full in the eye, and says in a loud voice, "I am James Shomate." The other generally gives his name in return. Risë welcomes him by it with a rush of affection.

According to Shomate, Risë's sense of geography is a panic. She is invariably expressing her pleasure at being in Idaho when she is really in Iowa. She keeps an eye out for strange trees, wondering if they would grow at her country place. In the experiments she has made with these discoveries, they have immediately died the death in the salt air of Westhampton, where even grass has a struggle. But her real elation comes at the sight of a river and a clump of trees.

"It's Delaware Water Gap!" she invariably cries, although they are somewhere in Kansas. In her youth she was once taken on a weekend to Delaware Water Gap and has never forgotten it.

Since they try to get in town two days before the performance, the first day is spent in going to the movies, strolling through the streets, and shopping. This latter habit is one of the pains of Walter's life. As the purchases roll into the New York apartment, he has the job of writing polite notes of regret. The object somehow doesn't fit in with their other possessions. Would they object too greatly if he returned it and asked for a refund? If he keeps something, the results are even worse.

"Where did you get these dishes?" demanded Risë at dinner one night after returning from a trip.

"You bought them at Marshall Field's," said Walter coldly.

"You know we don't need them," said Risë, with perfect logic. "Send them back."

But some of her purchases are of a more elaborate nature. Talk of gushers in Texas once prompted her to buy part interest in an oil well just being drilled. If it came in, she made them promise to call it the Nicky well.

"Maybe it'll be a dry hole," suggested one of her friends.

"It won't matter," she shrugged. "I've done plenty of dry auditions."

It was a dry hole, and she lost her investment, but that didn't stop her. In Vancouver she saw a small island and marveled at its loveliness.

"You can have it for five thousand dollars," said her new acquaintance.

"Sold!" cried Risë.

Walter managed to get rid of it six months later for only a small loss.

During the war when meat was scarce, she conceived the idea of buying a Texas steer and having the meat shipped to her parents in New York. The intention was to keep it in a freezer in the apartment. The management put up a firm hand of refusal, stating that the burden of a freezer on the electric lines would would blow out all the lights north of the square. They paid rent for storing the meat with a butcher.

"I've figured it out," said Walter, "and can say with certainty that the meat cost only fifty cents more a pound than they could have bought it for in the black market."

Risë has clung stubbornly to her determination to have complete rest and quiet on the day of a concert performance. The operator is instructed to put all calls through to Jimmy Shomate. Risë locks her hotel door, reads a paper-back thriller, looks at television or listens to radio, does her nails, irons her concert gown. Local committees often fail to appreciate her efforts. They are giving a cocktail party for the board of directors, they want to drive her around to see their beautiful town, there are questions to be settled about her performance. One committee chairwoman persisted in demanding to talk with Risë. Shomate said it was impossible; the chairwoman said it was a matter of life or death. Risë came on the phone.

"Do you think red roses or white roses would be best for the platform tonight?" asked the lady.

Lucie Magee, a reporter for the Jackson (Mississippi) *News*, wasn't easily discouraged in her attempt to see Risë on the day of a concert. She went to the 5-&-10 store and bought a hank of lovely electric-blue wool. She sent it to Risë, along with a note.

> You knit for fun and for Christmas giving
> But the yarns I put together help make a living.
> Would you, please, ma'am, consider swapping yarns?

Shomate reported that Risë was asleep.

"Don't shoot—I surrender!" wrote Lucie in her column that afternoon.

One of Shomate's most important jobs on tour is helping Risë with her costumes. Because of her bad shoulder, she can't get into her gown without his help, and most assuredly can't get out of it. One night after a concert in Tulsa, they talked quietly for a while, and then he left for his room. Halfway down the corridor, he heard her galloping after him.

"You dog!" she cried. "Do you want me to sleep in this tin can all night?"

Once on the platform, Risë is very assured and confident. She likes people and is glad to be singing for them. From long experience she has learned how to warm up an audience quickly. This is important for a concert artist, and some singers never manage it. If she feels a wall of coldness or uncertainty before her, she has been known to stop in the middle of a number, laugh apologetically, and say: "That wasn't very good, was it? We'll try it again." If this doesn't thaw them out, they can't be thawed.

Nothing upsets her on the concert platform. One night in Nashville, Risë took the wrong end to a song, and Shomate couldn't follow her. They came to a jolting halt. Risë threw her head back and laughed. The audience, startled and apprehensive, joined her in a roar of relief.

"Sorta overslid second there, didn't we?" she said to Shomate. "Well, start her over again."

The gowns that Risë presses in her hotel room on the day of a performance are generally made for her by Madame Adriana Biglia, of Venice, Italy. They cost between $1000 and $2000, and Risë wears them only once before having them cleaned. This is done by a New York firm, at a cost of from $40 to $75 for each cleaning. One particular gown with elaborate beading cost $150 to clean. Risë's annual bill for cleaning runs between $4000 and $5000, and this doesn't include her personal garments or her Metropolitan costumes.

When a woman once asked Risë what her daughter needed to know to become an opera star, Risë's answer somewhat startled her.

"She will need a good voice and the ability to act," she said, "but there are a few practical things that can also help her greatly. She should learn the following things: (a) how to cook, (b) how to sew, (c) how to do dry cleaning, (d) how to pack dresses in a box, and (e) how to do her own hair and make-up, this to be learned from a full beauty-shop course."

She went to Max Factor's in Hollywood and learned beauty-shop technique from the ground up. She does her own nails; she cuts her own hair (and Nicky's, too, when he can't escape); she goes to a beauty parlor only twice a year, for permanents. For the new *Carmen* she tinted her hair so often in an attempt to get the right color that her scalp threatened to come off, but she got it as she wanted it. She is an admitted genius at packing her suitcases for travel. She learned this by going to I. Magnin in Beverly Hills, a department store, and working in the mailing room until she mastered the art. She will listen to any beauty expert but finds they are often wrong. She has fixed ideas on the subject of make-up.

"If you have a 'smart' hairdo, it's a failure," she says. "If the hair style is that obvious, it means the frame of the face is more important than the face."

Her own hair is worn short, with high bangs. It is a natural auburn in color. People often call her redheaded. She also has her own ideas about diet.

"A beautiful shape is all very well in opera," she says, "but if you diet too much, you find yourself pooping out in the third act. Singing an opera is like pitching a fifteen-inning game. Or working in the lead mines."

This is the practical side that always amazes people who think of her as a feather-brained and fuzzy individual. She is a highly complicated personality who happens to be both a prima donna and a wonderfully organized woman. She is meticulous about small things, she is always on time, her role in the opera is always fully prepared. When she works, she is all business. She has done *Rosenkavalier* at least a hundred times, but when a new member is listed for the cast, she insists on a rehearsal to fit him in. She takes no chances when she appears at the Metropolitan. Jennie stands in the wings with a second pair of shoes in case anything happens to the first pair.

"My idea of heaven would be an opera house full of Risë Stevenses," Mr. Bing once said.

He didn't mean that she sings better or acts better than her associates, but that she can do both of these superbly and also be depended on. There are no tantrums, there are no demands that an air-conditioned limousine meet her at Dallas on the spring tour, there are no backstage politics or maneuvers. She not only knows her own part, but she knows every other part in an opera. She knows stage lighting and stage direction. She understands the backstage mechanical miracles that make an opera possible. She suffers with the conductor and the chorus. Above everything else, she is a disciplined artist—and she sells tickets. And therefore she always heads the prevailant top fee of the house.

On the social side there are friends who kindly call her hazy when they secretly believe her a bit half-witted. At a party at her apartment a celebrated wit was well launched into what was intended to be a hilarious story. Risë seized this moment to move about the room, emptying the contents of ash trays into a silent butler. She was amazed to find that she had ruined the story. She will laugh uproariously at a funny joke, and be unable to remember it ten minutes later.

One morning Walter came down to breakfast with a bad hangover. Risë was immediately concerned.

"I'll get you an aspirin," she said sympathetically.

She went upstairs and came back two hours later, fully dressed for lunch. She had forgotten all about it.

But when Walter comes up against a tough business problem he can't solve, he turns it over to Risë. She has a hard, logical mind. She is not troubled by extraneous matters. She can plow through a forest of technical points and get to the main issue. Her judgments are sound, and she has the capacity of waiting patiently for the other side to weaken. She likes the story of the New Mexican law suit, which was being heard by a mixed jury of Anglos and Spanish-Americans. The case was intricate, and it was further muddled by a battery of smart lawyers.

"This is one case that'll be over the head of those dumb Spanish-Americans," chortled the Anglo jury members.

They were mistaken. In the jury room it was soon evident that the Spanish-Americans hadn't even heard the subtle legal arguments of the attorneys. They asked only one thing: "Who stole the hat?"

This is Risë exactly. She concentrates on the main chance and lets nothing distract her. Sometimes she can even go too far with it. At one period she was unhappy because she had heard that another singer on one of the television programs was getting a higher fee. The money didn't bother her, but she felt hurt in her pride. Walter said stoutly that it was one battle he didn't want to handle for her: she would have to fight it out with the sponsor herself. She marched in on the great man and presented her case with great detail and firmness. She wanted a higher fee.

"Why, of course; why didn't you say so?" said the sponsor easily. "You didn't expect me to chase you around with it, did you?"

Risë came out elated, deflated, and angry. She could hardly wait to get home to Walter.

"You big smartie," she said, darkly. "Why didn't you tell me it was going to be that easy?"

Along with her other qualities, Risë's courage must be mentioned. Her hypochrondia is notorious, but when a hard lump was found on her side a few years ago, she bore the blow stoically. The usual fears were entertained, and there was no possibility of taking it lightly. Her father had died of cancer. Walter made plans to cancel her engagements; Risë overruled the idea. Early examination by her doctors brought a non-committal verdict: nothing could be established definitely until there had been an exploratory operation.

"Must it be done right away?" asked Risë.

"Well, it should be," said the doctors, "but it could probably wait two or three months without any harm."

Risë decided to fill her opera and concert engagements. Not even Sadie was let in on the secret. Walter quietly made plans for the first operation; if a second and more serious one were needed, it would be done in Paris. The news would be kept out of the papers. After the first month the critics began noting that Miss Stevens' voice sounded a bit weak. It *was* weak, and audiences were beginning to comment on the quality of her singing. She was under an almost unbearable burden of fear and worry, but she carried her program on to the end.

Sadie only heard about her daughter's condition when Risë was in the hospital, waiting for the exploratory operation. She forced her way into Risë's room, frantic with fear. The emotional scene threw Risë into a state of shock. When Walter arrived with the thought that the operation would be over, he found that it hadn't begun. It was a terrible three-hour period of waiting before the verdict was handed down: the lump was a non-malignant tumor. Risë was back home in two days; the operation had turned out to be a minor event in her life. The chief victim remains Walter, who has never ceased to reproach himself for his handling of the situation.

"I should have told Sadie," he says. "I thought I was doing it for her good, but it was a cruel and foolish thing to do."

For years Risë's recordings were handled by Goddard Lieberson, head of Columbia Records. It was a warm relationship, based on friendship and success. In one year Risë was paid $60,000 in royalties on her classical recordings. When it came time to sign a new contract, a strict routine was followed: Lieberson hired one of the old horse and carriages in front of the Plaza Hotel, and they trotted leisurely through Central Park, talking of everything but business. When they came back, Risë invariably signed a new contract at the old price. Walter agreed that it was a nice ride but felt that the results didn't measure up to the pleasure.

"Oh, what difference?" Risë would say lightly. "We're doing all right, aren't we?"

A new factor now entered the picture in the person of Emanuel (Manie) Sacks, who had left Columbia Records to take up a position with RCA Victor. Victor felt its list needed strengthening; Sacks was there for that purpose. One night at a party he ran into Walter and immediately began talking about Risë's contract. Walter said the old one had run out, and a new one was being negotiated. Sacks nodded and wandered away. That night at two o'clock Walter was awakened by the telephone in his apartment. It was Sacks.

"We are prepared to offer Risë $150,000 as an advance on a new contract," he said.

Walter came awake with a start. He immediately put in a call for Little Rock, Arkansas, where Risë had been appearing in a concert. Risë, who loves sleep as others crave opium, was not pleased by the interruption.

"Oh, Walter," she said wearily, "you know how much I like Goddard. What's the use of it?"

"*Money,*" shouted Walter. "*That's* what's the use of it."

He repeated the figure, got in a small dig about the expensive buggy rides through the park, and added a reference to their present bank account.

"Well, all right," Risë finally conceded, "but it has to be $200,000. If we're going to be heels, let's be great big heels."

This began an association with RCA Victor that has been pleasant to the point of exaltation. The original deal was made with George Marek, vice-president of RCA Victor and the man who had urged the idea on Manie Sacks. Risë and Walter were represented in the negotiations by Harold Stern, their lawyer and personal confidant of many years' standing. What came out of it was a financial arrangement unique in musical circles. Risë was assured of a fixed annual payment for a period of twenty years. This took away the gamble for Risë, and it has worked out excellently for RCA Victor.

In making records Risë has worked closely with Alan Kayes and Richard Mohr. Kayes is a genius at arranging preliminary details for a recording session. Since the advent of the long-play records and the making of albums with operas done in their entirety, this requires attention to a thousand details. Mohr is in charge of the actual recording and has established an international reputation for the quality of his work.

Risë still has a guilty qualm about Goddard Lieberson. The only one who can talk her out of it is Lieberson himself. Columbia Records wasn't ruined by her defection, and he is now president of the very prosperous firm. He pats her kindly on the shoulder when they meet and asks her not to worry. It's all in the game of Big Business.

Her insecurity is a source of irritation to Walter and a matter of amazement for her friends. On coming into the drawing room at a big party, she can't help remarking: "Oh, I didn't know you were going to dress." Walter grinds his teeth and says to her under his breath: "Cut it out!" When he gets her alone, he says: "What do you care what they think? If you came in shorts, you'd still be a sensation." It is true that she dominates any room she enters, just as she dominates any stage she acts upon. But nothing will ever get her to believe it. She is grateful for small favors, she is indebted to people who are pleasant to her, and she keeps up a lengthy correspondence with unknown friends in all parts of the country because their letters have touched her heart.

But the Law of Compensation works in her favor. Because she is good to other people, there is a group devoted to her. For years the Risë Stevens Music Club has carried her banner proudly aloft. At intervals the fan club publishes a bulletin about her activities. When she sings at the opera, they attend in a body. They read every word written about her and buy every record she puts out. Once a year Risë gives a party for them at her apartment. At the last party one hundred members showed up, including a delegate from Australia and another from England.

But with all this adulation, Risë's sense of insecurity never leaves her. This was shown most spectacularly when Walter suggested that a portrait by Salvador Dali might immortalize her, as Sir Joshua Reynolds had placed Madame Siddons forever on a pedestal, and Goya had done as much for the Duchess of Alba. The price was to be $12,000, and matters had progressed to a point where there was a meeting between Risë and Dali. Risë had expressed her admiration for Dali's work (of which she knew nothing, according to Walter), and Dali spoke of his pleasure at hearing her at the opera (he had no idea who she was, says Walter). The deal was about to be settled, when Risë spoke up in a small wistful voice.

"I think I'd rather wear it around my neck," she said.

This was one time when Walter made no attempt to dissuade her. He knew immediately that it was a crisis. Her insecurity had reached a point where it needed bolstering of a concrete sort. The portrait might eventually hang in the lounge of the Metropolitan and be admired, but she would never see it. The jewels would prove to her that she had arrived. They would be plain evidence to her old Bronx friends that the stories about her success were not manufactured.

Walter went quietly to work having pieces made up. The first blob was a blue and yellow sapphire necklace. Before that she had worn great jewelry loaned by famous jewelers, but everybody could tell it was too good to belong to her. The receipt of her own necklace was too much for her; she broke down and cried. A week later Walter presented a 20-carat emerald brooch. Six weeks later came an emerald bracelet with diamonds. Then came another emerald and diamond necklace. In all Walter spent ten times as much as he would have paid for the Dali portrait.

"It was either that," he says now, "or a psychiatrist would have had her in a year."

Another instance of Risë's modesty came with the interview of Harry Conover by Edward R. Murrow on his "Person to Person" television program. Mr. Conover is head of the famous agency in New York which supplies beautiful models to advertisers. As an expert with years of experience with lovely women, his word on the subject carries conviction.

"Who do you consider the most beautiful woman in the world?" Mr. Murrow asked.

Mr. Conover took his time in answering, seeming to weigh the alternatives with care.

"Risë Stevens," he said.

Mr. Murrow appeared to be surprised; he pressed the point.

"It is the all-around woman who counts," explained Mr. Conover. "I take into consideration looks, manner, poise, dignity, and charm. Miss Stevens has them all."

Walter was in bed in New York when these words came over TV. He swears that the shock threw him out on the floor. Risë was in Grand Rapids, Michigan, for a concert with a men's choir. His attempt to reach her by telephone failed; Miss Stevens had retired for the night and had given strict orders that she was not to be disturbed. From this, it was rather plain to Walter that she had not heard the program.

This was true; Risë had not turned on the television at all that night. She had written letters and gone to bed early. There was a rehearsal at nine in the morning. It was against her principles to sing on the day of a concert, but this was a special case. Businessmen made up the choir, and it had been impossible to get them together at any other time. When she reached the theatre next morning, she was swamped by congratulations. She nodded and smiled, but Jimmy Shomate could see that she didn't know what it was all about.

"What's going on, Jimmy?" she whispered when she got to him. "What are they talking about?"

Shomate was equally surprised. He had taken it for granted she had heard the program. He explained about the Conover interview. Risë looked at him in amazement.

"*Me,* Jimmy?" she asked, unbelievingly. "Did he really mean *me?*"

Risë is still not convinced that the incident ever happened. She wouldn't have liked it if Conover had called her the homeliest woman in the world, but she wouldn't have been any more surprised. The family prefers to regard it as a joke. As they regard TV's Jack O'Brian's repeated reference to her as the Brigitte Bardot of the Met. They use it to keep her in her place.

"All right, Most-Beautiful," they will say at Westhampton. "What's for lunch? Get on the ball, will you?"

Chapter Eighteen

The difference between Risë's real life and her public life is startling. When General David Sarnoff makes appearances before dealer groups of his company, RCA Victor, he tries to arrange the dates so that Risë can be present. She will sing a few numbers, but he particularly wants her for the reception that follows. She is elegant, poised, and friendly in this setting. She remembers any face she has ever seen before, and in the confusion names are not needed. The odds are ninety-nine to one that she has seen the individual at a similar gathering in years past. This makes for warmth of greeting. From a look at her in the midst of this group, it would seem that she would be at ease anywhere.

This is true in the broader sense, no matter how insecure she may be feeling inwardly. There are competent critics who hold that she could have been a great actress if she had started in the theatre instead of at the opera. The ability to create another character for herself is important to her in her public appearances. Since she is in love with mankind generally, she has no trouble with reporters or local concert committees. With the greatest attention and politeness she will answer stale old reportorial questions for the five hundredth time. She genuinely likes committee members, but woe to the lady who seeks to put her off balance by a caustic or sly remark. She has mental tentacles a mile long to spot the bitchy female or the phony. Her response to an attack of that sort will be of a brilliance to amaze people who know her only as the amiable hostess of Westhampton Beach.

"She doesn't know herself where the words come from," says Walter, "but they are dingers."

Risë has always liked the Metropolitan spring tours, and the Metropolitan has liked her appearance on them still more. Flaming personalities in the company have alternated in drawing the hinterland crowds, but Risë has been one of the meal tickets of the organization. Consistently through the years her presence has meant sold-out houses. In the days when she traveled with the troupe in their special train, Risë considered the outing a romp. She still gets great pleasure out of it, even though she planes in for a performance and planes back home to await the next one. Associates, who knew her only as the dedicated artist of the opera house, were amazed at the bubbling Surovy combination, who got fun out of everything and drew the rest of the company along in their hilarious wake.

The famous Bond Show specials that cruised about the country during the war were even more fun. Hollywood provided most of the talent for these spectacular tours, and Risë might have been expected to take a back seat amid the shenanigans that took place, but she was right up with the leaders in this foolery. She had been promised that her nightly stint would be confined to a song or two, but with the troupe playing in monstrous cow palaces seating multitudes, the poor comedians had a feeling of talking into a well. More and more the burden was thrown on the singers, and Risë found herself putting on what might be termed a small concert. Risë had no objection and even listened attentively to comedians who wanted to get into the act. Harpo Marx appeared with a great idea.

"You're standing up there dressed like Mrs. Astor's horse," he whispered, insinuatingly. "I sneak around behind with a pair of scissors and start snipping off the tail of your dress. Every time you hit a high note I take another snip. Maybe it might even end as a strip tease. What do you think of it?"

He gave her an elfish leer which threw her into a paroxysm

of laughter, and there was never any need of an answer to a proposition that was meant to be ridiculous from the start.

With his more solemn brother, Groucho, Risë had struck up a warm friendship based on their childhood days in New York. When she once confided her Bronx fears to him, he gave an angry growl.

"Don't tell *me* about them," he said darkly. "Every morning I wake up thinking I'm back in that lousy apartment on East 93rd Street. Nobody's ever going to make *me* believe show business is going to last."

The Metropolitan's great problem is in finding roles for her. Although her repertory is immense, there are only a few mezzo-soprano parts that carry a production. Once the top was reached, Risë exercised the greatest care in seeing that she was not swallowed in an opera. Musicologists might hold that Amneris in *Aida* and Azucena in *Il Trovatore* were the essential roles in the opera, but the public did not hold with the idea. Risë is the first to admit that she has been lucky in her career; she has also seen to it that she has always had what the Germans call *"Interessantes Fächer"*—interesting roles.

The Metropolitan revived *Dalila* for her after a lapse of twenty-two years. They did it with trepidation, since the opera had never been outstandingly popular since the days of Caruso. It became one of Risë's most successful parts, drawing full houses whenever she appeared in it and being a sensation on the spring tours. The experience was repeated with *Orfeo,* which in the past had always confined its popularity to a small group of the *cognoscenti* but became one of the surprise successes in Metropolitan history with Risë in the title role.

She now confines herself at the Metropolitan to four great roles —*Rosenkavalier, Orfeo, Carmen,* and *Dalila.* Her Dalila has been characterized as "so sumptuously provocative that poor Samson never has a chance." In the same vein she has been called a "hot-as-a-firecracker Carmen." As one critic has pointed out, "She is an expert at interpreting beautiful bad girls with a vocal range that takes in soprano, mezzo, and contralto."

Frank Daniel, of the Atlanta *Journal-Constitution,* has written: "Of all the gal-in-pants roles, Octavian in *Rosenkavalier* is the biggest and most demanding. Octavian is a 17-year-old aristocratic boy, gallant enough to console a princess in her husband's absence, and beautiful enough to masquerade as a serving maid pretending to be responsive to his rival's rough wooing. Unless he looks and acts like a young man, the sentiments of *Rosenkavalier* are likely to get askew. The part is almost impossible to play convincingly—except in the rare instance of a trim and histrionic Miss Stevens."

In all these operas Risë has had the important help of Walter in her interpretations. His stage sense is unerring; his ability to analyze a role is uncanny. By an ironic coincidence he now wields his greatest influence at the opera house. The place he once avoided like the plague has become his stronghold. Down there they say about him: "The prima donna in that family is Surovy." When he comes backstage before a performance, they ask anxiously about *his* health; nothing is ever the matter with Risë. He knows what is happening in every part of the house; he loves to joke with his friend Francis Robinson, assistant to Bing and head of the box office and Public Relations; his relations with Bing are warm and friendly and are based on the fact that Risë produces.

Walter's mastery of the music business is so complete that other artists in the company depend upon him for advice. This is particularly true about television appearances or concerts. Aside from Risë's artistic affairs, he is concerned with their financial future. With the advice of Harold Stern and Kurt Weinhold he has outlined a plan that assures the Surovys a comfortable living for as far ahead as the human eye can see.

This interests Risë only incidentally; her major concern is her work. Walter sees that nothing goes wrong there. It has been a cardinal rule that a singer must not be disturbed during a performance. Walter has smashed the rule to smithereens. If Risë has not done well during the first act of an opera, he comes back at intermission and tells her so plainly.

"You're standing outside yourself," he will say bluntly. "You don't know who you are."

She shrank when this first happened; she is now accustomed to it. She knows what he means by standing outside herself; he leaves as soon as he has bawled her out; she settles down to getting into the right mood; the second act is always much better. When she sings *Carmen,* Walter stays outside the house until he knows she has finished the "Seguidilla."

"I know the minute I get inside how it's going," says Walter. "If the chorus people and stagehands welcome me with a smile and pat my shoulder as I go by, I know it's all right; if they seem to be looking off somewhere else, I know we're in trouble. You never fool that gang; they're always right."

He establishes an atmosphere at home that relaxes Risë after her hard work. Part of that is in the aforenoted dragging her off her pedestal and bringing her to earth with a bang. He considers hard, firm life as an essential for a serious artist. The closer she is to reality, the deeper her characterizations will be, the more exultant and poignant will be her singing. He is an irrepressible wit, a natural clown, an irreverent personality. One night at a Long Island party, when the host was trying to impress a group of important advertising clients, Risë and Walter put on a rumba exhibition. Risë was serious in her dancing; Walter had prepared beforehand, and wasn't. As they wiggled, his pants began to slip. They continued to slip, much to the consternation of the guests. They finally slipped down entirely. There was nothing on underneath. Risë wouldn't speak to him for a week.

But there was pride and solemnity in the household when Risë received the honorary degree of Doctor of Humanities (L.H.D.) at Hobart and William Smith colleges at Geneva, N.Y. Hobart is a historic old college in the lovely lake country of upper New York State. At the graduation services presided over by Rev. Louis M. Hirshson, president of the colleges, Risë was touched to the point of tears when her doctorate's hood was slipped over her head by Otto Schoen René, nephew of her wonderful old teacher. Dr. Schoen René assured her that he had not prompted the honor, hearing about it only when formal announcement was made to the press.

In the citation that accompanied the degree, President Hirshson paid tribute to the treasure of song in the history of mankind and said of Risë herself: "Dame Risë, *'Auf Flügeln Des Gesanges'* you have brought richness, joy, and understanding to our generation. You have sung to our hearts and from these hearts comes thanksgiving. Receive this symbol of our gratitude and join these colleges as Doctor of Humanities, *honoris causa*, by the authority of the board of trustees."

Since Nicky was in summer school and couldn't get away for the event, Walter decided that Risë should attend alone. It was her big day, and he didn't want the limelight diluted by his presence. The reunion with Dr. Schoen René was warm and touching; the faculty and students at the colleges couldn't have been kinder or more flattering. She was in her hotel room after dinner, still suffused with humility and joy, when a telegram was brought up from the desk.

"We are standing here hand in hand crying. We haven't made a joke all day.

Walter and Nicky."

Risë happily cried herself to sleep and hasn't allowed anyone since to belittle her honor. When a friend greeted her jocularly as "Dr. Stevens," she gave him a hurt sad look that froze the words on his lips. She never speaks about it, but in her mind is always the thought of the Bronx and the miracle of reaching her present place from where she started. Nobody could be more humble about her accomplishments, but she is not going to deny that she has attained them.

Along the way she has been greatly helped by people who have asked nothing in return but her friendship. From the start at the Metropolitan, she came under the wing of one of the most remarkable women who ever appeared at the opera house. This was Lotte Lehmann, the great German soprano, whose career is a high point in the history of the institution. Opera buffs still cherish individual Lehmann performances as jewels of perfection. There was never a cheap or tawdry or careless Lehmann appearance. There were great performances that are still spoken of with reverence by opera lovers.

Lotte Lehmann sang the role of Marschallin at Risë's first Metropolitan appearance in *Rosenkavalier*. Although German-trained and a veteran of the rivalries in continental opera houses, Madame Lehmann came to Risë's dressing room at the end of the performance and embraced her. For anyone who cares to hear, she said:

"This child will be the greatest Octavian the world has ever seen."

While Madame Lehmann remained with the company, Risë would never take an individual curtain call in any performance where Madame Lehmann appeared. From her she learned not only the subtleties of *Rosenkavalier* but was encouraged to attempt other roles which had been thought beyond her capacities. The friendship started in those early days has never for a moment been allowed to lapse. In the writing desk at her apartment Risë keeps one drawer for material which she considers particularly precious. Half of the items are telegrams or letters from Madame Lehmann, congratulating her on performances or bolstering her up for greater efforts.

During her days in Hollywood, Risë saw a great deal of Madame Lehmann, who had retired to an estate in Santa Barbara. To her doors came the great musical figures of the world. Risë sat like a mouse, and listened. Just hearing the talk of these famous personages was heaven enough for her. It was not enough for the kindly Lehmann.

"Speak up, speak up," she would say, with rough affection. "You're an artist as much as the others."

Risë was quite certain this was short of the truth, but she did manage to meet the others on a tentative footing. If they felt they were wasting their words on a pretty novice, they refrained from saying so out of respect for the angry glare in Lehmann's eyes. As between conductors and singers, Lehmann was always on the side of the singers. Others might feel that Risë was a bit naïve in her attitudes, but Madame Lehmann encouraged it. If Risë was a great "yes" and "no" person, with nothing in between, Madame Lehmann regarded it as a virtue.

But not everything heard by Risë at these meetings was pleasant to the ear. Fritz Reiner gave it as his considered opinion that she was a good Mignon but would always fall short as Octavian. Bruno Walter said: "Believe me, you are the ideal Octavian, but you will never be able to do *Carmen*.

"You would be the perfect Fidelio," he added.

"But how could I be?" said Risë. "I couldn't possibly sing the role."

This was an instance of Risë's inability to dissemble. She could easily have played along with the suggestion; instead she blurted out the truth. Mr. Walter turned away in anger; they have never spoken since.

"What difference does it make?" asked Madame Lehmann with irritation, when Risë reported the incident. "He conducts; you sing. How can he know what your voice can do? You must learn this from the start: don't worry about critics or conductors or management. Nothing you can do will ever change them, so ignore them. Do what your heart and head tells you to do. If that isn't enough, no amount of fawning or cringing will make up for it."

Risë wanted most earnestly to follow the advice, but it was not easy. Like any other artist, she was almost pathologically sensitive to criticism. Olin Downes once wrote in the New York *Times* of a *Rosenkavalier* performance that "It is a shame Miss Stevens' German is so bad." At a dinner party a week later Risë was placed at his side. She spoke to him in German.

"I'm sorry," said Mr. Downes, "but I don't speak German."

"Well, *I* do," said Risë, significantly.

Risë has always had close friends among the critics, but she has never for a moment succumbed to the illusion that friendship could somehow temper the critical storm. The artist has her problems; the critic has his. Once the curtains part at the opera, the critic is a judge, and often a harsh judge. He may admire the performer as an individual and a friend, but he will be compelled to report that, on this particular night, she has bleated like a lamb and sung outrageously off key.

"That's the only way it can be," says Risë, "and you've got to learn to take it. What if the critics suddenly became boosters and Pollyannas? Would they be fooling our audiences, which are the most discriminating and sophisticated in the world? Not for a minute. You'd simply be ruining criticism and doing the artist no good whatever."

Risë has long enjoyed the stimulating friendship of such critics as Howard Taubman, Virgil Thomson, Alfred Frankenstein, Alexander Fried, Emily Coleman, and Harriett Johnson, to mention only a few of the many she has met. She admires their musical knowledge and literary style; she reserves the right to differ with them on their judgments. This is what makes the American musical scene so lively. The critical blows are often heavy, but they have never killed a worth-while artist. The great American audience has an admirable habit of making up its own mind.

But if there is one feeling Risë has about New York critics, aside from admiration and occasional spells of rage, it is sympathy. New York has a great deal of music and too few critics. The result is that the poor harassed critic often spends his nights chasing desperately between a Bernstein concert at Carnegie Hall to the debut of a promising baritone at Town Hall to a snatch of the opera at the Metropolitan. He must then sit down and hastily bat out his reviews for the late editions of the morning papers. That the reviews can be so good under these conditions is a tribute to the critics, but it is not exactly an ideal situation for the reviewers themselves.

"I think I'm a good judge of a singer's performance," says Risë, "but I couldn't judge at all if I only heard a fraction of a performance, and I certainly couldn't judge it fairly if I had that deadline hanging over me. How can you report accurately on a Boris if you've missed the great death scene at the end? How can you know the merits of a Donna Anna without hearing the final and most difficult aria?"

Risë has never understood why musical reviews couldn't wait until a day later. Unlike the legitimate theatre and the movies, music is not concerned with immediate box-office reaction. She finds that many critics agree with this thesis and pray only that their publishers will someday see the light, but the mechanics of publishing are esoteric by their very nature and yield grudgingly to change. Short of leading a demonstration of protest, there is little Risë can do about it, and she is not precisely the martyr type.

"I take it out in feeling sorry for my friends, the critics," says Risë. "They're the most overworked men in the world and surely must be among the greatest. How they can function under that pressure is beyond me."

For years at the Metropolitan, Risë had looked longingly toward one thing: a chance to do Gluck's *Orfeo ed Euridica*. She had sung it in Prague, Cairo, Alexandria, and Buenos Aires. It was her favorite role, but she soon learned to keep quiet about it around the opera house. The box-office men blanched at the mere mention of the subject. *Orfeo* was as good as a fire alarm in emptying a theatre. Gluck had written it two hundred years ago; it was the first modern opera, a revolutionary work that had set the path for all opera that was to follow. Opera previously had been an excuse for a series of set pieces for singers, accompanied by tiresome ritornelles. Gluck, for the first time, wrote music to fit the words. *Orfeo* is one of the loveliest of operas; some authorities consider it the greatest of operas. Gluck produced miracles of orchestration that have not been excelled even by Mozart, Verdi, and Wagner. The work was a complete departure from anything going before; it met with great resistance from public and critics. Its success in Paris in 1774 was due to the backing of Marie Antoinette, who had sat at Gluck's feet as a child in Vienna, when he was *Kapellmeister* for the court of her mother, Maria Theresa.

But the fact remained that at the Metropolitan in the past, the boxes in the Diamond Horseshoe on *Orfeo* nights had been filled with remote second cousins and members of the box holders' domestic staff. Risë had discussed *Orfeo* with Mr. Bing at intervals, but he had merely shaken his head ruefully. He was quite prepared to throw an occasional sop to the experts, longhairs and dilettantes, but a look at the old box-office figures invariably gave him a touch of vertigo. Then, after a lapse of thirteen years, rumors began to circulate that a revival of *Orfeo* was being considered. Risë's heart leaped. It was ominous that Mr. Bing had said nothing to her, but perhaps his plans weren't complete. Risë and Walter discussed the matter. Walter counseled patience; when the right time came, she would be hearing from Bing.

"No, I can't wait," said Risë. "We've never done this before, but I want you to ask him for something now."

Walter's interview was painful. Bing confirmed the reports that there was to be a revival of *Orfeo*, but unfortunately it was not for Risë. The part had been given to Giulietta Simionato, a new acquisition of the Metropolitan, who had been acclaimed in the part in Europe.

"It was a low point in Risë's life," says Walter. "When I told her she folded up into a little figure."

But Risë's luck was to save her again. As the time neared for the *Orfeo* rehearsals, word came from Italy that Simionato would be unable to fill her contract because of illness. Walter waited calmly for Bing's phone call, which followed closely on the announcement. He arrived at the Metropolitan to find Bing harassed and apologetic.

"I throw myself on your mercy again," said Bing. "I'm afraid I made it all too plain that Risë was second best. Would she take it to help us out?"

"Don't worry; she'll take it," said Walter. "She's not a *gekränkte Leberwurst*."

Bing laughed with relief. Not only was he off the hook, but the phrase was rich with Viennese overtones. *Gekränkte Leberwurst* . . . indignant sausage . . . haughty . . . nose in the air.

But other obstacles were still ahead. The production was to be in charge of Pierre Monteux, the great French conductor. Through a series of unfortunate circumstances, Risë had previously had a serious quarrel with Mr. Monteux over a performance of *Carmen*. Monteux had done the old *Carmen* hundreds of times; he saw no need to change it. But the Tyrone Guthrie *Carmen* was now established at the Metropolitan, a standard by which all future productions of the opera were to be judged. It was an impasse. Mr. Bing backed Risë staunchly in her determination that the new *Carmen* be done; Monteux stuck to his guns. At the dress rehearsal there was a blowup. Risë was at the end of her rope.

"I can't do it," she cried finally. "It's impossible this way."

Without a word Monteux placed his baton on the desk, turned away through the little door leading to the musicians' room under the stage, and left the theatre. A truce was patched up in time to allow the performance to be given, but deep wounds were left behind. There is good evidence for believing that Simionato's contract had been a result of the incident. Monteux's presence as conductor was almost obligatory; he was the supreme interpreter of Gluck's works. He would hardly want a repetition of the *Carmen* trouble.

With Simionato's defection Monteux was in an embarrassing position. His contract would not allow him to reject Risë, but he probably awaited her arrival at the first rehearsal with no pleasure. One glance was enough to tell him that he was meeting a new Risë. *Carmen* was bred into her bones; it would have taken a tearing of tendons to change it. She approached *Orfeo* with reverence, and Monteux was the keeper of the holy flame.

"I am in your hands, Maestro," she said softly.

The breach was healed; the success of the opera was historic.

In 1956, Dino Yannopoulos, stage director of the Metropolitan and a Greek by birth, recruited a company for a summer season of opera in Athens. In addition to Risë, there were Eleanor Steber, Blanche Thebom, and Dimitri Mitropoulos. The performances were given in the old amphitheatre of Herodes Atticus at the foot of the Acropolis. It had been built by the wealthy merchant in A.D. 161 and was now in ruins. Yannopoulos had no scenery but produced miracles of stagecraft by the use of old shattered pillars and blocks of marble. Greek tragedies had been acted in this very setting centuries before. It was the great moment of Risë's life when she first appeared in *Orfeo* before an audience of descendants of the great figures of old. Risë was to write about it later in a magazine article.

"When I reached the famous aria in which Orpheo laments the death of his wife Euridice, the moon came out. It bathed the scene in an eerie, silvery light. The shadows of the Acropolis slanted toward me in the mist; the ghosts of history seemed to envelop me. And then it happened. I lost all touch with reality, with singing and acting. I felt I was in ancient Greece, mentally and *physically*. I actually seemed to be living a former life, one in which I had acted on this very stage.

"As in a trance I finished the aria, then fell prostrate on the body of Euridice. What happened next, I had to be told later—first silence, then five minutes of thunderous applause. It was this noise that gradually wakened me. Dazed, uncertain, I made my way back to the present. My whole life seemed to whirl through my mind—my early struggles and failures, my later successes, my marriage, the death of my brother, events both happy and unhappy. All this took but a moment, but it left me emotionally exhausted.

"When the performance ended, I pondered this experience. Illusion, fainting spell—whatever it was, I had 'lived' for a moment in the remote past. Returning to the present, I had seen the crises of my life flash by like pictures. How? Why? Perhaps I would never know. But this I did know: when you view the events of your life in the light of centuries, how tiny, how unimportant they are! That, at least, was something to hang on to. So far as I am concerned, it always will be."

Risë finishes each season with a sigh of relief. She is going out to Westhampton Beach and sleep for a month. She never wants to see a concert platform or an operatic stage again. For the first week, she lies in the sun on the terrace, wrapped protestingly in the garments Walter has provided for her. When the weather warms up, she goes out to her boat and paddles around in the water. She attends cocktail parties, she goes to lunch with friends, she shops at Bohack's for grocery bargains, she cleans out the bureau drawers and moves the furniture. During the whole period, she bangs around in the kitchen like an Escoffier. But there comes a time when none of this is enough. She gets Jimmy Shomate on the phone in New York and asks him furiously what he thinks he's doing: why isn't he out there? They begin on next year's concert program.

During the winter when Risë is in New York, and not on concert tours, she goes two or three times a week to Vera Schwarz's studio on 57th Street. The session begins on a social note: they sit around a pot of coffee and gossip. By degrees the real work starts. Risë begins to vocalize, she stops to chat, she takes another sip of coffee, she vocalizes some more. From that, they go into the hard problems. Miss Schwarz has noticed something in Risë's last performance; it must be cleared up. Risë works incessantly on the interpretation of her concert numbers. Although her great operas would seem to be set by long tradition, she never allows them to grow stale.

"Others I urge to work," sighs Miss Schwarz, "but not this one; she wears me out with it."

The association has been long and friendly; the results have been outstanding. For Miss Schwarz, friendship alone would not have been enough. She had been a *prima donna assoluta*, one of the most famous in Europe. Like Madame Schoen René and all other great teachers, art comes before all else with her. As a friend, her relations with Risë are warm and tender; as a teacher, she is stern and relentless.

"Even if I wanted to go easy," says Miss Schwarz, "this one would not have it. She is a great artist; she has the demon within her that all great artists must have. It is the supreme pleasure when this relationship exists between artist and teacher. I see my own life relived again. Art is a re-creation; what satisfaction it is when an artist can hand the flame on to another."

Looking over her artistic career, Risë feels she owes a great deal to the late Edward Johnson, of the Metropolitan, and Kurt Weinhold, her concert manager. Although there was a low period in their relationship during the "cold war" episode, Mr. Johnson saw to it that she had star parts from the first and was given every chance to develop with the company. As a fine actor himself during his operatic days, he could see Risë's dramatic possibilities from the start and assisted her greatly with his advice. In his retirement Mr. Johnson was the same gay and lively figure of his singing days. The friendship of Risë and Mr. Johnson had grown warmer with the years.

In her personal life Risë's best friend remains her earliest friend. Florence Hynes is now Mrs. George Glynn, a happily married woman who has no regrets for the musical career she surrendered. Her pride in Risë is constant; their meetings are frequent; they fight over the old Bronx days with glee.

The paramount interest of Risë and Walter a year ago was getting Nicky into a good preparatory school. At least, that was Walter's idea, and he worked on it so hard that Risë hadn't the heart to discourage him. She felt Nicky was doing well at Browning in New York and should stay another year. Walter said, nonsense; the boy needed to get away from home. In the process of gathering information for the change, he became possibly the greatest authority on preparatory schools in the history of the nation. The final choice fell on Choate School, at Wallingford, Connecticut. Surovy proposed; Choate demurred. Its standards were forbiddingly high, a fact that Walter knew and which accounted for his choice. Master Nicolas Vincent Surovy would have to take an examination for admittance and would then only be accepted for summer school. His work there would determine whether he should go further.

Risë was apprehensive, tearful, and furious at Walter for putting her dear one through such an ordeal. Nicky went off to Choate for a two-day examination. They waited at home on tenterhooks. At the slam of the apartment front door on the third day Risë and Walter came running. They could tell from Nicky's look that it was all right.

"You've made it!" cried Risë elatedly. "How did you ever do it?"

Nicky put up a nonchalant hand to ward off her caresses.

"Oh, it was simple enough," he said easily. "Every school needs at least one idiot."

Risë let forth a scream which could be taken as either joy or anger. She seized Nicky roughly around the waist with her left arm; at the same instant she seized Walter with the right arm. She shoved them precipitately onto the divan, holding them there with a grip of iron. She fell to her knees between them, never relaxing her hold.

"You are charming, you are delightful, you are impossible," she said tensely. "I have prayed, I have fought, but it is no use. I give in. From now on I'm going to be Hungarian like the rest of you!"

With a whoop she rumpled them together like a ball and threw herself on top of them. They laughed till the tears ran down their cheeks, they laughed till there was no breath left in them.

On this pleasant note, the curtain descends.

References:

 Shakespeare p.37
 Rena + Walter p.100
 pregnant — p.127
 former admirations of opera stars p.143
 engagement at Purdue 145
 side lines of the trade p.218

 personality p.219, 224

lucky circumstance <u>but</u>
key note — work + discipline
     see also p.219